Lecture Notes
in Business Information Processing   199

T0233891

Torgeir Dingsøyr   Nils Brede Moe
Roberto Tonelli   Steve Counsell
Cigdem Gencel   Kai Petersen (Eds.)

Agile Methods

Large-Scale Development, Refactoring, Testing, and Estimation

XP 2014 International Workshops
Rome, Italy, May 26-30, 2014
Revised Selected Papers

 Springer

Volume Editors

Torgeir Dingsøyr
SINTEF, Trondheim, Norway
E-mail: torgeir.dingsoyr@sintef.no

Nils Brede Moe
SINTEF, Trondheim, Norway
E-mail: nils.b.moe@sintef.no

Roberto Tonelli
University of Cagliari, Italy
E-mail: roberto.tonelli@dsf.unica.it

Steve Counsell
Brunel University London, Uxbridge, UK
E-mail: steve.counsell@brunel.ac.uk

Cigdem Gencel
Free University of Bozen-Bolzano, Italy
E-mail: cigdem.gencel@unibz.it

Kai Petersen
Blekinge Institute of Technology, Karlskrona, Sweden
E-mail: kai.petersen@bth.se

ISSN 1865-1348   e-ISSN 1865-1356
ISBN 978-3-319-14357-6   e-ISBN 978-3-319-14358-3
DOI 10.1007/978-3-319-14358-3
Springer Cham Heidelberg New York Dordrecht London

Library of Congress Control Number: 2014957488

Typesetting: Camera-ready by author, data conversion by Scientific Publishing Services, Chennai, India

Printed on acid-free paper

Springer is part of Springer Science+Business Media (www.springer.com)

Preface

We are very happy to present the proceedings from the workshops held in conjunction with the 15th International Conference on Agile Software Development, XP 2014. This is the first time that revised and extended articles from scientific workshops at the conference are published in a separate proceedings volume. This book contains articles from three workshops: (1) the Workshop on Principles of Large-Scale Agile Development; (2) the International Workshop on Refactoring & Testing (RefTest); and the (3) First International Workshop on Estimations in the 21st Century Software Engineering (EstSE21).

The Workshop on Principles of Large-Scale Agile Development received 11 submissions, which were reviewed by three or four Program Committee members. Three articles were accepted and three conditionally accepted for the proceedings. The selected articles were revised and extended and went through a second review process. We are very grateful to the following Program Committee members for helping us in the second review phase: Steve Adolph, Siva Dorairaj, Philippe Kruchten, Sridhar Nerur, Jaana Nyfjord, and Helena Holmström Olsson. We have also included an article from an invited keynote at the workshop by Maarit Laanti. The organization of the workshop was supported by the SINTEF internal project "Agile Project Management in Large Development Projects" and by the project Agile 2.0, which is supported by the Research council of Norway (grant 236759/O30), and by the companies Kantega, Kongsberg Defence & Aerospace, and Steria.

The Workshop on Refactoring & Testing (RefTest) received 12 submissions, which were examined by three or four referees of the Program Committee. Six papers were selected for the conference presentations by the reviewers. Among the six presented, four received full consideration for the proceedings, and two were conditionally accepted. After a second review process, where each paper was reviewed by two referees, five articles, revised and extended, were accepted for the proceedings. We are indebted to all the Program Committee members for their contribution and their care in the first and second round reviews: Giulio Concas, Giuseppe Destefanis, Dongsun Kim, Stephen Swift, Ewan Tempero, Bartosz Walter, Marco Zanoni, Hongyu Zhang, Hubert Baumeister, Theodore D. Hellmann, Kieran Conboy, Laurent Bossavit, and Augustin Yague.

The First International Workshop on Estimations in the 21st Century Software Engineering (EstSE21) received five submissions, reviewed by three reviewers of the Program Committee. Based on the reviews, two submissions were accepted for publication and presentation at the workshop. The authors used the reviews and the discussions during the workshop to improve and extend their submissions.

Finally, we would like to thank Michele Marchesi, the academic program chair, for help with organizing the scientific workshops at the conference.

September 2014

Torgeir Dingsøyr
Nils Brede Moe
Steve Counsell
Roberto Tonelli
Cigdem Gencel
Kai Petersen

Workshop Organization

Workshop on Principles of Large-Scale Agile Development

Primary Organizers

Torgeir Dingsøyr   SINTEF, Norway
Nils Brede Moe   SINTEF, Norway

Program Committee

Steve Adolph	WSA Consulting, Canada
Ali Babar	The University of Adelaide, Australia
Venugopal Balijepally	Oakland University, USA
Jan Bosch	University of Gothenburg, Sweden
Mohammad Dadashzadeh	Oakland University, USA
Jerry DeHondt	Oakland University, USA
Siva Dorairaj	Software Education, New Zealand
Tore Dybå	SINTEF ICT, Norway
Jutta Eckstein	IT Communication, Germany
Elke Hochmüller	Carinthia University of Applied Sciences, Austria
Mark Kilby	Leading Agile, USA
Philippe Kruchten	University of British Columbia, Canada
Parastoo Mohagheghi	Norwegian Labour and Welfare Administration
Sridhar Nerur	University of Texas at Arlington, USA
Jaana Nyfjord	SICS Swedish ICT, Sweden
Helena Holmström Olsson	Malmö University, Sweden
Maria Paasivaara	Aalto University, Finland
Ken Power	Cisco, Ireland
Vijayan Sugumaran	Oakland University, USA
Eva Amdahl Seim	SINTEF Technology and Society, Norway
Rini van Solingen	Delft University of Technology, The Netherlands
Hans van Vliet	Vrije Universiteit Amsterdam, The Netherlands

International Workshop on Refactoring & Testing (RefTest)

Primary Organizers

Francesca Arcelli Fontana	University of Milan-Bicocca, Italy
Steve Counsell	Brunel University, UK
Alessandro Murgia	University of Antwerp, Belgium
Roberto Tonelli	University of Cagliari, italy

Program Committee:

Giulio Concas	University of Cagliari, Italy
Giuseppe Destefanis	University of Cagliari, Italy
Dongsun Kim	Hong Kong University of Science and Technology, Hong Kong
Stephen Swift	Brunel University, London, UK
Ewan Tempero	The University of Auckland, New Zealand
Bartosz Walter	Poznan University of Technology, Poland
Marco Zanoni	University of Milano Bicocca, Italy
Hongyu Zhang	Tsinghua University, Beijing, China
Hubert Baumeister	Technical University of Denmark
Theodore D. Hellmann	University of Calgary, Canada
Kieran Conboy	National University of Ireland, Galway
Laurent Bossavit	Institut Agile, France
Mika Mantyla	University of Aalto, Finland
Agustin Yague	Universidad Politecnica de Madrid, Spain

First International Workshop on Estimations in the 21st Century Software Engineering (EstSE21)

Primary Organizers

Cigdem Gencel	Free University of Bozen-Bolzano, Italy
Kai Petersen	Blekinge Institute of Technology, Sweden
Luca Santillo	Agile Metrics, Italy

Program Committee

Pekka Abrahamsson	Free University of Bozen-Bolzano, Italy
Alain Abran	École de technologie supérieure, Canada
Stefan Biffl	TU Wien, Austria
Luigi Buglione	ETS Montréal / Engineering.IT, Italy
Maya Daneva	University of Twente, The Netherlands
Christof Ebert	Vector Consulting Services, Germany
Magne Jørgensen	Simula Research Laboratory, Norway
Emilia Mendes	Blekinge Institute of Technology, Sweden
Jürgen Münch	University of Helsinki, Finland
Barış Özkan	Atılım University, Turkey
Charles Symons	Common Software Metrics Consortium (COSMIC), UK
Ayca Tarhan	Hacettepe University, Turkey
Oktay Türetken	Technische Universiteit Eindhoven, The Netherlands
Xiaofeng Wang	Free University of Bozen-Bolzano, Italy

Table of Contents

Estimations in the 21st Century Software Engineering

Towards Principles of Large-Scale Agile Development

A Summary of the Workshop at XP2014
and a Revised Research Agenda

Torgeir Dingsøyr[1, 2] and Nils Brede Moe[1, 3]

[1]SINTEF,
NO-7465 Trondheim, Norway
torgeird@sintef.no
[2] Department of Computer and Information Science,
Norwegian University of Science and Technology
[3] Blekinge Institute of Technology
SE-371 79 Karlskrona, Sweden
nils.b.moe@sintef.no

Abstract. Large projects are increasingly adopting agile development practices, and this raises new challenges for research. The workshop on principles of large-scale agile development focused on central topics in large-scale: the role of architecture, inter-team coordination, portfolio management and scaling agile practices. We propose eight principles for large-scale agile development, and present a revised research agenda.

Keywords: Large-scale agile software development, architecture, portfolio management; project management, scaling, inter-team coordination, software engineering.

1 Introduction

Since the formulation of the agile manifesto in 2001, agile methods have transformed software development practice by strongly emphasizing change tolerance, evolutionary delivery and active end-user involvement [1]. Agile development has received widespread interest, resulting in a shift of patterns of thought. Scrum is now a de facto standard for development in many countries, and other methods like extreme programming (XP) and elements of lean software development such as Kanban are in widespread use. Rajlich describes agile development as a paradigm shift in software engineering that "brings a host of new topics into the forefront of software engineering research" [2].

In the first special issue on agile development, in *IEEE Computer*, Williams and Cockburn [3] stated that agile methods "best suit *collocated teams* of about *50 people or fewer* who have easy access to user and business experts and are developing projects that are not life-critical". The success of agile methods for small, co-located teams has inspired use in new domains: Companies increasingly apply agile practices to large-scale projects.

T. Dingsøyr et al. (Eds.): XP 2014 Workshops, LNBIP 199, pp. 1–8, 2014.

However, there are challenges with achieving the same productivity gains in these areas, as in the "home ground" of agile methods. Agile methods are based on the idea that high-quality software can be developed by small teams using the principles of continuous design improvement and testing based on rapid feedback and change [4]. As agile development techniques are used on large-scale projects, new challenges arise. "Agile in the large" was voted "top burning research question" by practitioners at the XP2010 conference [5].

Fundamental assumptions in agile development are severely challenged when using these practices in large-scale projects. Self-management is a central principle in agile methods, but studies from other fields than software development indicate that self-management can reduce the ability to effectively coordinate across teams [6]. Also while the teams need to self-manage, team members need to have an effective knowledge network and collaborate closely with experts outside the team in large-scale agile [7]. To have an emerging architecture could hamper project progress when many teams are working in parallel, and some practices like the scrum of scrum has been found to be inefficient in large projects [8]. An international survey on agile adoption[1] shows that agile practice has primarily been successful in small teams.

To address these challenges with agile methods in large projects, we organized a workshop at XP2013 which resulted in a suggested research agenda [9]. At XP2014, we wanted to strengthen this line of research and organized a workshop on "Principles of Large-Scale Agile Development." The aims of this workshop were to create a community of researchers interested in this topic, to deepen the knowledge through identifying potential principles of large-scale agile development and to revisit the research agenda defined in 2013.

The workshop included a keynote on "Characteristics and principles for large-scale agile development" by Maarit Laanti [10] and a second keynote on "The leader role in large-scale agile development" by Lars-Ola Damm. All workshop members were asked to define what they meant by 'large-scale agile.' Further, we had paper presentations and group discussions on four topics: Architecture, inter-team coordination, portfolio management and scaling. The assignment for groups during discussion was to identify main principles within each core area. After these discussions we revisited the research agenda and did a voting on what should be high priority topics.

In this summary of the workshop discussions and introduction to the papers from the conference, we start by defining what we mean by large-scale agile development, then introduce the papers in this post-conference proceedings and add results from the workshop discussions to propose principles in the four areas architecture, inter-team coordination, portfolio management and scaling. Finally, we present the revised research agenda defined at the workshop. We hope this summary will inspire further research and provide valuable pointers to relevant research areas.

---

[1] Scott Ambler: Agile Adoption Rate Survey 2008, http://www.ambysoft.com/surveys/agileFebruary2008.html

2   What is Large-Scale Agile Development?

The term 'large-scale agile development' has been used to describe agile development in everything from large teams to large multi-team projects to making use of principles of agile development in a whole organization.

There is an established discussion on what constitutes agile software development, with Conboy [11] providing the most thorough discussion. He defines agility as the continuous readiness "to rapidly or inherently create change, proactively or reactively embrace change, and learn from change while contributing to perceived customer value (economy, quality, and simplicity), through its collective components and relationships with its environment."

How participants at the workshop defined large-scale agile development is shown in Table 1. We see that many focus on aspects of size such as number of people involved in the development, lines of code in the solution, number of development sites, number of teams, to definitions such as "agile in larger organizations." Arguments for a definition based in the number of teams is presented in [12], where large-scale agile is defined as *"agile development efforts with more than two teams."*

This definition excludes agile methods applied in large organizations from 'large-scale agile', and we propose that this is considered as a research direction on its own.

Table 1. Definitions by workshop participants at XP2014

Definitions of large-scale agile development
Over 50 developers OR 1/2 million lines of code OR more than 3 sites / time zones.
Over 50 persons, over 5 teams, developing together the same product / project using agile method.
Agile being applied to more than one team, one project, one product.
Agile applied on the organisational level.
Truly agile development in a context of more teams than one person can manage, and larger products than few teams can handle.
When coordination of teams can be achieved in a new forum like a Scrum of Scrum forum.
Several arenas are needed for coordination, like multiple Scrum of Scrums.
Large teams — how to get everyone on board with framework.
Big projects / Many people / Crucial to organisation / Customer focused / Flexible change / Many projects.
It is when you don´t know everyone else working in the same project/product.
Large-scale agile success depends on having the right structures in place "freedom to perform".
Agile organisations are those that learn fast and are effective in creating value.
Multiple teams working together in order to deliver software artefacts.
When the values/principles or practices scale, extends to other functions, units of a company, i.e. beyond team and projects (+ how it is done).
Driven by many needs and challenges in organisations.
Emergent complex and adaptive approach, cultural based – a mind-set.

3   Towards Principles of Large-Scale Agile Development

The workshop focused on four aspects of large-scale agile development: Architecture, inter-team coordination, portfolio management and scaling:

Architecture
Some of the critique of agile development and in particular of large-scale agile development has been how architecture is managed in such development efforts. Nord et al. [13] takes the position that agility is enabled by architecture, and architecture is enabled by agility. Architects work on three key concerns: Architecture of the system, the structure of the development organization and the production infrastructure. They identify a set of architectural tactics, which guide the alignment of the three concerns. Further advice to organising architectural work in large-scale agile development is provided by Eckstein [14], who argue that architectural work should be organized, depending on the number of changes and the level of uncertainty. Based on the above mentioned arguments and discussions at the workshop, we propose the following principles:

1. Architecture has a key role in defining how work is coordinated in large-scale development efforts.
2. The level of change and level of uncertainty will influence how the architecture work should be organized.

Inter-Team Coordination
A number of measures are important to coordinate teams in large-scale development efforts. Paasivaara et al. focus on the importance of defining common values through a study of an agile transformation project [15]. The article describes how value workshops were used to define common values, agree on interpretations and define behavioural implications. A similar approach is described by Nyfjord et al. [16], who focus on establishing common norms or conventions like "speaking the teams language". At the workshop, discussions in several groups focused on the importance of knowledge networks to achieve inter-team coordination.

In large-scale development, the needs for coordination of work appear on two levels – the team's level and between the team and the rest of the organization. Team members need to collaborate effectively within the team to accomplish their tasks, but also with experts outside the team, e.g. designers, architects, infrastructure personnel, and other stakeholders. Large-scale development needs an effective knowledge network.

Based on the articles and discussions at the workshop, we propose the following principles to achieve inter-team coordination in addition to standard mechanisms like the scrum-of-scrum meetings:

3. Common norms and values facilitate inter-team coordination.
4. Effective knowledge networks are essential in large-scale development due to the knowledge-intensive nature of software development.

Portfolio Management

Agile project portfolio management is about handling several agile projects in the same portfolio. In traditional project portfolio management, the portfolio consists of a set of projects executed in isolation from each other and the changing environment [17]. However, in agile software development this is not valid as projects are flexible, feedback driven, and embracing change even at the end of the project. A new request from a client on a single project, may affect the portfolio as a whole.

Controls are essential when managing a project portfolio. Controls can be understood as an attempt by the organization to influence people to take actions and make decisions, which are consistent with the goals of the organisations. Controls can be formal and informal. The informal control is contained by the development group (clan) and the individual's ability to monitor and evaluate it selves according to the acceptable behaviour.

Agile project portfolio management can also be seen as handling a dynamic non-linear system. The theory of Complex-adaptive systems (CAS) can be used to study such systems [17]. In CAS self-organization emerges as agents interacts through simple rules that can change and adapt. Feedback is the driving force of change.

Based on the article by Sweetman et al. and the discussion in the workshop, we propose the following principle of large-scale agile portfolio management:

   5. Continuously feedback from the portfolio to project levels enables the teams and project members to take decisions that are consistent with the goals of the large-scale agile portfolio.
   6. Continuously feedback from the project level to the portfolio level enables changing the portfolio to optimise the value of the large-scale agile portfolio.

Scaling

Applying principles of large-scale agile development, requires an understanding of the term "scaling". Without a proper understanding of the term, inappropriate methods may be applied. Power [18] argues that there are three contexts of agility and scale: 1) agile use in a large organisation 2) agile used in a large development effort in a large organizations, and 3) the large organization it selves is agile. Understanding the context is essential when choosing the right approach for improving the agility of the teams and organization.

Eklund et al. [19] argues that scaling agile software development in embedded systems is a question of scaling agile in two dimensions: First increasing the involved number of teams and utilize agile practices for mid- and long-range planning such as release planning and road mapping. Second, scaling the system engineering activities executed in each sprint, to a truly iterative practice instead of a stage-gated planned approach. A cross-functional team must have the ability or support to perform activities at several abstraction levels in a systems engineering V-model in each iteration or sprint.

Based on the article by Power [18] and Eklund et al. [19] and the discussion in the workshop, we propose the following principle of large-scale agile portfolio management:

7. Describing the context for agility and scale is essential for understanding how to improve agility in large-scale agile.
8. For large-scale embedded systems development, agility should scale both with respect to the number of involved teams, and the systems engineering activities in each iteration due to the co-dependency of software and hardware development.

4   Revised Research Agenda

In the workshop, the researchers and practitioners revisited the research agenda defined in 2013 [9]. The research agenda was first presented and then the topics where discussed both from an academic and a practitioner perspective. The research agenda was then modified before topics were given priority by the workshop participants. The topics included on the agenda were categorized as high or medium priority.

Table 2. Revised research agenda for large-scale agile software development

Priority	Topic	Description
High	Organisation of large development efforts	Organizational models, portfolio management, governance, project management, agile product-line engineering.
	Variability factors in scaling	Identify what factors are important in large projects that influence the development process.
	Inter-team coordination	Coordination of work between teams in large-scale agile development.
	Key performance indicators in large development efforts	Identify appropriate metrics are to monitor progress and support transparency.
	Knowledge sharing and improvement	How to ensure feedback for learning, use of knowledge networks and learning practices.
	Release planning and architecture	Coordinating and prioritizing functional and non-functional requirements, continuous delivery, minimizing technical debt.
Medium	Customer collaboration	Practices and techniques for product owners and customers to collaborate with developers in large-scale projects.
	Scaling agile practices	Determine which agile practices scale and which do not. Understand why and when agile practices scale.
	Agile contracts	Understand if contracts can change the mind-set of customers from upfront planning to agile principles. Uncover what legal limitations exist in contracts that reduce agility in large projects.
	Agile transformation	Efficient adoption of agile practices in large projects.
	UX design	Integration of user experience design in large projects

With the suggested research agenda in Table 2, we hope this will foster a continuous discussion over research agenda, and be an inspiration for future research.

Acknowledgement. The work on this article was supported by the SINTEF internal project "Agile project management in large development projects", by the Swedish Knowledge Foundation under the KK-Ho☐g grant 2012/0200, and by the project Agile 2.0 which is supported by the Research council of Norway through grant 236759/O30, and by the companies Kantega, Kongsberg Defence & Aerospace and Steria. We are grateful to Tor Erlend Fægri at SINTEF for comments on an earlier version of this article, and to all workshop participants for engaging discussions.

References

[1] Dingsøyr, T., Nerur, S., Balijepally, V., Moe, N.B.: A Decade of Agile Methodologies: Towards Explaining Agile Software Development. Journal of Systems and Software 85, 1213–1221 (2012)

[2] Rajlich, V.: Changing the paradigm of Software Engineering. Communications of the ACM 49, 67–70 (2006)

[3] Williams, L., Cockburn, A.: Agile Software Development: It's about Feedback and Change. IEEE Computer 36, 39–43 (2003)

[4] Nerur, S., Mahapatra, R., Mangalaraj, G.: Challenges of migrating to agile methodologies. Communications of the ACM 48, 72–78 (2005)

[5] Freudenberg, S., Sharp, H.: The Top 10 Burning Research Questions from Practitioners. IEEE Software, 8–9 (2010)

[6] Ingvaldsen, J.A., Rolfsen, M.: Autonomous work groups and the challenge of inter-group coordination. Human Relations 65, 861–881 (2012)

[7] Moe, N.B., Smite, D., Sablis, A., Børjesson, A.-L., Andréasson, P.: Networking in a large-scale distributed agile project. presented at the Proceedings of the 8th ACM/IEEE International Symposium on Empirical Software Engineering and Measurement, Torino, Italy (2014)

[8] Paasivaara, M., Lassenius, C., Heikkila, V.T.: Inter-team Coordination in Large-Scale Globally Distributed Scrum: Do Scrum-of-Scrums Really Work? In: Proceedings of the ACM-IEEE International Symposium on Empirical Software Engineering and Measurement (ESEM 2012), pp. 235–238 (2012)

[9] Dingsøyr, T., Moe, N.B.: Research Challenges in Large-Scale Agile Software Development. ACM Software Engineering Notes 38, 38–39 (2013)

[10] Laanti, M.: Characteristics and Principles of Scaled Agile. In: Dingsøyr, T., Moe, N.B., Counsell, S., Tonelli, R., Gencel, C., Petersen, K. (eds.) XP 2014 Workshops. LNBIP, vol. 199, Springer, Heidelberg (2014)

[11] Conboy, K.: Agility From First Principles: Reconstructing the Concept of Agility in Information Systems Development. Information Systems Research 20, 329–354 (2009)

[12] Dingsøyr, T., Fægri, T.E., Itkonen, J.: What is Large in Large-Scale? A Taxonomy of Scale for Agile Software Development. In: Profes 2014, Helsinki (accepted for publication at, 2014)

[13] Nord, R.L., Ozkaya, I., Kruchten, P.: Agile in distress: Architecture to the rescue. In: Dingsøyr, T., Moe, N.B., Counsell, S., Tonelli, R., Gencel, C., Petersen, K. (eds.) XP 2014 Workshops. LNBIP, vol. 199, Springer, Heidelberg (2014)

[14] Eckstein, J.: Architecture in Large Scale Agile Development. In: Dingsøyr, T., Moe, N.B., Counsell, S., Tonelli, R., Gencel, C., Petersen, K. (eds.) XP 2014 Workshops. LNBIP, vol. 199, Springer, Heidelberg (2014)

[15] Paasivaara, M., Väättänen, O., Hallikainen, M., Lassenius, C.: Supporting a Large-Scale Lean and Agile Transformation by Defining Common Values. In: Dingsøyr, T., Moe, N.B., Counsell, S., Tonelli, R., Gencel, C., Petersen, K. (eds.) XP 2014 Workshops. LNBIP, vol. 199, Springer, Heidelberg (2014)

[16] Nyfjord, J., Bathallath, S., Kjellin, H.: Conventions for Coordinating Large Agile Projects. In: Dingsøyr, T., Moe, N.B., Counsell, S., Tonelli, R., Gencel, C., Petersen, K. (eds.) XP 2014 Workshops. LNBIP, vol. 199, Springer, Heidelberg (2014)

[17] Sweetman, R., O'Dwyer, O., Conboy, K.: Control in Software Project Portfolios: A Complex Adaptive Systems Approach. In: Dingsøyr, T., Moe, N.B., Counsell, S., Tonelli, R., Gencel, C., Petersen, K. (eds.) XP 2014 Workshops, vol. 199, Springer, Heidelberg (2014)

[18] Power, K.: A Model for Understanding When Scaling Agile is Appropriate in Large Organizations. In: Dingsøyr, T., Moe, N.B., Counsell, S., Tonelli, R., Gencel, C., Petersen, K. (eds.) XP 2014 Workshops, vol. 199, Springer, Heidelberg (2014)

[19] Eklund, U., Olsson, H.H., Strøm, N.J.: Industrial challenges of scaling agile in mass-produced embedded systems. In: Dingsøyr, T., Moe, N.B., Counsell, S., Tonelli, R., Gencel, C., Petersen, K. (eds.) XP 2014 Workshops, vol. 199, Springer, Heidelberg (2014)

Characteristics and Principles of Scaled Agile

Maarit Laanti

Nitor Delta, Finland
Maarit.Laanti@nitor.fi

Abstract. The Agile Manifesto and Agile Principles are typically referred to as the definitions of "agile" and "agility". There is research on agile values and agile practises, but how should "Scaled Agility" be defined, and what might be the characteristics and principles of Scaled Agile? This paper examines the characteristics of scaled agile, and the principles that are used to build up such agility. It also gives suggestions as principles upon which Scaled Agility can be built.

Keywords: large-scale agile software development, agile methods, software engineering, project management, portfolio management, Scaled Agile.

1   Background and Models for Scaled Agile

Scaled agile has been an interest of the agile community for some years now [1]. Although there exists already research on agile values [2] and practices [3], the agile community is wondering if the principles listed in the agile manifesto scale as such or if something else is needed [1].

The first models for scaling agility to the whole organization already exist. Scaled Agile Framework [4, 5] was introduced to a wide audience in the Agile 2013 conference in August 2013 [6] and Disciplined Agile Delivery (DAD) [7] by Ambler in the International Conference of Software Engineering in May 2013 [8]. Also other frames for scaling agile are emerging, such as the Agility Path by Schwaber [9]. All the above-mentioned models have been created by practitioners.

Scaled Agile and Agile Organizations have become hot topics since the launch of the Scaled Agility Big Picture that describes an operational model for an Agile Organization, and the Scaled Agile Academy that delivers certified training courses for Scaled Agility. The Scaled Agile Framework (SAFe) is in use in multiple companies, including BMC Software, Mitchell International, Trade Station Technologies, Discount Tire, John Deere, Valpak, Infogain and SEI [10], and has become very popular. Scaled Agile Academy won the North American Red Herring 100 competition that ranks new start-ups based on their success [11].

Early adopters of Scaled Agile Framework have reported significant improvement in terms of productivity and quality. Improving productivity and quality is a key concern of any organization, but there are also some global trends that amplify the reasons why organizations are looking into ways to boost their performance.

1. Change or die. New innovations and new technologies come to markets with increased speed. [12, 13]

T. Dingsøyr et al. (Eds.): XP 2014 Workshops, LNBIP 199, pp. 9–20, 2014.

2. Constant need for further innovations. What is there is quickly copied – a need for constant innovation to enable competitiveness. [14, 15]
3. Transaction cost is small or almost missing compared to traditional settings. Publishing new (software) versions in the cloud is "free" once the cloud and the continuous deployment infrastructure is there. This leads to a faster ROI circulation. [16, 17]
4. Markets are more unpredictable than before. There is a need to be flexible with investments and capacity. [18, 19]

2   Principles Behind Scaled Agile Framework

Agile Software Development is most typically defined via the "Manifesto for Agile Software Development" [20, 21]. When agile methods are taken into use in other organizational disciplines (other than software development) it is typical to rely on other principles that are compatible with Agile Principles. SAFe e.g. has practices that cover the Portfolio level responsible for investments, Program level responsible for the execution of the planned initiatives and Team level.

The Team level can work using Scrum method, Kanban method or their combination that means that the SAFe Team level practices are compliant with Agile Principles like Scrum and Kanban are. But the Agile Principles are not enough to tell how to most efficiently organize Portfolio and Program levels. Thus SAFe builds on 2nd generation of Lean: Principles of the Product Development Flow as defined by Reinertsen [16] to define new way of working practices that are compliant with agile Team level practices for Program and Portfolio levels. Agile changes when it scales, and lean principles provide a good source for this. For example, a single agile team typically needs to worry only about one value chain, but lean principles advice how to manage multiple value chains, which is an organizational level problem. On Portfolio level the question is whether the organization has the right number of projects that represent the best mix of opportunities [22].

2.1   Aspects of Scaled Agile

However, Scaled Agile means more than adding Adaptivity to Program and Portfolio level. From various other sources we can find also other Aspects of Organizational-level agility, see Table 1.

One could argue that in Table 1 the first three aspects (Strategic Agility, Business Agility, and Agile Organization) are actually the same, only observed from different angles or viewpoints. The list could also contain Agile Innovation [30] as one agile aspect. Oza and Abrahamsson [30] define Agile Innovation as an aspect that combines innovation processes with agile processes. Here it is omitted because creativity and innovation are seen as an outcome of a Complex System tolerating internal conflicts [31]. Creativity and innovation can thus be understood as intrinsic qualities of such an Agile Organization, and they could thus be derived from other Agile Aspects as a result.

Table 1. Different Aspects of Agility, detected in large organizations

	Agile Aspect	Definitions
1	Strategic Agility	The ability to continuously redirect and reinvent the core businesses without losing momentum (in contrast to traditional portfolio restructuring) by maintaining balance with strategic sensitivity (awareness and attention), leadership unity (collective commitment), and resource fluidity (people rotation and organizational structures), working as an integrated real-time system [23].
2	Business Agility	The marriage of strategy (awareness) and agility (tactics) in order to create a responsive organization for business benefit [24] or a sum of process agility and technical agility or a sum of speed and flexibility that we can then, e.g., use to enable mobile business solutions [25]. Hugos [24] states that all products have two components: the actual product and an information component that adds value to a customer. The information component can be understood as covering all the immaterial benefits that the user gets when purchasing the specific product in question. A product ecosystem provides similar (immaterial) added value to the customer; thus here the additional value provided by a product ecosystem is included in the Business Agility aspect.
3	Agile Organization	The well-working combination of Informal Networks and the Formal Organizational structure, for which agility is key and pervading, trust a necessity [26].
4	People Agility	The ability to shuffle work around the organization when the priorities or focuses change — this is roughly similar to the "Resource Fluidity" [23].
5	Tools Agility	The ability to have tools that support the agile way of working and can easily be modified for a new purpose as the process changes [27].
6	Organizational Culture	The competing different organizational values and cultures related to agile values and agile culture [28].
7	Agility of the Product that is Built	The ability to modify, version, personalize, configure, or refresh the product to reach new customer groups or please the existing user [29].
8	Agility of payoff functions	Options thinking in regarding new investments. Balancing capacity into most profitable work, instead of having people to work on designated areas only. Prioritizing work based on future value [5].

3   Definition for Scaled Agile

When studying the different Aspects of Large-Scale Agile the common nominator is that people have used agile thinking to solve problems in different disciplines, such as Architecting, Design, Marketing, Portfolio Management or Program Management.

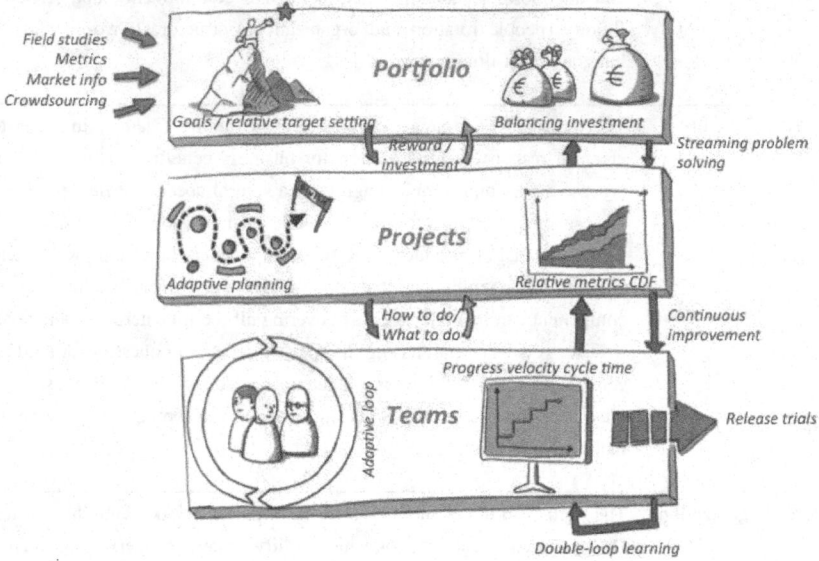

Fig. 1. Model for an Adaptive Organisation

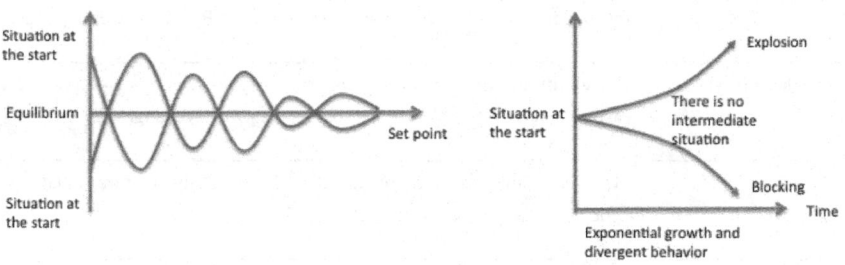

Fig. 2. Left. Negative feedback system behaviour in electrical circuits. Right. Positive feedback system behaviour in electrical circuits.

How different disciplines would be enhanced by agile thinking could be a way to define what Scaled Agile is, i.e. we would be adaptive on all levels of the organization, see Figure 1. That would mean we set goals to an organization that are relative, and balance the investments between various initiatives. We would use rolling forecasting and adaptive planning and flow-based, cumulative metrics. Teams would plan their work using increments or limiting the work-in-progress, and follow-up with relative metrics.

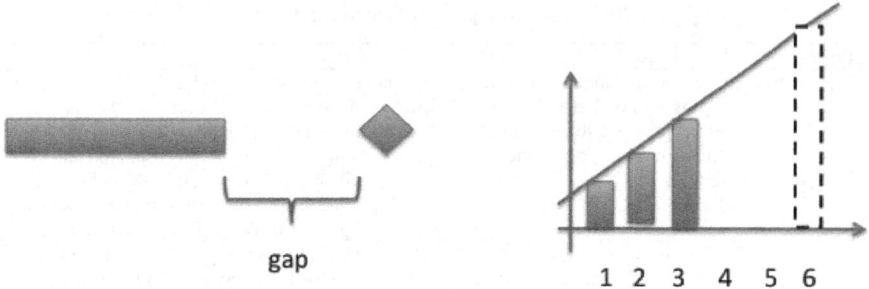

Fig. 3. Left. Negative feedback systems look for conformance. Right. Positive feedback systems measure progress and direction.

Traditionally, we have steered companies and projects by setting a target, creating a plan and then measuring the gap between the progress and the plan. In electrical circuit design this is known as a negative feedback loop, looking for a conformance and stability, see figure 2. A system operating under conformance can never produce more than was originally planned. An adaptive system on the contrary is a positive feedback system that measures the output and the direction. These kinds of systems tend to either grow or shrink exponentially, being thus more suitable for volatile markets. See Figure 3.

An agile organization may be better at adapting to its surroundings. This is a compatible view with Goldman's [63] definition of agility:

"a comprehensive response to the business challenges of profiting from rapidly changing, continually fragmenting, global markets for high-quality, high-performance, customer-configured goods and services. It is dynamic, context-specific, aggressively change-embracing, and growth-oriented. It is not about improving efficiency, cutting costs, or battening down the business hatches to ride out fearsome competitive "storms", it is about succeeding and about winning: about succeeding in emerging competitive arenas, and about winning profits, market share, and customers in the very center of the competitive storms many companies now fear."

4   Principles for Scaled Agile

The Scaled Agile Framework builds on Principles of Lean Flow thinking, but does not cover all of the mentioned Aspects of Agility. The Agile Aspects and various other compatible sources of Principles could be a source for new process innovations. The possible sources for Principles of Scaled Agile are e.g. Toyota Principles [32, 33], or Lean [34] or Beyond Budgeting Principles [35] that cover both leadership principles and process principles, or various strategic principles such as Blue Ocean [36]. See Appendix A for list of these related principles.

But what principles should we choose? One could also find a number of potential principles for Scaled Agile by studying the values (if not the principles) of companies that people identify as agile-minded. An alternative way is to discuss with the people in organizations who have some experience in Scaled Agility and derive the principles from this experience. In Table 2 we present the list of principles we believe could form the principles for Scaled Agile. This list has been peer-reviewed and suggestions incorporated from some experienced practitioners. For each principle, the origins of thought are also presented.

Table 2. Principles of Scaled Agile

	Principle	Explanation	Origins
1	The content is the key	Use the feedback from user and the intrinsic knowledge based on expertise and experience to create the best you can dream of. Delighting the user is key to success.	This principle combines Agile Principle of Working software is the primary measure of progress [20] with the first values (Focus on the user and all else will follow) of Google [37] and the first value (Empathy for Customers/Users) of Apple [38]. Great design as well as great user experience can only be created iteratively. Denning [39] emphasizes NPS as primary metrics that correlate with business success.
2	Co-creation	Groups are faster solving problems than individuals. Let the software evolve together, as the sum of the whole is more than its parts. Software Development is a Co-operative Game.	This principle combines the idea that groups are faster solving problems than individuals [40, 41] with Cockburn's research [42] that Software Development is a co-operative game. The co-creation is a synergistic, rather than a reductionistic view.
3	Feedback is the fuel to learning	Use rapid and concrete feedback on all work done. Study what creates success and do more of that.	Reinertsen [16] emphasises fast feedback . The plan-do-check-act is the essence of all lean improvement actions.
4	Business Agility	Releases generate revenue. The business model must dictate the release rate and user interest defines the business model. A pay per month basis business can only be based on continuous releasing. Release less often when the transaction cost is high.	See Reinertsen [16] on transaction and holding costs. Business model refactoring [43] discusses different ways of generating money in software business.
5	Use of Automation as Leverage	Use automation to leverage the manual effort needed. Develop the system, so that it gives a better leverage for the work unit done.	Use of autonomination is one key idea of Taiichi Ohno from Toyota [44]. The idea of depeloping a system, rather than people, comes from Deming [45].
6	Scale Using Fractals	Fractals are nature's way to scale, and fairly permanent structures. Use higher abstraction levels and nested systems, such as nested control loops.	Refer to ideas of Panarchic systems [46].
7	Avoid Combinatorial Explosions	Complexity is best tamed by splitting it to smaller pieces. Internal releases must be as small as possible.	Adding more people to project slows down the progress, as need for communication grows almost exponentially when the number of interfaces increases [47]. Combinatorial explosions come from mathematics [48, 49].
8	Sequence for maximal throughput	Modular architecture increases speed. Find the maximum throughput for your portfolio by balancing what can be done in parallel, and what must be done in sequence.	Refer to theories of value chain, and value chain analysis [40]. Per researcher's experiences [5].
9	Appreciate deep knowledge	Only more than five years experience creates deep knowledge. Use the best experts to tackle the most important and wicked problems. Check what new is learned and that your knowledge is still deep. Give creativity room.	Per researcher's experiences. Also Apple [38], Facebook [50] and Netflix [51] are known to value experience.

Table 2. (*Continued*)

10	Work Leveling	Even distribution of work and elimination of unnecessary work and waiting time based on measured performance. Work prioritization and Kanban are the tools here.	According to lean thinking, muri (uneven distribution of work) creates mura (overburden) that creates muda (waste). According to researcher's experience, the concepts are applicable to both humans and machinery [52].
11	Simplicity	Seek simplicity in solutions.	Simplicity is one of the Agile Principles [20].
12	Situationality	Use Pareto principle to avoid making processes overly complex. Not all cases need to be treated equally.	Refer to Beyond Budgeting Principles [35].
13	Control process, not items	Create simple rules for decision-making, instead of controlling each decision individually. Make clear game rules.	Refer to Reinertsen [16] and Beyond Budgeting [53] for distributed decision-making.
14	Growth mindset	Do more of what created success. Best leaders do not reject faulty attempts, but instead twist them to create more success. Have a growth mindset and improve what originally created success. Failures are the secret source of success.	Systematic on actions. Refer how Pixar works [54]. Refer to Mindset [55].
15	Listen to employees, they know all the problems	Value is created in the front-line. The rate at which you are able to remove impediments of progress or service correlates with the improvement done for business. Understand the problem you are solving.	Unused employee creativity is one form of waste [56]. Your people create the service, the rest of the organization is there to help them [57].
16	Detect and use patterns	Use and apply patterns. Your problems have already been solved by someone and somewhere.	Refer to TRIZ for patterns to solve product engineering problems [58].
17	Cost innovation	Ease the user's burden with a solution that costs less. Provide better service or fill the gaps between value chains. Do not tie capital, allow flexibility in investments and option thinking in portfolio level. Optimize cost of portfolio.	For cost innovation, refer to [14]. For value chains refer to [40]. For agile portfolio and cost thinking, refer to [59].
18	Utilize tacit knowledge.	Crowdsource the strategy. Use tacit knowledge of people to tell if you are heading in the right direction or not. When people feel proud of the outcome, you are heading in the right direction.	According to researcher's experience. The idea is similar to lean Niko-niko tables [60]
19	Learning happens between teams	Create collective knowledge that share the same vision and ambition. Collective must have multitalented semi-permanent teams combined with deep individual knowledge.	See organizational learning theories [61].
20	Fast is better than perfection.	Maximize the work undone. If it is not broken, do not fix it. Tolerate small imperfections. Fast is better than perfection. The best is the enemy of the good.	Lean startups are good when quickly trying new ideas [62].
21	Prevent problems when small.	Success hides small problems. In order to stay successful do not become ignorant for small problems.	See Creativity, Inc. [54]

5   Conclusions

This paper has examined Scaled Agile from Agile Aspects point of view, and presented a set of Principles for Scaled Agile. Simply put, Scaled Agility can be understood as an attempt to solve process problems other than software development on team level using agile mind-set and tools (adaptivity).

The new kind of emerging and disappearing opportunities, shortening cycles times, constant need for further innovations and disappearing transaction costs combined with cloud technologies may make future organizations as growing and shrinking adaptive fractals. This metaphor of an adaptive fractal may replace the old metaphor of an organization as a hierarchy over time.

References

1. Dingsøyr, T., Moe, N.: Reserach Challenges in Agile Software Development. In: ACM SIGSOFT Software Engineering Notes, vol. 38(5) (September 2013)
2. Fagerholm, F., Pagels, M.: Examining the Structure of Lean and Agile Values among Software Developers. In: Cantone, G., Marchesi, M. (eds.) XP 2014. LBIP, vol. 179, pp. 218–233. Springer, Heidelberg (2014)
3. Doyle, M., Williams, L., Cohn, M., Rubin, K.S.: Agile software development in practice. In: Cantone, G., Marchesi, M. (eds.) XP 2014. LNBIP, vol. 179, pp. 32–45. Springer, Heidelberg (2014)
4. Leffingwell, D.: Agile Software Requirements: Lean Requirements Practices for Teams, Programs, and the Enterprise. Addison-Wesley (2011) ISBN-10: 0-321-63584-1, ISBN-13: 978-0-321-63584-6
5. Laanti, M.: Agile Methods in Large-Scale Software Development Organizations. Applicability and model for adoption. Dissertation. University of Oulu (2013) ISBN 978-952-62-0033-0
6. Blog post by Dean Leffingwell, Agile 2013 conference schedule (2013), http://scaledagileframework.com/safe-at-agile-2013/, http://agile2013.agilealliance.org/program/sessionschedule/ (accessed on July 1, 2014)
7. Ambler, S.: Disciplined Agile Delivery: A Practitioner's Guide to Agile Software Delivery in the Enterprise. IBM Press (2012) ISBN-13: 978-0132810135
8. Brown, A.W., Ambler, S., Royce, W.: Agility at scale: Economic governance, measured improvement, and disciplined delivery. In: Proceedings of the 2013 International Conference on Software Engineering, pp. 873–881 (2013)
9. https://www.scrum.org/About/All-Articles/articleType/ArticleView/articleId/691/The-Path-to-Agility (accessed on July 01, 2014)
10. http://scaledagileframework.com/case-studies/ (accessed July 01, 2014)
11. http://www.prweb.com/releases/2014/05/prweb11892399.htm
12. Moore, G.: Escape Velocity: Free Your Company's Future from the Pull of the Past. Harper Business (2011) ISBN-13: 978-0062040893
13. Hitt, M.A., Keats, B.W., Demarie, S.M.: Navigating the new competitive landscape: Building strategic flexibility and competitive advantage in the 21st century. The Academy of Management Executive 12(4), 22–42 (1998)
14. Zeng, M.: Dragons at your door: How Chinese Cost Innovation Is Disrupting Global Competition. Harvard Business Review Press (2007) ISBN-13: 978-1422102084

15. Zhou, K.Z.: Innovation, imitation, and new product performance: The case of China. Industrial Marketing Management 35(3), 394–402 (2006)
16. Reinertsen, D.: The Principles of Product Development Flow. Second Generation Lean Product Development. Celeritas Publishing (2009) ISBN-10: 1935401009
17. Abrahamsson, P.: Speeding up embedded software development. ITEA Innovation report (2007)
18. Christopher, M.: The Agile Supply Chain. Industrial Marketing Management 29, 37–44 (2000)
19. Stalk, G.: Time – the next source of competitive advantage. Harward Business Review (July/August 1988)
20. Agile Manifesto (2001), http://www.agilemanifesto.org (accessed on July 2011 and May 2012)
21. Fowler, M., Highsmith, J.: The Agile Manifesto. Software Development (August 2001)
22. Stettina, C.J., Hörz, J.: Agile Portfolio Management: An empirical perspective of practice in use. International Journal of Project Management (April 2014)
23. Doz, Y., Kosonen, M.: Fast Strategy. How Strategic Agility will help You Stay ahead of the Game. Wharton School Publishing (2008) ISBN: 978-0-273-71244-2
24. Hugos, M.H.: Business Agility. Sustainable Prosperity in a Relentlessly Competitive World. Microsoft Executive Leadership Series. John Wiley & Sons, Inc. (2009) ISBN 978-0-470-41345-6
25. Evans, N.D.: Business Agility. Strategies for Gaining Competitive Advantage through Mobile Business Solutions. Prentise Hall (2002) ISBN-0-13-066837-0
26. Atkinson, S.R., Moffat, J.: The Agile Organization: From Informal Networks to Complex Effects and Agility. Information Age Transformation Series. Library of Congress Cataloging-in-Publication Data (2005) ISBN 1-893723-16-X
27. West, D., Hammond, J.: The Forrester Wave: Agile Development Management Tools, Q2 2010. Forrester Research (2010)
28. Iivari, J., Iivari, N.: Organizational Culture and the Deployment of Agile Methods: The Competing Values Model View. In: Agile Software Development, Current Research and Future Directions. Springer (2010) ISBN 978-3-642-12574-4
29. Grant, T.: Tech Vendors Supporting Agile Must Be Adaptive. For Technology Product Management & Marketing Professionals. Forrester Research (2010)
30. Oza, N., Abrahamsson, P.: Building Blocks of Agile Innovation. Booksurge Llc. (2009) ISBN-10: 1439260982, ISBN-13: 978-1439260982
31. Appelo, J.: Management 3.0. Leading Agile Developers, Developing Agile Leaders. Addison-Wesley (2011) ISBN-10: 0-321-71247-1, ISBN-13: 978-0-321-71247-9
32. http://www.toyota-global.com/company/vision_philosophy/guiding_principles.html / (accessed September 08, 2014)
33. Spear, S.J.: Learning to Lead at Toyota. Harvard Business Review 82(5), 78–91 (2004)
34. Poppendieck, M.: Principles of Lean thinking. IT Management Select 18 (2011)
35. Beyond Budgeting Principles, http://www.bbrt.org/beyond-budgeting/bb-principles.html (accessed July 22, 2014)
36. Kim, W.C.: Blue Ocean Strategy: How to Create Uncontested Market Space and Make Competition Irrelevant. Harvard Business Review Press (2005) ISBN-13: 978-1591396192
37. Google values, http://www.google.com/about/company/philosophy/ (accessed July 05, 2014)
38. Apple values, http://www.seanet.com/~jonpugh/applevalues.html (accessed July 05, 2014)
39. Denning, S.: Leader's Guide to Radical Management Reinventing the Workplace for the 21st Century. JosseyBass (2010) ASIN: B00CNWRJS4

40. Poppendieck, M., Poppendieck, T.: Lean Software Development: An Agile Toolkit. Addison Wesley (2003) ISBN-0-321-15078-3
41. Surowiecki, J.: The Wisdom of Crowds. Anchor (2005) ISBN-13: 978-038572707
42. Cockburn, A.: Agile Software Development: The Cooperative Game, 2nd edn. Addison-Wesley (2006) ISBN-10: 0321482751
43. Osterwalder, A.: Business Model Generation: A Handbook for Visionaries, Game Changers, and Challengers. John Wiley and Sons (2010) ISBN-13: 978-0470876411
44. Ohno, T., Miller, J.: Taiichi Ohno's Workplace Management. Gemba Press (2007) ISBN-13: 978-0978638757
45. Lazko, W.J., Saunders, D.: Four Days with Dr. Deming: A Strategy for Modern Methods of Management. Prentice Hall (1995) ISBN-13: 978-0201633665
46. Holling, C.S.: Understanding the complexity of Economic, Ecological, and Social Systems
47. Brooks, F.: The Mythical Man-Month: Essays on Software Engineering. Addison Wesley (1995) ISBN-13: 978-0201835953
48. Krippendorff, K.: Combinatorial Explosion. Web Dictionary of Cybernetics and Systems. Principia Cybernetica Web (accessed on July 03, 2014)
49. Grindal, M.: Handling Combinatorial Explosion in Software Testing. Linköping Studies in Science and Technology. Dissertation, 1073 (2007)
50. Facebook values, https://www.facebook.com/careers/ (accessed on May 25, 2014)
51. Netflix values http://jobs.netflix.com/ (accessed on May 25, 2014)
52. Smits, H.: The impact of scaling on planning activities in an agile software development center. In: 40th Annual Hawaii International Conference on System Sciences, HICSS 2007, pp. 274c–274c. IEEE (2007)
53. Bogsnes, B.: Implementing Beyond Budgeting: Unlocking the Performance Potential (2008) ISBN-13: 978-0470405161
54. Catmull, E., Wallace, A.: Creativity, Inc.: Overcoming the Unseen Forces That Stand in the Way of True Inspiration (2014) ISBN-13: 78-0812993011
55. Dweck, C.: Mindset: How you can fulfill your potential. Amazon Digital Services, Inc. ASIN: B005RZB65Q
56. Cawley, O., Wang, X., Richardson, I.: Lean Software Development–What Exactly Are We Talking About? In: Fitzgerald, B., Conboy, K., Power, K., Valerdi, R., Morgan, L., Stol, K.-J. (eds.) LESS 2013. LNBIP, vol. 167, pp. 16–31. Springer, Heidelberg (2013)
57. Vineet, N.: Employees First, Customers Second: Turning Conventional Management Upside Down. Harvard Business Review Press (2010) ISBN-13: 978-1422139066
58. Gadd, K.: TRIZ for Engineers: Enabling Inventive Problem Solving. Wiley (1887) ISBN-13: 978-0470741887
59. Laanti, M., Sirkiä, R.: Lean and agile financial planning, BBRT research paper, work in progress
60. Medinilla, Á.: Self-Organization. In: Agile Management, pp. 99–117. Springer, Heidelberg (2012)
61. Argyris, C.: On Organizational learning. Wiley-Blackwell (1999) ISBN-13: 978-0631213093
62. Ries, E.: The Lean Startup: How Today's Entrepreneurs Use Continuous Innovation to Create Radically Successful Businesses. Crown Business (2011) ISBN-13: 978-0307887894
63. Goldman, S., Naegel, R., Preiss, K.: Agile Competitors and Virtual Organizations: Strategies for Enriching the Customer. Wiley (1994) ISBN 0471286508

Appendix A. List of Related Principles

	Source	Principles
1	Toyota [32]	1. Honor the language and spirit of the law of every nation and undertake open and fair business activities to be a good corporate citizen of the world. 2. Respect the culture and customs of every nation and contribute to economic and social development through corporate activities in their respective communities. 3. Dedicate our business to providing clean and safe products and to enhancing the quality of life everywhere through all of our activities. 4. Create and develop advanced technologies and provide outstanding products and services that fulfill the needs of customers worldwide. 5. Foster a corporate culture that enhances both individual creativity and the value of teamwork, while honoring mutual trust and respect between labor and management. 6. Pursue growth through harmony with the global community via innovative management. 7. Work with business partners in research and manufacture to achieve stable, long-term growth and mutual benefits, while keeping ourselves open to new partnerships.
2	Lean Thinking [34]	1. Specify value from the standpoint of the end customer by product family. 2. Identify all the steps in the value stream for each product family, eliminating whenever possible those steps that do not create value. 3. Make the value-creating steps occur in tight sequence so the product will flow smoothly toward the customer. 4. As flow is introduced, let customers pull value from the next upstream activity. 5. As value is specified, value streams are identified, wasted steps are removed, and flow and pull are introduced, begin the process again and continue it until a state of perfection is reached in which perfect value is created with no waste.
3	Beyond Budgeting [35]	*Governance and transparency*

		1. Values	Bind people to a common cause; *not a central plan*
		2. Governance	Govern through shared values and sound judgement; *not detailed rules and regulations*
		3. Transparency	Make information open and transparent; *don't restrict and control it*
		Accountable teams	
		4. Teams	Organize around a seamless network of accountable teams; *not centralized functions*
		5. Trust	Trust teams to regulate their performance; *don't micro-manage them*
		6. Accountability	Base accountability on holistic criteria and peer reviews; *not on hierarchical relationships*

	Goals and rewards	
	7. Goals	Set ambitious medium-term goals, *not short-term fixed targets*
	8. Rewards	Base rewards on relative performance; *not on meeting fixed targets*
	Planning and controls	
	9. Planning	Make planning a continuous and inclusive process; *not a top-down annual event*
	10. Coordination	Coordinate interactions dynamically; *not through annual budgets*
	11. Resources	Make resources available just-in-time; *not just-in-case*
	12. Controls	Base controls on fast, frequent feedback; *not budget variances*

| 4 | Blue Ocean [36] | 1. Reconstruct market boundaries. This principle identifies the paths by which managers can systematically create uncontested market space across diverse industry domains, hence attenuating search risk. Using a Six Paths framework, it teaches companies how to make the competition irrelevant by looking across the six conventional boundaries of competition to open up commercially important blue oceans. |

2. Focus on the big picture, not the numbers. This principle, which addresses planning risk, presents an alternative to the existing strategic planning process, which is often criticized as a number-crunching exercise that keeps companies locked into making incremental improvements. Using a visualizing approach that drives managers to focus on the big picture, this principle proposes a four-step planning process for strategies that create and capture blue ocean opportunities.

3. Reach beyond existing demand. To create the greatest market of new demand, managers must challenge the conventional practice of aiming for finer segmentation to better meet existing customer preferences, which often results increasingly small target markets. Instead, this principle, which addresses scale risk, states the importance of aggregating demand, not by focusing on the differences that separate customers but rather by building on the powerful commonalities across noncustomers.

4. Get the strategic sequence right. The fourth principle describes a sequence that companies should follow to ensure that the business model they build will be able to produce and maintain profitable growth. When companies follow the sequence of (1) utility, (2) price, (3) cost, and (4) adoption requirements, they address the business model risk.

The remaining two principles address the execution risks of blue ocean strategy.

5. Overcome key organizational hurdles. Tipping point leadership shows managers how to mobilize an organization to overcome the key organizational hurdles that block the implementation of a blue ocean strategy. This principle mitigates organizational risk, outlining how leaders and managers can surmount the cognitive, resource, motivational, and political hurdles in spite of limited time and resources.

6. Build execution into strategy. This principle introduces fair process to address the management risk associated with people's attitudes and behaviors. Because a blue ocean strategy represents a departure from the status quo, fair process is required to facilitate both strategy making and execution by mobilizing people for the voluntary cooperation needed for execution. By integrating execution into strategy formulation, people are motivated to act.

Architecture in Large Scale Agile Development

Jutta Eckstein

Independent, Gaussstr. 29, 38106 Braunschweig, Germany
Jutta@JEckstein.com

Abstract. In order to welcome changing requirements (even late in development) agile development should enable the architecture to incorporate these changes and therefore to emerge over time. This implies not finalizing the architecture upfront. Moreover, in small agile teams it is assumed that there is no dedicated role for an architect – instead the whole team should be responsible for the architecture. In large-scale agile development the requirement for an emergent architecture still holds true. However, it is unrealistic to ask members of e.g. ten teams to be equally responsible for the architecture. Moreover, the role and support for the architecture depends not only on the degree of the size but as well on the degree of complexity. In this paper I report on the experience using different models for supporting emergent architecture in large environments that take the degree of complexity into account.

Keywords: agile methods, architect, change, chief architect, complexity, community of practice, emergent architecture, large-scale agile software development, project management, software engineering, technical consulting team, technical service team, uncertainty.

1   Introduction

Agile development focuses on maximizing the business value at all times. In small agile development this is addressed by a cross-functional team, which Scrum called a Scrum Team [1]. The developers on such a team encompass all competencies, skills, and know-how needed to deliver frequently product increments. There are no explicit roles like tester or database expert for the developers in order to stress the joint responsibility for the delivery. This structure allows such a team to work independently in a self-organized manner.

Scaling up agile development does not change the goal of maximizing the business value continuously. However, for large-scale agile development it is crucial to provide a supporting team structure. Thus, instead of structuring teams according to know-how (like user interfaces or databases), activities (like business analysis or testing), or components (as defined by i.e. architectural layers), teams have to be structured –cross-functional– around the business value. Only this allows teams in large-scale agile development to self-organize and to deliver business value frequently and regularly. Such teams are called domain or feature teams [2, 3] and are defined by Larman and Vodde as:

T. Dingsøyr et al. (Eds.): XP 2014 Workshops, LNBIP 199, pp. 21–29, 2014.

> "A *feature team* [...] is a long-lived, cross-functional, cross-component team
> that completes many end-to-end customer features–one by one." ([2], p. 549).

This inherent focus on business value by the team's structure contrasts structuring teams based on components as suggested by Leffingwell, who states:

> "Components are the architectural building blocks of large-scale systems. Agile teams should organize around components, each of which can be defined/built/tested by the team that is accountable for delivering it." ([4], p. 204).

Thus, instead of structuring the teams around the business value, Leffingwell suggests to structure them around architectural components. Consequently, he suggests for scaling-up and implementing what he calls an architectural runway to add more component teams. Yet, large-scale agile development should concentrate on delivering primarily customer value and not primarily components.

However, focusing on the business value still requires an architecture that allows adding features over time. Ideally, we would know upfront what kind of features will have to be added later by knowing the *intent* of the product [5]. Yet, as Kruchten clarifies:

> "In reality, in most software development projects, we define Intent gradually, and it tends to evolve throughout the project under various pressures and demands for changes." ([5], p. 7)

This implies that it is not possible to finalize the architecture upfront because the added features might force an architectural change. Thus, focusing on the business value requires that the architecture emerges or rather changes over time. In small agile teams, it is the whole team's responsibility to ensure the evolvement of the architecture without a dedicated role for an architect [1]. In large-scale agile development it is unrealistic to ask all members of the undertaking to decide on architectural issues jointly, because this could be a hundred-plus people.

In this paper, I will examine the different possibilities for supporting emergent architecture in a large environment. The architecture is labeled as emergent, for emphasizing the understanding that it is not possible to stabilize the architecture at the beginning of the undertaking. This means the architecture will change over time. After clarifying architectural complexity, section two will focus on three different models: First on the support of a relatively stable architecture which will only have to adjust to a few changes, thus on low complexity; Next on the opposite–the support for the creation of a new architecture which is accompanied by high uncertainty and frequent changes and therefore on high complexity; And finally on the complexity in between–the support for an architecture that needs to be adaptive in order to deal with some changes and a medium degree of uncertainty. In section three further issues are discussed and section four provides a final conclusion.

2   Supporting Architecture

As Leffingwell mentions:

> *"The larger and more complex the system and the higher the criticality of failure, the more the teams will need to base their daily decisions on an agreed-upon and intentional architecture [...]."* ([4], p. 202).

Leffingwell does not explain what is meant by complex, yet the statements still holds true. For example, it makes a difference if the system a team is working on is about to be created, still tremendously changing, or if it is quite stable. These differences mark the complexity of the system and subsequently as well of the architecture [6]. Kruchten emphasizes moreover, that among others the pre-existence of a stable architecture and the rate of change are important dimensions that define the context for a project [5]. The complexity that is important for addressing architectural support is expressed by the relationship between the required changes and the existing uncertainties (see Fig. 1).

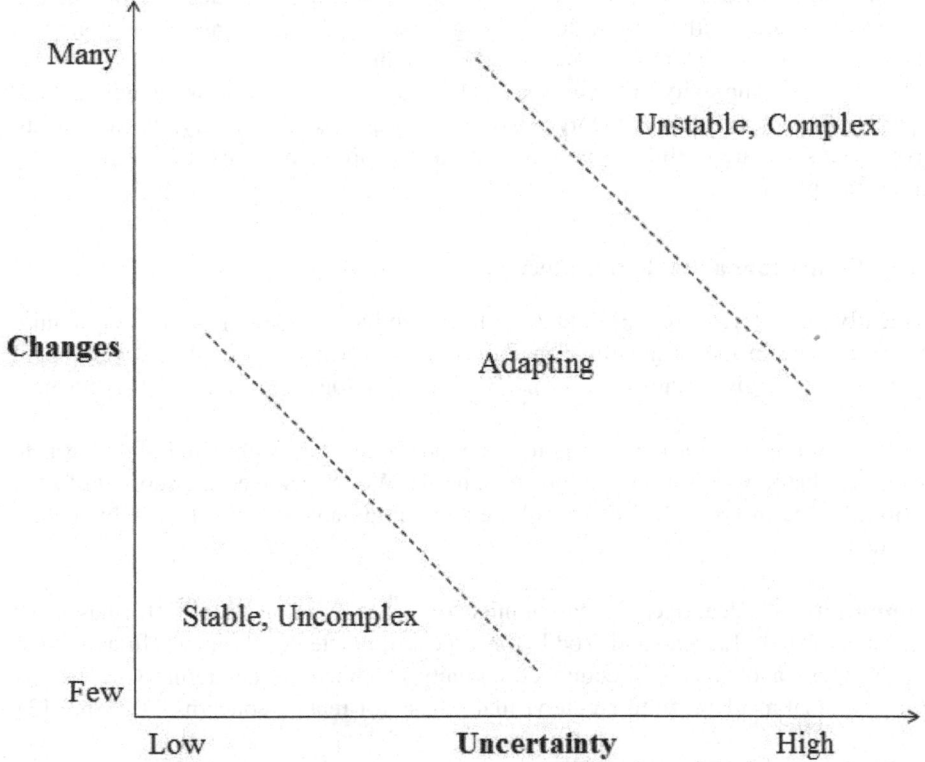

Fig. 1. Complexity of architecture based on changes and uncertainties

This expression of complexity is related to the so-called Landscape Diagram [7] which has originally been created by Stacey [8] and then further developed by Zimmerman, Lindberg, and Plsek [9]. The three subsequent models presented below, deal with those different kinds of architectural complexity.

As figure 1 shows, the complexity of the architecture is defined on the one hand by the uncertainty (x-axis) and on the other hand by the requests for changes (y-axis). According to Kruchten, uncertainty is defined by the uncertainty in the intent, e.g. the business domain; in the work, e.g. the tools or environment; the people, e.g. the know-how; and the final product [5]. For example, the business domain could be new to the developers and/or to the customer, in case the customer wants to enter a new market segment. The technology used to implement the product could be new to the team and could be additionally of cutting-edge without a lot of experiences by other projects, people, or companies. In these cases, it is very likely that uncertainty is experienced as high. The rate of change, mainly in terms of changing (business) requirements, but also in terms of tools or people influences the stability of the architecture. Thus, the architecture will be the more unstable and complex, the more changes and the higher the uncertainties are.

Subsequently will be examined what kind of support is useful for an architecture that falls in an area with only a few changes and low uncertainties; for one that is located in the area with a high rate of changes and uncertainties; and finally one that sits in between with moderate changes and uncertainty.

Examining complexity this way shall help to decide on the necessary architectural support. Thus, in relation to George Box' famous quote: "Essentially, all models are wrong, but some are useful." –here different models are more or less useful depending on the complexity.

2.1   Supporting a Stable Architecture

Typically, long-term projects and long-term product development do not require severe changes in the architecture once they are on track[1]. This kind of development is marked by high certainty in terms of the technology used and of the business requested.

Very often the major concern is to keep the architecture stable and allowing it to evolve gradually with subsequent business needs. We have solved the support of such an architecture in two different ways by either a community of practice or by a chief architect:

Community of Practice. A community of practice (CoP, see [10]) has been suggested also by Larman and Vodde for large scale agile development. In particular, they propose a design/architecture community of practice and define CoP as "an organizational mechanism to create virtual groups for related concerns." ([2], p. 313).

---

[1] Thanks to Philippe Kruchten for the following additional remark that even for the ones that are not on track, typically no severe changes are required, because performing the changes is too costly and risky (Kruchten's comment while reviewing an earlier version of this paper).

The idea is that every cross-functional feature team covers the role of an architect. This is a role and is therefore not bound to a specific person. However, in practice quite often only a few team members are willing and skilled for taking this role. Whenever an architectural decision has to be made, these "architects" of the diverse feature teams assemble (this could as well happen virtually) and decide upon the request. Sometimes the feature teams decide that the CoP meets regularly in order to monitor any changes and possible improvements within the architecture.

Chief Architect. Instead of a CoP a single person can provide the main support for the architecture. Next to being technologically skilled, the main requirement for this person is to be as well socially skilled. The chief architect (sometimes also called architecture owner) needs to work closely with all different feature teams, which requires architecting by wandering around [11]. This approach allows the chief architect (a) to understand the needs of the teams; (b) to ensure the teams understand the architecture; and (c) to help improving the architecture.

2.2 Supporting an Unstable Architecture

Starting a new project or creating a new product involves most often many uncertainties. Those uncertainties refer to the technology used, the understanding of the requirements, and making the "right" decisions both business and technology wise.

Additionally very often this uncertainty is accompanied by the fact that the team is newly assembled and has to go through different phases until it performs [12]. Moreover, if the undertaking would be started by e.g. ten teams the system would as well be split technology-wise into ten parts [13]. Thus, starting from day one e.g. with ten feature teams is not recommended.

Instead in order to scale, the system has to be enabled to scale. The recommended model for an unstable and heavily changing architecture is to establish a technical service team:

Technical Service Team. Instead of spreading the support for the architecture across all feature teams by a CoP or by asking a single person to provide that support as the chief architect, this role is taken in the context of high complexity by a specific team: A technical service team [3]. The key is that this team provides a service to the feature teams – or in other words, the customers of this team are the feature teams. This means in turn that the feature teams have to act as well as a customer and provide a product owner for that team, who decides on the priorities of the (technical) stories the feature teams require. This is the big difference to a non-agile architecture team which defines the architecture upfront (and sometimes also builds it) but is not driven by the feature teams' requests. Such kind of a non-agile architecture team is often regarded as being disconnected from reality and project members think of them of being located on an ivory tower far away from the actual needs of the projects.

Sometimes the technical service team is as well the starting team [14]. In such a situation, this team creates the base architecture founded on i.e. three key user stories which will be implemented as well by this team. Only after implementing the base architecture along with these i.e. three user stories, the feature teams will join the undertaking. Then still, depending on the complexity either the technical service team remains as described above and will be guided by a product owner representing the feature teams or the technical service team dissolves in the diverse feature teams.

2.3   Supporting an Adaptive Architecture

If both the requested changes and the uncertainty are moderate, the architecture needs as well moderate support in order to being adaptive. In this situation the architecture is not really stable.

Therefore, it needs more attention than just by a single person as the chief architect. The burden would also be too high for a CoP, because the members of the CoP would be required to synchronize continuously and to focus almost only on architectural issues. As a result, the feature teams would not be able to concentrate on the business value, because at least one of their members would have to concentrate on the architecture at all times. Thus, the recommended model is to establish a technical consulting team:

Technical Consulting Team. This is a mix of the chief architect or the CoP and the technical service team. So like the chief architect, the individual members of this team provide their support by wandering around. And like the CoP, the individual members of the technical consulting team will most often offer their support (in terms of consulting, coaching, mentoring, and pair programming) to a specific feature team during an iteration. Thus, a member of the technical consulting team will act as a regular feature team member during the course of an iteration and is as such as responsible for (or committed to) the iteration goal as every other feature team member. Yet, for the next iteration this person might support a different feature team.

But unlike the CoP, the technical consulting team is typically smaller in number than the amount of feature teams involved in the undertaking. E.g. in one project we had fifteen feature teams, yet only seven team members in the technical consulting team. Thus, not every feature team had the support of a technical consulting team member in each and every iteration. Supporting every feature team in each iteration this is typically not needed for an architecture of medium complexity.

In case a major change in the architecture is required, the technical consulting team provides this change as a service to the feature teams by implementing it, just like the technical service team.

3   Discussion

Different levels of complexity require different models for supporting the emergence of the architecture. See figure 2 for an overview of these different models.

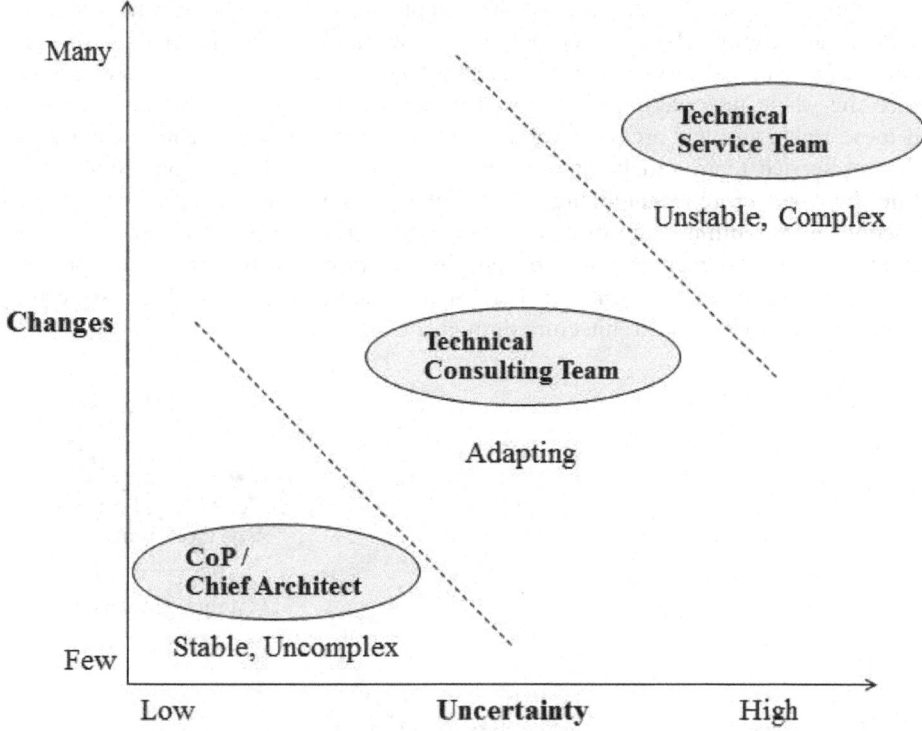

Fig. 2. Different models for architectural support depending on the complexity

The consequences of using the different models in other circumstances than recommended should not be underestimated: For example, if the system experiences many changes accompanied with high uncertainty, a single chief architect would be overwhelmed with the demands. For the feature teams this would mean, either to wait for a decision or to come up with an own one. The latter is not per se a bad idea, yet it could create the problem that different feature teams come up with contradicting solutions to similar problems. This results in breaking the conceptual integrity which in turn makes it harder for both implementing new functionality and maintaining the system.

The diverse teams (technical service team, technical consulting team, or CoP) that support the architecture can organize themselves in different ways. Some of those teams might decide on requiring a leader for the team. This person is then often perceived as the chief architect. However, it is important to distinguish this role from the chief architect in a stable environment who is not the leader of a particular team.

In many cases the complexity will change over time (see Fig. 3). Different developments of the complexity can happen, yet most often the complexity will decrease over time [5]. Most likely the uncertainty will lower, because the business domain and the technology will be better known. Frequently this results in fewer changes, because the uncertainty decreases for the customer as well over time.

As figure 3 shows, the decrease of the complexity over time affects the required architectural support. Thus, often large-scale agile development starts with the support of a technical service team. This team might even be the single starting team before the whole undertaking will be scaled up. As the architecture is getting more and more stable and less architectural services are required for the feature teams, the technical service team will be shrunk and turned into a technical consulting team. While the architecture is stabilizing even more and even fewer changes are required, the technical consulting team disappears – maybe one member remains as the chief architect, maybe all members will become members of the diverse feature teams. Either those people or different members of the feature teams will then ensure the conceptual integrity of the architecture through a CoP.

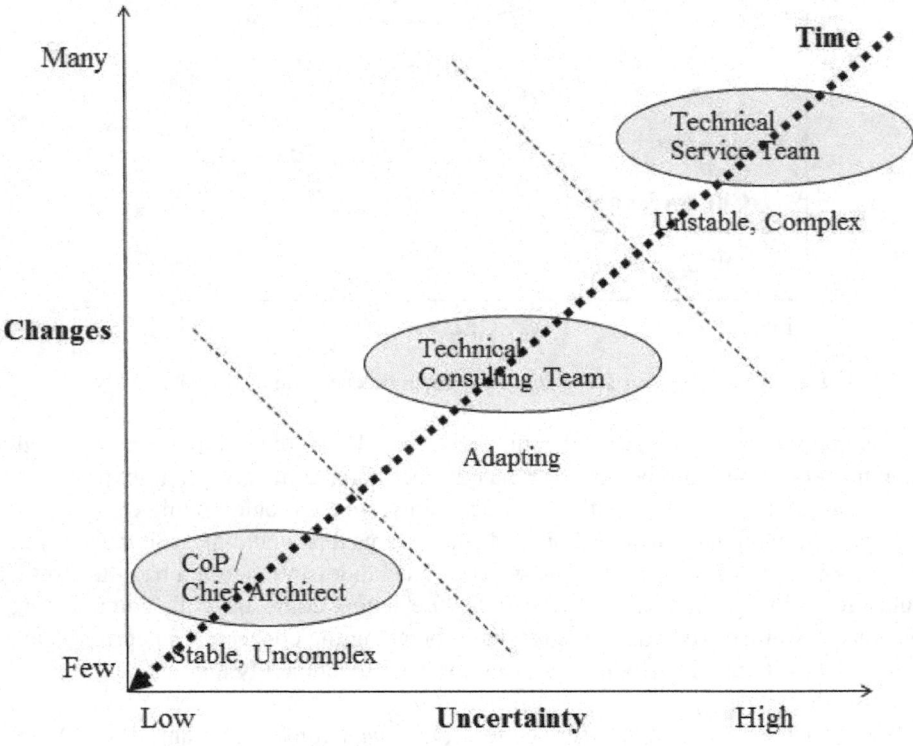

Fig. 3. Complexity decreases over time

4 Closing

Depending on the complexity –defined by the degree of uncertainty and requested changes– different models have been presented for supporting architectural support in large-scale agile development. All of these models have been applied by the author. Those models have not only been used when working on project or product development, yet as well when scaling to product line development or supporting an organization-wide architecture. Therefore, these models have as well been proven in praxis when scaling up to the whole organization and combining the efforts on supporting different architectures on a higher level.

For large-scale agile development it is essential to provide architectural support without losing focus on the business value. Yet, concentrating on the business value only leads to the loss of conceptual integrity. Thus, both dimensions –business and technology (the latter in terms of architecture) – have to be taken into account for large-scale agile development.

References

1. Sutherland, J., Schwaber, K.: The Scrum Guide. The Definitive Guide to Scrum: The Rules of the Game,
   https://www.scrum.org/Portals/0/Documents/Scrum%20Guides/2013/Scrum-Guide.pdf
2. A survey of current research on online communities of practice. Harvard Business School Press, Boston (2002)
3. Larman, C., Vodde, B.: Practices for Scaling Lean & Agile Development: Large, Multisite, and Offshore Product Development with Large-Scale Scrum. Addison-Wesley, Upper Saddle River (2010)
4. Eckstein, J.: Agile Software Development in the Large: Diving into the Deep. Dorset House Publishing, New York (2004)
5. Leffingwell, D.: Scaling Software Agility: Best Practices for Large Enterprises. Addison-Wesley, Upper Saddle River (2007)
6. Kruchten, P.: The frog and the octopus: A conceptual model of software development (2011), http://arxiv.org/pdf/1209.1327 (last accessed: June 18, 2014)
7. Eckstein, J.: Roles and Responsibilities in Feature Teams. In: Šmite, D., Moe, N.B., Ågerfalk, P.J. (eds.) Agility Across Time and Space: Implementing Agile Methods in Global Software Projects, pp. 289–299. Springer, Heidelberg (2010)
8. Holladay, R., Quade, K.: Influencing Patterns for Change. CreateSpace Independent Publishing Platform (2008)
9. Stacey, R.D.: Strategic Management and Organizational Dynamics, 2nd edn. Pitman Publishing, Berlin (1996)
10. Wenger, E.C., McDermott, R., Snyder, W.M.: Cultivating Communities
11. Zimmerman, B., Lindberg, C., Plsek, P.: Edgeware: lessons from complexity science for health care leaders. V H A Incorporated (Curt Lindberg, Plexus Institute) (2008)
12. Peters, T., Waterman, R.H.: Search of Excellence, 2nd edn. Profile Books Ltd. (2004)
13. Tuckman, B.: Developmental sequence in small groups. Psychological Bulletin (63) (1965)
14. Conway, M.E.: How Do Committees Invent? Datamation 14(4) (1968)
15. Eckstein, J.: Agile Software Development with Distributed Teams: Staying Agile in a Global World. Dorset House Publishing, New York (2010)

Industrial Challenges of Scaling Agile in Mass-Produced Embedded Systems

Ulrik Eklund[1], Helena Holmström Olsson[1], and Niels Jørgen Strøm[2]

[1] Dept. Computer Science, School of Technology, Malmö University
SE-205 06 Malmö, Sweden
{ulrik.eklund,helena.holmstrom.olsson}@mah.se
[2] Grundfos A/S
DK-8850 Bjerringbro, Denmark
njstroem@grundfos.com

Abstract When individual teams in mechatronic organizations attempt to adopt agile software practices, these practices tend to only affect modules or sub-systems. The short iterations on team level do not lead to short lead-times in launching new or updated products since the overall R&D approach on an organization level is still governed by an overall stage gate or single cycle V-model.

This paper identifies challenges for future research on how to combine the predictability and planning desired of mechanical manufacturing with the dynamic capabilities of modern agile software development. Scaling agile in this context requires an expansion in two dimensions: First, scaling the number of involved teams. Second, traversing necessary systems engineering activities in each sprint due to the co-dependency of software and hardware development.

Keywords: software engineering, agile development, agile methods, large-scale agile software development, project management, embedded systems, embedded software, software and hardware co-dependency.

1   Introduction

The embedded systems industry is currently in significant transition, i.e. markets becoming more fast-changing and unpredictable, customer requirements becoming increasingly complex, rapidly advancing technologies and the constant need to shorten time-to-market of new products. Moreover, while the ability to manufacture high-quality mechanical systems is still critical, it is no longer the only differentiator and what makes a company competitive. During the last two decades, electronics and software have been introduced into many products, and embedded systems companies are becoming increasingly software-intensive with software being the key differentiator [1]. This requires a significant shift in the ways-of-working within these companies, and currently many large companies within the embedded systems domain struggle with the alignment of hardware and software development cycles and practices [1].

T. Dingsøyr et al. (Eds.): XP 2014 Workshops, LNBIP 199, pp. 30–42, 2014.

In response to this, agile methods advocating flexibility, efficiency and speed are seen as an increasingly attractive solution [2], and highly relevant also in the embedded Systems domain [3]. Typically, agile methods emphasize the use of short iterations and incremental development of small features, with the intention to increases the ability for companies to accommodate fast changing customer requirements as well as turbulent and fluctuating market needs [2,4].

However, when agile practices are introduced for software teams in a mechatronics environment without careful consideration it just results in different development cycle-times for hardware, and even more so in mechanics, compared to software development, with the longest cycle determining the lead-time for the complete product. For production equipment depending on the product design it becomes even worse, because investments and lead-times for the manufacturing setup are even more difficult to do with short iterations. This is the main difference between scaling agile in domains where only software teams are concerned, and in embedded domains also concerned with mechanical design and manufacturing.

This position paper presents a set of research challenges relevant when agile practices are scaled beyond a single team in organisations developing and delivering mass-produced embedded systems and into combining mechanical, hardware and software disciplines in the agile practices. The challenges are based on concerns of member companies in a Nordic research partnership with eight international industry companies and three universities.

2   Empirical Data

The main empirical data source for the challenges identified in this paper was a workshop conducted within a Nordic software research partnership[1] in November 2013, where seven companies presented their most important research challenges within software engineering. Three of the companies mentioned a set of challenges with agile development in large organisations as a top priority for future research within the partnership. The challenges presented in this paper are a synthesis of these presented challenges, elucidated by examples from two of the companies; Grundfos and Volvo Cars.

Grundfos is the world's largest manufacturer of circulator pumps, many controlled by embedded software. The examples provided for this paper from Grundfos serves to highlight the challenges all companies experienced in combining agile and waterfall development in a mechatronics environment; where there are different development cycle-times for hardware, and even more so in mechanics, compared to software. For production equipment depending on the product design it becomes even worse because investments and lead-times for the manufacturing setup are even more difficult to do with short iterations.

The synthesized challenges were also corroborated by data from three in-depth case studies on agile development at Volvo Cars, another of the partnership companies; the cases being published in e.g. [5].

---

[1] http://www.software-center.se

3   Background

3.1   Software in Embedded Products

Software is prevalent in many products manufactured today; cars, washing machines, mobile phones, airplanes, satellites and industrial devices, e.g. pumps [6]. The embedded software controls the behaviour of the product and is most often critical for the success of the product. Typically these products are developed in large, and sometimes very complex, industrial projects with a more or less elaborate R&D process governed by a stage gate model to arrive at the finished design of the product. Even though many companies are in a transition towards delivering services deployed on already delivered hardware and mechanics, they still heavily rely on the financial transaction taking place when the physical product goes from the company to the customer.

The software in an embedded system increases in size exponentially over time [6], and software is increasingly so being a crucial element and one of the most important drivers for innovations, e.g. in the car industry [7] and the pump industry. But the manufacturing and delivery setup of a new car or pump model is presently still a heavier investment than the software budget. A product example from Grundfos shows that the software budget for a new pump was between 5 and 10% of the total project investments.

The most common approach to develop embedded software, according to a mapping study [8], is to use an integration-centric approach, summarized as: Early in the development cycle requirements are allocated to software and hardware components. This is usual done by a central systems engineering team or architect. A number of development teams then implement the requirements allocated to their component. All of the teams are usually synchronized according to a common project model. After the finalization of the components the integration phase starts where all components are integrated to form the complete systems and system level testing takes place, where most integration problems are found and resolved [9]. This cycle may repeat 1-5 times, and it is common that the integration points in time are scheduled according to a stage-gate model [10]. An integration cycle is typically six months or more, meaning that a development project can have a lead-time of multiple years.

Example from the Pump Domain. Grundfos typically defines 4 to 6 review series of a PCB design to ensure quality before launching a new product. This approach is agile on the team level, and every cycle takes between 4 and 8 weeks dependent on complexity and where in the process the cycle takes place.

At the system integration level (integrating the product with other related products in a system) an example from Grundfos of a complex system showed a total integration and test phase of 9 months with additional bug fix cycles afterwards - giving a single integration and test phase of approximately a year. This leads to a lead-time before production could start measured in years, rather than months.

3.2   Mechanical and Hardware Development

The typical culture of company with a heavy tradition of mechanical engineering is to focus on predictability and doing so by trying to foresee activities many months ahead because of the constraints linked to mechanical manufacturing. Traditionally mechatronics manufacturing companies freeze the design at a certain point in a stage-gate model and after that the mechanical design does not change, instead focus it's activities on optimizing the manufacturing, sales and delivery processes. The purpose of the stage gate model is, at certain stages, to ensure the feasibility of releasing large investments, not only for development but in particular for manufacturing. Developing a mechanical part for a product often includes developing and investing in very expensive manufacturing tools with long lead times, expanding the development cycle for mechanics to up to 12 months or more. If the company is already established in a mature domain, e.g. the car industry, these type of activities are highly optimized, with much know-how of the company directed to running such projects.

Software may be strongly dependent on mechanical structures because of software modelling etc. and since there is a very weak link between software and mechanics cycle times (typically weeks vs. many months) the final verification of the software/mechanics interface cannot take place until much later, even if models, simulations and fast prototyping such as e.g. 3D printing is utilized. Sometimes this late verification can lead to less optimal solutions where issues are solved in software even though they would have been better solved in mechanics, had it been possible to use an agile approach.

3.3   Agile Software Development

For more than a decade, agile development methods have gained much popularity and become widely recognized within the field of software engineering. The methods promise shorter time-to-market, as well as higher flexibility to accomodate changes in requirments and thereby, increase companies' ability to react and respond to evolving customer and market needs [4,11,12]. While there are a number of different agile methods, they typically emphasize close customer collaboration, iterative development and small cross-functional development teams. Also, team autonomy and end-to-end responsibility are reported as important characteristics permeating the methods [13]. As recognized by Kettunen and Laanti [14], the concept of agile is multi-dimensional, and there are many reasons for companies to adopt agile ways-of-working. Typically, most companies introduce agile methods to increase the frequency in which they release new features and new products, and as a way to improve their software engineering efficiency. According to Dingsøyr et al. [15] agility embraces lean processes with an emphasis on realizing effective outcomes, and common for agile methods is that they entail the ability to rapidly and flexibly create and respond to change in the business and technical domains [15].

Today, there exist a number of different agile methods, with Extreme programming (XP) and Scrum being the two most common ones. XP focuses on the programming practice itself and prescribes a set of practices for developers, e.g. pair programming and continuous unit testing. In addition, it includes practices such as user stories and iterative planning as a support for management in their requirements prioritization processes [16]. Scrum, on the other hand, focuses more on the process for the development team, i.e. how to prioritize, track and optimize team performance, and how to continuously evaluate and follow-up with the customer what is being implemented [17]. Although different in focus, both these methods emphasize the importance of working in short sprints, to constantly reprioritize what is being developed, and to test and validate new software functionality in rapid cycles.

Originally, agile methods evolved to meet the needs of small and co-located development teams [14]. Currently, and due to many successful accounts [18,19] agile methods have become attractive to a broad variety of companies, including companies involved in large-scale development of embedded systems, and there are attempts such as Industrial XP and Scrum of Scrums aiming at scaling agile methods [20]. However, with characteristics such as hardware-software interdependencies, heavy compliance to standards and regulations, and limited flexibility due to real-time functionality [21], development of embedded systems challenges the traditional concept of agile practices.

3.4   Agile Development of Embedded Software

Currently, companies producing embedded systems are in the process of deploying agile methods, and several attempts to scale agile methods to include development of mass-produced systems can be identified [22,20,23].

Some organizations developing mass-produced system have successfully introduced agile development on the team level where individual teams are allowed to define their own ways of working to facilitate speed, short iterations and delivery quality when developing their components. The experiences of doing this are generally positive according to two literature studies by [3] and [24].

However, the applicability of agile methods is not without challenges in large-scale development of software intended for mass-produced systems [25]. Companies also often discover misalignments between the agile methods and their already established ways-of-working when attempting to adopt agile practices in a large-scale setting [26]. One reason is that many large-scale development companies practice agile in a way that is not consistent with the original agile ideas, and that the translation of the original ideas to a context of mass-production is difficult.

Ronkainen and Abrahamsson [27] identified four main characteristics that would affect adoption of agile methods under strict hardware constraints, typical of most embedded systems:

- Meeting hard real-time requirements, e.g. performance
- Experimenting is part of the systems development, many technological constraints are difficult to ascertain until actual hardware and mechanics is available.

- High-level designs and executable documentation are not sufficient, information shared between teams tend to be detailed and implementation-specific
- Embedded development is test driven by nature, but some of the core ideas of
agile are problematic to implement when doing software/hardware co-design
(e.g. write tests first, run every unit test at least daily)

Greene [28] describes how elements from Scrum and XP were used in a firmware project to deal with changing hardware interfaces for a new family of 64-
bit microprocessors. Some of the constraints they had to satisfy were; consistent
firmware interfaces across the entire processor family, architecture features that
are better, cheaper, or more flexibly implemented in firmware than hardware,
and workarounds for processor errata. Some of the challenges they had to deal
with were

- Turnaround time for silicon from the factory of more than a month.
- Detailed quarterly planning of schedules, which quickly became obsolete.
- Too specialized team members will little cross-domain firmware knowledge.
- lack of test coverage, and no regression tests when changes were made. Re-
liance on outside groups to find problems.
- Poor code maintainability, due to overly optimized and complex code.

Cordciro et al. [29] proposes an agile method for developing embedded software under stringent hardware constraints. The aim to: Resolve the trade-off
between flexibility and performance, fulfill hardware constraints, support a flow
from specification to implementation, propose novel test techniques, and use an
incremental approach where the developer can validate a system specification
in each iteration. They solve this by proposing three sets of parallel processes
organized in three process groups: System Platform Processes, Product Development Processes, and Product Management Processes. The method assumes
that a system designer chooses the system components from an already existing
platform library to instantiate a given product. Both this and the previous example only concerned a very limited number of involved developers, less than 10
developers in 1-2 teams.

A conclusion is that teams in an integration-centric organization that attempt
to adopt agile software practices have difficulties in scaling them beyond the team
level. The adopted agile practices typically only affect modules or sub-systems,
as seen in figure 1 below. The product as a whole is still developed with an
integration-centric approach, as described in section 3.1, with the mechanics
and manufacturing schedules also controlling the software development.

Even if agile teams try to follow a platform-oriented approach focusing on
developing prioritized cross product features, individual stage-gate projects still
require a certain amount of functionality bound to product-specific hardware
and mechanics. This makes the agile overall prioritization process difficult to
perform. One or two major products with large investments can draw all the
attention making it difficult to do the right prioritization of feature development
across the full range of products.

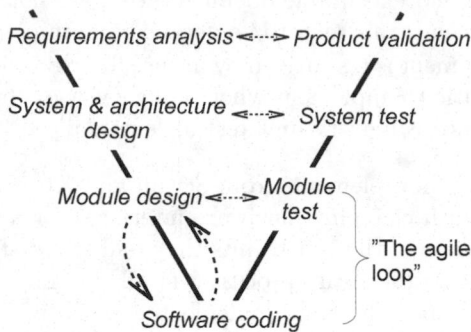

Fig. 1. The agile iteration on team level seen in the context of a typical systems engineering approach

The shift towards agile is complex for companies developing embedded systems since they are often used to heavyweight sequential processes also outside of R&D; additional challenges are e.g:

- dependencies to a number of suppliers and sub-contractors [5], with some software subcontractors tied up in sourcing agreements,
- software interfacing with hardware and mechanics, and
- certification processes.

As a result the development teams need to spend effort to align the internal team practices to the overall product development and release processes (see e.g. [30]). All this also means that the short iterations on team level do not lead to short lead-times in launching new or updated products.

4   Industrial Challenges of Scaling Agile

The key agile principle of delivering software frequently [31] contrasts with the situation described in section 3.4.

The long-term prediction and associated lead-times forced upon software development teams in this context leads to lack of flexibility in case market needs change during the development project. If an organisation was fully adhering to all agile principles it would in theory be possible to deploy new software throughout the entire life-cycle of the product if economically viable.

Not being able to exploit agile software development and adapting stage-gate models to agile software development also leads to a continuation of notoriously poor predictability when developing software, something which is prevalent also for embedded software.

4.1   Challenge of Uniting Agility with Stage-Gate Development

The principal challenge is how to combine the planning and achieved predictability associated with mechanical manufacturing with the dynamic planning capabilities of modern agile software development; in practice this means large mechatronics companies need to solve the challenge of how to scale agile software development beyond short iterations on the team level.

This challenge is a major obstacle to allowing differentiated lead-times towards start of production (SOP) depending on the size or complexity of the wanted software features rather than depending on investments in mechanical manufacturing according to a stage-gate process. Rephrased; it means that while the start of the product project is demanded by the activities necessary for mechanical and manufacturing development, the development of a specific software feature can start independently of this while still aiming at the same SOP, as seen in figure 2.

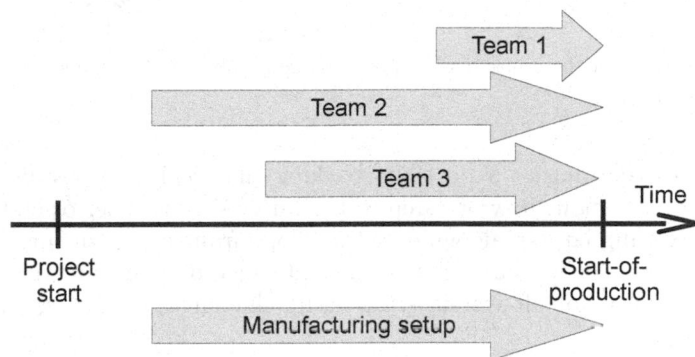

Fig. 2. Different sub-projects are allowed differentiated lead-times towards Start-of-Production (or start-of-deployment)

4.2   Challenge of Scaling the Number of Involved Teams

Scaling agile in this context is a challenge in two dimensions, as seen in figure 3: First, scaling the number of involved teams, this is usually what ?scaling? in the context of agile means. Second, scaling up the necessary system engineering activities in the iterations/sprints prescribed by different agile methodologies.

A complex product today, e.g. a car, has up to a hundred development teams doing software and embedded development, and twice that numer of teams doing mechanical development. Currently these teams are synchronized by all adhering to the same schedule according to a stage-gate process. The need for such large-scale development requires mid range and long range planning mechanisms beyond the standard sprint pattern of plan/commit, execute, and demo/adapt used for individual teams [32]. Typically such mechanisms involve release planning and road mapping of product portfolios, as described by the Scaled Agile Framework [32] or by Disciplined Agile Delivery [33].

The Scaled Agile Framework[2] presents guidelines on how to plan releases when demanded, while the individual teams work and deliver continuously in agile iterations. The involved teams are part of an agile release train that provides the program-level value according to the program backlog. These program backlogs

---

[2] http://scaledagileframework.com/

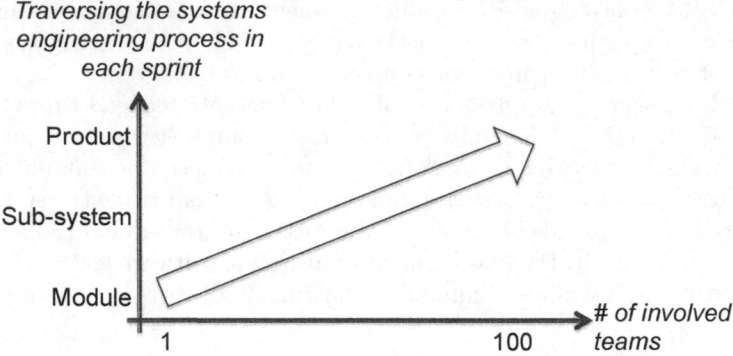

Fig. 3. Scaling agile in the context of mass-produced embedded systems is a challenge in two dimensions

are prioritized according to a portfolio backlog that realize the value streams that proved a continuous flow of value to the business, customer or end user.

However, existing large-scale agile methodology frameworks such as these do not address the challenges particular to the embedded domain (identified by e.g. [27]), and especially not all system engineering challenges regarding large-scale manufacturing.

4.3   Challenge of Scaling System Engineering Activities

The second dimension in figure 3 is traversing the systems engineering process in each sprint, i.e. not being confined to iterate each module separately in each sprint, but also allow re-prioritization of system-wide features and properties. This means that each team must have the ability or support to perform activities at all abstraction levels in the V-model in figure 1, for example doing system wide tests. This second dimension is what distinguishes agile development in mass-produced embedded systems, and can be considered the novel research challenge.

A trivial example of a system engineering activity in a sprint would be if it is necessary to have access to a physical property, such as fluid flow or temperature, in order to realize a specific feature. A system engineering choice would be to either try to estimate this based on other data or to use a sensor to directly measure the physical value with higher accuracy. The former choice could be implemented purely in software, while the latter would entail a change in the physical and electronics design of the system, incurring a cost, and possibly a lead-time, penalty. In a safety-critical system both choices may be necessary to implement for redundancy.

A related difficulty in this dimension concerns cross-functional team expertise and component interdependencies [25]. Usually, organizations realize that many components in a large-scale system are technically very difficult and interdependent, and require years of experience to be fully understood by developers. To solve this they therefore often organize in specialist or component teams with exclusive access rights to key components occasionally leading to bottle-neck situations. This is in contrast with the basics of agile where teams are self-contained and are able to solve their tasks independently in each sprint. As a result, many large-scale organizations experience long lead times before the development teams can implement anything useful in a component.

5 Discussion on Solutions

Our preliminary assumption is that the solutions to the challenges above not only lies within the process dimension, it is a question of implementing agile practices on an enterprise scale. We therefore expect a holistic approach is needed, weighing in business, architectural, and organizational aspects, besides scaled processes.

Typical software architectures for embedded systems are monolithic, having a static structure for every instantiation and variation is achieved by variation points in the components, usually by de-selecting code. An architecture that supports continuous integrations, including system tests, must probably be based on composition instead, allowing a creative selection and configuration of components and most of the tailoring towards specific products is achieved through different component configurations developed by various agile teams.

Some other architectural patterns supporting large-scale agile systems development would be suitable hardware device abstractions, and mechanism allowing for device composition supporting necessary security and safety integrity levels. However, monitoring of architectural and/or organizational dependencies and subsequent actions to resolve these dependencies is necessary. For example, even if proper hardware abstractions are made, new functionality may require new low level features to be implemented by the aforementioned component/specialist team causing dependency problems to the team implementing a new customer feature. Causes for this could both be architectural and organizational. Remedies to consider for mitigating this could be refactoring, spreading the necessary knowledge, establishing mentors to be able to immediately stand in and facilitate what is necessary, establish task force capacity, and these activities need to be iterative as well.

Martini et al. [34] identifies factors that inhibit the speed of organisations with a large number of small, independent and fast teams. The teams suffer from excessive inter-team interactions, which may lead to paralysis. Some of their recommendations to manage such factors, complementing current agile practices, are establishing cross-team roles with part-time domain experts and architects, and allow for programmed available time for other concerns, and not only synchronizing e.g. planning among SCRUM masters.

6 Summary

Mechanical and manufacturing development have very long lead-times compared to software development iterations of 2-6 weeks, reconciling this is a challenge when shortening lead-times towards start-of-production. The goal would be to allow differentiated lead-times towards SOP depending on the size or complexity of the wanted software features, i.e. the development of a specific software feature can start independently of other features while still aiming at the same SOP. Related to this overall challenge we identified a number of additional challenges:

- Embedded system companies have already established ways-of-working for systems engineering which need to be considered.
- Individual stage gate product projects still require a certain amount of functionality bound to product-specific hardware and mechanics making a platform approach with agile overall prioritization difficult to perform.

Scaling agile software development in this context is then a question of scaling agile in two dimensions: First increasing the involved number of teams and utilize agile practices for mid- and long-range planning such as release planning and road mapping. Many large-scale development companies practice agile in a way that is not consistent with the original agile ideas, and that the translation of the original ideas to a context of mass-production is difficult. This is already a growing research field, as seen in [35], which gives some examples of smaller challenges:

- To coordinate work between agile teams.
- To effectively structure the organization and collaborate in large projects, especially when the organization is distributed.
- To plan large projects and control the scope.
- To understand the role of architecture in large-scale agile.

Second, scaling the system engineering activities executed in each sprint, to a truly iterative practice instead of a stage-gated planned approach. A cross-functional team must have the ability or support to perform activities at several abstraction levels in a systems engineering V-model in each iteration or sprint. This is a novel challenge, particular to the embedded domain. We can see a set of associated challenges that needs to be addressed in this domain, regardless of project size:

- Embedded systems have specific product requirements, e.g. safety, which are not obviously addressed by agile practices such as XP or Scrum.
- The feedback loop with customers and management is quite long due to the business model of delivering physical products in exchange of a financial transaction, and manufacturing constraints how short this can be.
- Mechanical and manufacturing development emphasises long-term predictability, and is usually successful in achieving this. This contrasts with the desire of short-term agility and poor long-term predictability of software development.
- Component interdependencies affect cross-functional teams requiring special expertise. Components in a large-scale system are technically very difficult and interdependent, and require years of experience to be fully understood by developers.

The call to action is to broaden the research on scaling agile to address the identified challenges particular to developing mass-produced embedded systems, and thus solving actual industrial needs.

References

1. Bosch, J., Eklund, U.: Eternal embedded software: Towards innovation experiment systems. In: Dingsøyr, T., Moe, N.B., Counsell, S., Tonelli, R., Gencel, C., Petersen, K. (eds.) ISoLA 2012, Part I. LNCS, vol. 7609, pp. 19–31. Springer, Heidelberg (2012)

2. Dzamashvili Fogelström, N., Gorschek, T., Svahnberg, M., Olsson, P.: The impact of agile principles on market-driven software product development. Journal of Software Maintenance and Evolution: Research and Practice 22(1), 53–80 (2010)

3. Albuquerque, C.O., Antonino, P.O., Nakagawa, E.Y.: An investigation into agile methods in embedded systems development. In: Murgante, B., Gervasi, O., Misra, S., Nedjah, N., Rocha, A.M.A.C., Taniar, D., Apduhan, B.O. (eds.) ICCSA 2012, Part III. LNCS, vol. 7335, pp. 576–591. Springer, Heidelberg (2012)

4. Williams, L., Cockburn, A.: Agile software development: It's about feedback and change. Computer 36(6), 39–43 (2003)

5. Eklund, U., Bosch, J.: Applying agile development in mass-produced embedded systems. In: Wohlin, C. (ed.) XP 2012. LNBIP, vol. 111, pp. 31–46. Springer, Heidelberg (2012)

6. Ebert, C., Jones, C.: Embedded software: Facts, figures, and future. Computer 42(4), 42–52 (2009)

7. Broy, M.: Challenges in automotive software engineering. In: Proceedings of the International Conference on Software Engineering, Shanghai, China, pp. 33–42. ACM (2006)

8. Eklund, U., Bosch, J.: Archetypical approaches of fast software development and slow embedded projects. In: Proceedings of the Euromicro Conference on Software Engineering and Advanced Applications, Santander, Spain, pp. 276–283. IEEE (2013)

9. Bosch, J., Bosch-Sijtsema, P.: From integration to composition: On the impact of software product lines, global development and ecosystems. Journal of Systems and Software 83(1), 67–76 (2010)

10. Cooper, R.: Stage-gate systems: A new tool for managing new products. Business Horizons 33(3), 44–54 (1990)

11. Larman, C., Vodde, B.: Scaling Lean & Agile Development: Thinking and Organizational Tools for Large-Scale Scrum, 1st edn. Addison-Wesley Professional (2008)

12. Highsmith, J., Cockburn, A.: Agile software development: The business of innovation. Computer 34(9), 120–127 (2001)

13. Dybå, T., Dingsøyr, T.: Empirical studies of agile software development: A systematic review. Information and Software Technology 50(9-10), 833–859 (2008)

14. Kettunen, P., Laanti, M.: Combining agile software projects and large-scale organizational agility. Software Process: Improvement and Practice 13(2), 183–193 (2008)

15. Dingsøyr, T., Nerur, S., Balijepally, V., Moe, N.B.: A decade of agile methodologies: Towards explaining agile software development. Journal of Systems and Software 85(6), 1213–1221 (2012)

16. Beck, K.: Extreme programming: A humanistic discipline of software development. In: Astesiano, E. (ed.) ETAPS 1998 and FASE 1998. LNCS, vol. 1382, pp. 1–6. Springer, Heidelberg (1998)

17. Schwaber, K.: Scrum development process. In: Proceedings of the ACM Conference on Object Oriented Programming Systems, Languages, and Applications, pp. 117–134 (1995)

18. Abrahamsson, P., Warsta, J., Siponen, M., Ronkainen, J.: New directions on agile methods: A comparative analysis. In: Proceedings of the International Conference on Software Engineering, pp. 244–254 (2003)
19. Holmström Olsson, H., Alahyari, H., Bosch, J.: Climbing the "stairway to heaven". In: Proceeding of the Euromicro Conference on Software Engineering and Advanced Applications, Cesme, Izmir, Turkey (2012)
20. McMahon, P.: Extending agile methods: A distributed project and organizational improvement perspective. In: Systems and Software Technology Conference (2005)
21. Kaisti, M., Mujunen, T., Mäkilä, T., Rantala, V., Lehtonen, T.: Agile principles in the embedded system development. In: Cantone, G., Marchesi, M. (eds.) XP 2014. LNBIP, vol. 179, pp. 16–31. Springer, Heidelberg (2014)
22. Kerievsky, J.: Industrial XP: Making XP work in large organizations. Executive Report. Cutter Consortium, 6(2) (2005)
23. Lagerberg, L., Skude, T., Emanuelsson, P., Sandahl, K., Stahl, D.: The impact of agile principles and practices on large-scale software development projects: A multiple-case study of two projects at ericsson. In: ACM/IEEE International Symposium on Empirical Software Engineering and Measurement, Baltimore, MD, USA, pp. 348–356 (2013)
24. Shen, M., Yang, W., Rong, G., Shao, D.: Applying agile methods to embedded software development: A systematic review. In: Proceedings of the International Workshop on Software Engineering for Embedded Systems, pp. 30–36. IEEE (2012)
25. Heikkilä, V.T., Paasivaara, M., Lassenius, C., Engblom, C.: Continuous release planning in a large-scale scrum development organization at ericsson. In: Baumeister, H., Weber, B. (eds.) XP 2013. LNBIP, vol. 149, pp. 195–209. Springer, Heidelberg (2013)
26. Badampudi, D., Fricker, S.A., Moreno, A.M.: Perspectives on productivity and delays in large-scale agile projects. In: Baumeister, H., Weber, B. (eds.) XP 2013. LNBIP, vol. 149, pp. 180–194. Springer, Heidelberg (2013)
27. Ronkainen, J., Abrahamsson, P.: Software development under stringent hardware constraints: Do agile methods have a chance? In: Marchesi, M., Succi, G. (eds.) XP 2003. LNCS, vol. 2675, pp. 73–79. Springer, Heidelberg (2003)
28. Greene, B.: Agile methods applied to embedded firmware development. In: Proceedings of the Agile Development Conference, pp. 71–77. IEEE Computer Society (2004)
29. Cordeiro, L., Mar, C., Valentin, E., Cruz, F., Patrick, D., Barreto, R., Lucena, V.: An agile development methodology applied to embedded control software under stringent hardware constraints. SIGSOFT Softw. Eng. Notes 33(1), 5:1–5:10 (2008)
30. Karlström, D., Runeson, P.: Integrating agile software development into stage-gate managed product development. Empirical Software Engineering 11(2), 203–225 (2006)
31. Beck, K., Beedle, M., van Bennekum, A., Cockburn, A., Cunningham, W., Fowler, M., Grenning, J., Highsmith, J., Hunt, A., Jeffries, R., Kern, J., Marick, B., Martin, R.C., Mellor, S., Schwaber, K., Sutherland, J., Thomas, D.: Manifesto for agile software development (2001)
32. Leffingwell, D.: Agile Software Requirements: Lean Requirements Practices for Teams, Programs, and the Enterprise, 1st edn. Addison-Wesley (2011)
33. Ambler, S.W., Lines, M.: Disciplined Agile Delivery, 1st edn. IBM Press (2012)
34. Martini, A., Pareto, L., Bosch, J.: Improving businesses success by managing interactions among agile teams in large organizations. In: Herzwurm, G., Margaria, T. (eds.) ICSOB 2013. LNBIP, vol. 150, pp. 60–72. Springer, Heidelberg (2013)
35. Dingsøyr, T., Moe, N.B.: Research challenges in large-scale agile software development. SIGSOFT Softw. Eng. Notes 38(5), 38–39 (2013)

Agile in Distress: Architecture to the Rescue

Robert L. Nord[1], Ipek Ozkaya[1], and Philippe Kruchten[2]

[1] Carnegie Mellon Software Engineering Institute, Pittsburgh, PA, USA
{rn,ozkaya}@sei.cmu.edu
[2] Electrical & Computer Engineering, University of British Columbia, Vancouver, Canada
pbk@ece.ubc.ca

Abstract. For large-scale software-development endeavors, agility is enabled by architecture, and vice versa. The iterative, risk-driven life cycle inherent in agile approaches allows developers to focus early on key architectural decisions, spread these decisions over time, and validate architectural solutions early. Conversely, an early focus on architecture allows a large agile project to define an implementation structure that drives an organization into small teams, some focusing on common elements and their key relationships and some working more autonomously on features. Architects in agile software development typically work on three distinct but interdependent structures: architecture of the system, the structure of the development organization, and the production infrastructure. Architectural work supports the implementation of high-priority business features without risking excessive redesign later or requiring heavy coordination between teams. Architectural *tactics* provide a framework for identifying key concerns and guide the alignment of these three structures throughout the development life cycle.

Keywords: agile, architecture, organizational structure, production infrastructure, large-scale agile software development, software engineering, project management.

1   Introduction

Agile software-development approaches have provided notable improvements over more rigid, phased, document-intensive approaches. This should not be surprising: many of the practices that the Agile Manifesto encourages had existed for a while, but first the mindset of software design and development practitioners had to shift. These approaches now emphasize trust, face-to-face communication, and less formal artifacts coupled with new technologies for computer-supported communication and development environments. Agile approaches work well for projects in a "sweet spot" with certain enabling characteristics: small teams of 5–12, preferably collocated; a stable underlying architecture; frequent deliveries; and low to medium criticality of the system. But the question "how do we scale 'agile' to larger, bolder software-development endeavors?" is still repeatedly asked.

In this paper, we define *large scale* by scope of the system, team size, and project duration. At a large scale, the scope of the system touches several domains and has

T. Dingsøyr et al. (Eds.): XP 2014 Workshops, LNBIP 199, pp. 43–57, 2014.
© Springer International Publishing Switzerland 2014

some combination of interoperability, security, and performance concerns. The size of a development team is more than 18 people, partitioned into a few teams, and likely to be geographically distributed. And the duration of the development typically extends beyond a year.

There are many possible answers to the questions "how do we scale agile up?" and "how do we use it outside of its sweet spot?" They often take the form of modifying an agile practice to make it work "at scale." The typical example is the daily standup meeting, or *Scrum*, scaled up to a *Scrum of Scrums*. But this may be a solution to a different problem. The real problem is how to be agile at the organization level, not simply how to scale individual practices (even if the latter may support the former).

In this paper, we demonstrate that an early and continuous focus on the *architecture* of the system enables scaling up agile development and minimizing unanticipated roadblocks. If we define *agility* as the ability of an organization to rapidly react to change in its environment [1], [2], then we can restate the problems as follows:

- Can the architecture of the product support multiple waves of enhancements, to accommodate a constant flow of new needs?
- Can the architecture evolve continuously to support enhancements?
- Does the architecture allow teams to organize the work so that they feel as if they were in the sweet spot and allow them to take advantage of agile practices?
- Can the organization avoid the extra work generated by repetitive handover from a development team to an operations group?

2 Why Scale Necessitates Architecture

Architecture is the high-level structure of a software system, the discipline of creating such a high-level structure, and the documentation of this structure [3]. The architecture of a software system is a metaphor, analogous to the architecture of a building [4]. Agile teams sometimes fear architecture as a remnant of some ugly past, decry it as "big design upfront" (BDUF), and naïvely hope that a suitable architecture will gradually emerge out of weekly refactorings. While "refactoring has emerged as an important software engineering technique, it is not a replacement for sound architectural design; if an architecture is decent you can improve it, but refactored junk is still junk" [5]. We know that at-scale development needs a healthy, proactive, and early focus on both system architecture and software architecture.

Architecture provides a way to partition work around large chunks of software development, guiding the organization into teams. This often takes the form of one or more "infrastructure" teams supporting one or more "feature" teams. Conflicts in software development are reduced when there is an overall socio-technical congruence between the structure of the system and the structure of the teams. This allows the creation of islands of stability in which teams can operate in a mode that is closer to the agile sweet spot, and possibly at a faster iteration rhythm. But architecture also provides other benefits to a large, distributed project:

- a common vocabulary and a common culture to speak about the system and how it functions. This was the intent of the "metaphor" practice of the original XP.
- a systematic way to control dependencies—of code, data, timing, and requirements—which tend to grow uncontrolled in large projects.
- a way to keep technical debt in check, by identifying and gradually reducing technical debt at the structural or architectural level, which is the second type of debt in McConnell's taxonomy [6].
- a guide for release planning and configuration management.

When projects scale up on all three dimensions of scope, team size, and duration, software developers need tools to organize the work, make the right decisions, communicate these decisions, implement and validate them, and define guidelines and processes applicable across the project. These tools do not exist in the traditional toolkit of Scrum, XP, and lean, but they can be found in the architects' toolkit.

When working at scale, the agile community begins in small ways to acknowledge the need for architecture, and even sometimes for an architect (or "architecture owner," as a counterpart to the "product owner"), as, for example, in Cockburn's Walking Skeleton [7] and the architectural runway of the Scaled Agile Framework [8]. We have seen increasing evidence in practice where successful teams tailor architecture with agile approaches [9], [10], [11].

In practice, architects in agile software development typically work on three distinct but interdependent structures (Fig.1):

- The *Architecture* (A) of the system under design, development, or refinement, what we have called the traditional system or software architecture.
- The *Structure* (S) of the organization: teams, partners, subcontractors, and others.
- The *Production infrastructure* (P) used to develop and deploy the system, the last activity being especially important in contexts where the development and operations are combined and the system is deployed more or less continuously.

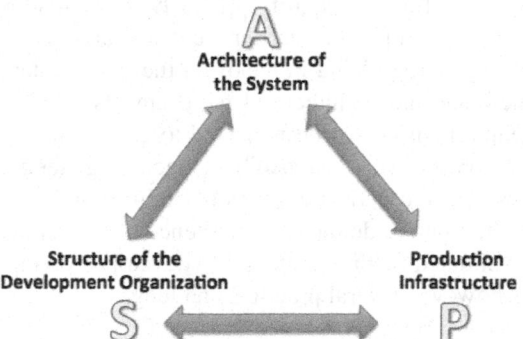

Fig. 1. System architecture (A), organizational structure (S), and production infrastructure (P)

These three structures must be kept aligned over time to support agility. In this paper, we examine the alignment of these structures from the perspective of A and the role of the architect in an agile software-development organization. The relationship of A to S is known as *socio-technical congruence* [12] and has been extensively studied, especially in the context of global, distributed software development. It is very pertinent at the level of the static architectural structure (development view), where a development team wants to avoid conflicts of access to the code between teams and between individuals, while having clear ownership or responsibility over large chunks of code. When A is lagging, we face a situation of technical debt [13]; when S is lagging, we have a phenomenon called "social debt," akin to technical debt, which slows down development [14].

The alignment of A with P is seeing renewed interest with increased focus on continuous integration and deployment and the concept of "DevOps" [15]: combining the development organization with the operations organization, and having the tools in place to ensure continuous delivery or deployment, even in the case of very large online, mission-critical systems (e.g., Netflix, Facebook, Amazon). When P is lagging, we witness a case of "infrastructure debt" as described by Shafer [16], which is another source of friction in software development.

A, S, and P must be "refactored" regularly to be kept in sync so that they can keep supporting each other. Too much early design in any of the three will potentially result in excessive delays, which will increase friction (by increased debt), reduce quality, and lead to overall product delivery delays.

3   How Architecture Benefits from Agility

Given that software designers and developers increasingly recognize the importance of architecture in supporting large-scale agile development, the challenge is no longer about whether architecture is needed but about *when* is it needed, how often, and when the misalignment of A with S and P should trigger a large or small refactoring of the whole A-S-P triad. Designing an architecture in one large increment upfront could delay feedback on the requirements and technical risks of the system.

Architectural design benefits from agility primarily through shorter iterations that produce smaller increments and provide earlier feedback: architectural design and the gradual building of the system go hand in hand. As the stakeholder needs evolve, the designers extract functional and architectural requirements. Dependencies between these two kinds of requirements must be managed to ensure that necessary elements of the architecture are present (or "stubbed") in upcoming iterations. This skeletal foundation must be woven into early iterations of architectural and functional increments. This approach facilitates a deliberate emergence of an architecture over several iterations, constantly validated by the functionality developed on top of it.

This process raises however several practical challenges:

- How do we pace ourselves? What is an appropriate increment? In which order do we work on the functionality and architecture to produce an increment of value to the user while managing costs of rework and delay?
- How do we use iterations to also refine and evolve both S, the structure of the development organization, and P, the production infrastructure.

We've described this approach using the "zipper" metaphor [17]; see Fig. 2. As the requirements are being developed and refined, the architect identifies and extracts architecturally significant requirements (in red); more feature oriented, or functionally oriented, requirements (in green); as well as dependencies between them: *to start building story card X, we need architectural support Y that is at least prototyped (e.g., an API and a stub).* Small iterations are used to design, build, and test a few of the architectural elements and the features that depend on them. By starting with the most critical or challenging requirements, we force the architects to think about the more fundamental aspects early. Whatever they design in the architecture (A) is validated not by some abstract test but by a product embryo of actual functionality.

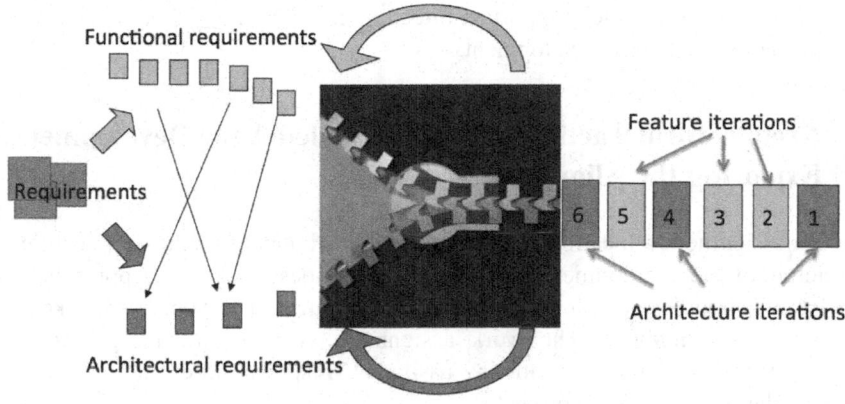

Fig. 2. The zipper model [17]

Some functional and architectural requirements can be in the same iteration, or we can alternate some iterations focusing on architecture and some focusing on more user-facing functionality. Architecture-only iterations may be necessary if some significant refactoring of the emerging architecture is needed, disrupting work on new features to rework existing code.

Many agile practices will therefore contribute to helping architects do a better job of producing more value by reducing waste: frequent communication among the architect, the teams implementing the architecture, and the teams working on features; early realistic testing of certain architectural aspects; reflection and rapid feedback on the suitability or performance of the architecture, allowing for improvements or change of approach; and reduced amount of documentation produced and handed over (compared with an early and more massive architectural undertaking).

This iterative approach, with a clear focus on producing production-quality code early, will also push the architect to pay attention to the allocation of the architecture to the organization and production infrastructure. As the team grows and its structure evolves, the need to improve direct, rapid communication between team members will lead to frequent adjustments of the team structure (S), such as changing the composition of the teams, redefining responsibilities, re-arranging the office layout, adopting "information radiators" or web-based communication tools, and other modifications. This is self-organization in action.

The emphasis on executable code at each iteration will drive the team to experiment early with creating a viable production and delivery environment (P) and evolve it, working early with the people in charge of operations.

The zipper model is far from the antipattern of BDUF and its associated problems:

1. Architecture? – Done.
2. Development of the function can now start.
3. Oops, the architecture does not support all these functions? – It's a bit late to tell us; the architects have moved on to the next project.

Agile practices and principles support architecture in a tight, integrated fashion, which in turn enables scaled agile development.

4   Architectural Tactics to Support Scaled Agile Development: Exploring the Alignment of A and S

The work assignment allocation view captures the alignment of the architecture and the structure of the development organization [3]. It describes the mapping between the software's modules and the people, team, or organizational work units tasked with developing those modules. The work assignment view helps with planning and managing team resource allocations, assigning responsibilities for builds, and explaining the structure of the project.

Architectural tactics enable a simultaneous focus on architecture and agile development by aligning feature-based development and system decomposition to minimize coupling between teams [18]. The tactics we explore for improving the alignment of the architecture of the system and the development of the organization include vertical and horizontal decomposition of the architecture to enable alignment of the teams accordingly as well as matrix augmented-role team structures.

4.1   Vertical and Horizontal System Decomposition

The system decomposition tactic allows assigning responsibilities to the development teams according to the stage of the development effort and the need to focus on features or infrastructure.

The work assignment view gives each team its charter. A common charter for agile teams is to give them responsibility for every piece of implementation for developing a feature, so they do not have to wait until someone else has finished other work. We call this *vertical decomposition* because every component of the system required for realizing the feature is implemented only to the degree required by the team.

An alternative charter is to give teams responsibilities based on system infrastructure. We call this *horizontal decomposition*, an approach in which an agile team bases system decomposition on the architectural needs of the system, focusing on a framework of common services and variability mechanisms. To develop a feature, the team implements only the logic of that feature using the frameworks. The frameworks and common services have already taken care of the logic of integrating the new pieces of code into the system. This type of architecture minimizes the dependencies between different feature implementations so that different teams can implement features without coordination.

The larger the system to be developed and the more agile development teams there will be to develop it, the more the underlying architecture has to support independent development teams. A development effort with only one collocated team may not need explicit architecture design and documentation tasks, and the amount of rework when letting the architecture emerge might be acceptable. With more teams involved, the coordination required between teams starts hindering progress. Each time teams have to coordinate with each other, they may have to wait, which increases the risk of not finishing a task as planned. According to Conway's Law [19], minimizing coordination between teams requires an architecture that is designed to have loosely coupled components so that the team structure can be aligned along those components.

Another factor that makes architecture tasks more important in a large-scale development is the discovery and creation of reusable code, such as common services. If agile development teams are organized to work according to user-visible features (vertically), then the potential of code pieces being reused across features is difficult to evaluate. In this situation, every team is rapidly developing their features, but altogether the teams could have been more efficient if someone would have spent the time discovering and creating a common service (horizontally).

The goal of creating a feature-based vertical decomposition for alignment between architecture and team structure is to decouple teams and architecture to ensure parallel progress where teams are organized in a Scrum of Scrums. Defining the appropriate architecture is key to the success of large-scale software-development projects where there is the need to manage multiple agile teams concurrently over many years. Feature-based vertical decomposition is the preferred approach for assigning tasks to teams. This approach requires minimizing the number of technical and social dependencies to achieve appropriate productivity of the agile development teams.

Two generic examples of such architectures are shown in Fig. 3. Here we have an architecture consisting of three layers. Those three layers contain the common services. Every layer also has either a framework or a plug-in interface defined that implements the control logic of that layer. To develop a feature, only the logic of that feature has to be implemented in each layer using the frameworks or plug-in interfaces. This focuses the development on only what is needed for the feature implementation. All the logic of how to integrate the new pieces of code into the system, such as using the intra-layer communication protocols, is already taken care of by the frameworks and the common services. This type of architecture also minimizes the dependencies between different feature implementations so that different teams can implement features without coordination.

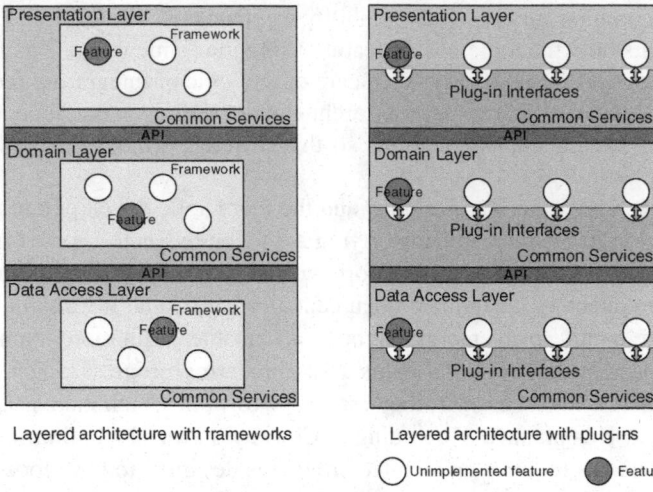

Layered architecture with frameworks   Layered architecture with plug-ins

⃝ Unimplemented feature   ● Feature

Fig. 3. Layered architecture supporting feature-based development

Horizontal decomposition of the system and alignment of the teams to the architecture accordingly is most useful when the skeleton of the system is being developed. As teams create a platform containing commonly used services and development environments, either as frameworks or platform plug-ins to enable rapid feature-based development, it is best to focus their effort on the development of those layers rather than on functionality that will cross over multiple aspects of the system. Another key activity that requires horizontal decomposition is when the stable interfaces between key system elements are being defined. When the commonly used services and development environment are sufficiently in place, then the teams can change their focus to features that span the system.

In every agile project that we analyzed [10] [18] [20], we observed a strong desire to achieve vertical decomposition and team alignment. But especially in the beginning of a project, there is also a strong need for horizontal decomposition and alignment to ensure the teams build components that support later feature development. Horizontal alignment is mostly seen as a temporary phase to achieve the "desired state" of vertical alignment. The Eclipse plug-in framework architecture can be viewed as an example of this balance between horizontal and vertical alignment of teams to the architecture. The existing architecture framework, created over multiple releases by the internal team, enables external organizations and teams to develop features on the framework. The existence of such an infrastructure allows for rapid development. The goal of agile teams that need to operate at scale should be to establish such a supportive infrastructure, which evolves over time yet still supports rapid development.

4.2   Matrix and Augmented Team Structures

The matrix teams tactic allows introducing specialized roles, such as the architect, seamlessly to the agile development effort.

Coordination and *congruence* tactics provide the context for achieving successful matrix and augmented team structures. In its simplest instantiation, a Scrum development environment consists of a single co-located Scrum team with the skills, authority, and knowledge required to specify requirements, architect, design, code, and test the system. As systems grow in size and complexity, however, the single Scrum team model may no longer meet development demands. Information about complexity and uncertainty can supplement the work assignment view (to produce what Herbsleb calls the *coordination view* [3] [21]) to provide more detail about which teams need how much communication, collocation, or both, and how that communication will influence which strategy to use to affect project structure. Achieving *congruence*, then, is matching coordination requirements and coordination capabilities.

A number of different strategies can be used to scale up the overall development organization while maintaining an agile Scrum-based development approach. One approach is replication, essentially creating multiple Scrum teams with the same structure and responsibilities, sufficient to accomplish the required scope of work. This approach works only to some extent, as typically scale issues are not resolved simply by a Scrum of Scrums, in other words, by more of the same scaling. Successful scaling and alignment of the development organization with the system is mostly achieved by a hybrid approach. The hybrid approach involves Scrum team replication but also changes the nature of the Scrum teams in a number of ways. For example, teams aligned horizontally could use the Scrum of Scrums to coordinate vertical issues; later, as the teams move alignment vertically, the role of the Scrum of Scrum changes to coordinate horizontal issues. Another example is to supplement Scrum teams with traditional function-oriented teams, such as using an Integration and Test team to merge and validate code across multiple Scrum teams or dynamically allocating teams depending on the nature of high-priority tasks. (In purist Scrum circles, the hybrid approach would most likely be labeled an example of "ScrumBut.") At scale, the tasks assigned to teams also need to focus on the alignment. In addition, at scale we often observe the breaking of the self-organization of the teams and a balance between a hierarchical ownership structure and small teams in which roles might be more fluid.

5   Architectural Tactics to Support Scaled Agile Development: Exploring the Alignment of A and P

The install allocation view captures the alignment of the architecture and the production infrastructure [3]. It describes the mapping between the software's components and structures in the file system of the production environment. Understanding the organization of the files and folders of the installed software can help developers, deployers, and operators create build-and-deploy procedures, update and configure files of multiple installed versions of the same system, and design and implement an "automatic updates" feature. With the increasing need to focus on continuous integration and multiple deployment contexts and the growing DevOps movement, this view is becoming more dominant. The alignment of the architecture and the production infrastructure becomes critical to articulate.

The tactics that improve the alignment of architecture and production infrastructure are those that extend the concept of the runway beyond the skeletal architecture stubs to include the tooling infrastructure as well as those that include automated deployment and integration support. The more stable the supporting architecture and infrastructure (platform, frameworks, tools), the more teams can be aligned vertically. The less stable the infrastructure at the onset, the more team members have the responsibility to create parts of that architecture and production infrastructure (necessitating a focus on horizontal decomposition of the system).

5.1   Architecture and Infrastructure Runway

The runway-building tactic applies when there is a need for an architecture and infrastructure sufficient to allow incorporation of near-term needs without potentially introducing delays or extra work. One way to manage the alignment of A and P to enhance agility is to reassess the meaning of the architecture runway. Dean Leffingwell [8] describes his concept of architecture runway as follows: "Architectural runway is the answer to a *big* question: *What technology initiatives need to be underway now so that we can reliably deliver a new class of features in the next year or so?*" As such, establishing the runway is often interpreted as the first iteration of the architecture, selecting the frameworks, packages, and so on. Leffingwell and colleagues also make the statement that the bigger the system, the longer the runway.

Leffingwell, Martens, and Zamora [22] explain the role of intentional architecture as one of the key factors to successfully scaling agile. Building and maintaining architectural runway puts in place a system infrastructure sufficient to allow incorporation of near-term product backlog without potentially destabilizing refactoring.

For systems with a smaller scope (and a smaller team size), a shorter runway—that is, architectural infrastructure to support the present iteration or release cycle—may be all that is needed. Especially in the face of uncertain requirements for technology or features, it may be more efficient for the team to try something out, get feedback, and refactor as needed, rather than to invest more time up front in trying to discern requirements that are in flux.

For systems with increasing scope (and larger teams), a longer runway is needed. Building and re-architecting infrastructure takes longer than a single iteration or release cycle. Delivering planned functionality is more predictable when the infrastructure for the new features is already in place. This requires looking ahead in the planning process and investing in architecture by including infrastructure work in the present iteration that will support future features the customer needs.

However, the meaning of runway must expand to encompass the production infrastructure as well. Often such tasks are covered under the planning phase. Articulating the production environment requires defining the alignment with the architecture to be among the main tasks of the runway construction.

Aligning the teams horizontally and focusing on horizontal decomposition of the system are good practices during the early stages of a project as the architectural runway is created, while vertical alignment works well during feature development. Between those two states, we find matrix structures in which the teams are either horizontally or vertically aligned while some members within those teams have opposite responsibilities. Fig. 4 shows an example of this. Here three teams are horizontally aligned to the layers of the architecture to fulfill their primary responsibility to build infrastructure. However, some team members from each team have the responsibility to develop features, and they coordinate with each other in the Scrum of Scrums.

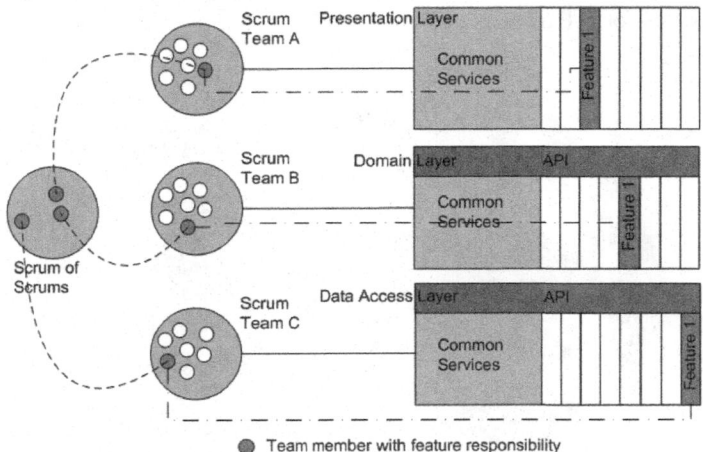

● Team member with feature responsibility

Fig. 4. Progressing architecture and feature development in parallel

5.2   Deployability Tactics

Deployability tactics are those that will make the tooling and deployment environment and alignment run smoothly and at ease. The most relevant tactics include parameterization, self-monitoring, and self-initiating version-update support. While these tactics are also relevant in building the system architecture, they become more significant when managing the alignment of the architecture with the production environment and supporting large-scale operations [23].

Parameterization focuses on environmental variables relevant to the production infrastructure such as databases and server names. This allows deferring binding time and changing aspects of the build and production environment without having to change the build.

Self-monitoring allows for monitoring the system performance and faults as it runs and when it gets out of sync. Both the production infrastructure and the architecture of the system can take advantage of load balancing, logging, and redundancy tactics to realign the allocation and improve system behavior.

Self-initiated version update allows running scripts that update the relevant versions of the software in production. This becomes an issue particularly at scale and when continuous integration and deployment is a goal. The clients and the main applications may get out of sync as well as the supporting tooling environment.

All of these tactics require relevant architecting to influence the allocation relationship between architecture and production infrastructure and to check that the alignment is still in sync.

6   Using the Tactics in Concert to Achieve A-S-P Alignment

In this section, we explore a subset of tactics that can help keep the architecture of the system (A), the structure of the organization (S), and the production infrastructure (P) aligned to achieve agility at scale. Fig. 5 summarizes the tactics that we explored. We did not include tactics related to S-P because we positioned this paper from the perspective of the architecture (A). A complete picture would necessitate exploring alignment tactics for S-P as well as for A-S and A-P.

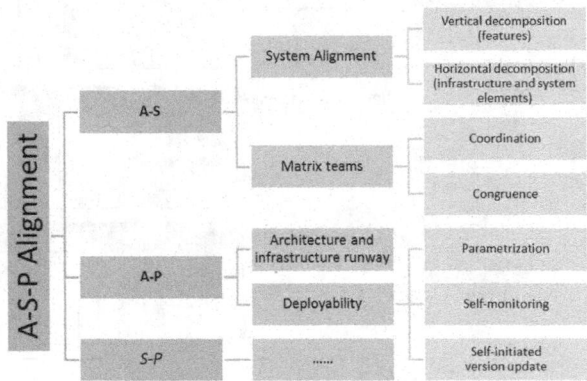

Fig. 5. Summary of the A-S-P alignment tactics

Different phases in a system's life cycle require different tactics. An example walk-through might look like the following:

At the start of a project, it makes sense to organize the teams horizontally. Most of the team's responsibilities focus on making the supporting infrastructure stable enough for feature development to start. This includes activities related to building the architecture elements (A), understanding the key quality attributes, and establishing the build and deployment infrastructure (P), hence building the architecture runway. Team members create a rough sketch of the architecture, make technology decisions, establish the tool environment, and select relevant deployability tactics. Typically, teams use a small subset of basic features to guide the creation of the development infrastructure, but they may not implement those features during this phase.

As soon as the most important interfaces are defined, some team members start developing features. At this point, a matrix organization is established, focusing on coordination requirements and congruence needs. Most team members still have component-oriented responsibilities; therefore, the teams are still horizontally organized. Now, however, some team members start implementing features using the development infrastructure built so far. For example, in a Scrum of Scrums the team members assigned to implement features coordinate with each other to ensure on-time delivery of the features. This helps stabilize the interfaces and provides the first sketches for implementation frameworks that will be helpful for feature development.

As the interfaces become more stable, most of the teams switch to vertical (feature-oriented) development. Some team members still have horizontal responsibilities because the development of common services as well as framework and interface enhancements is performed continuously.

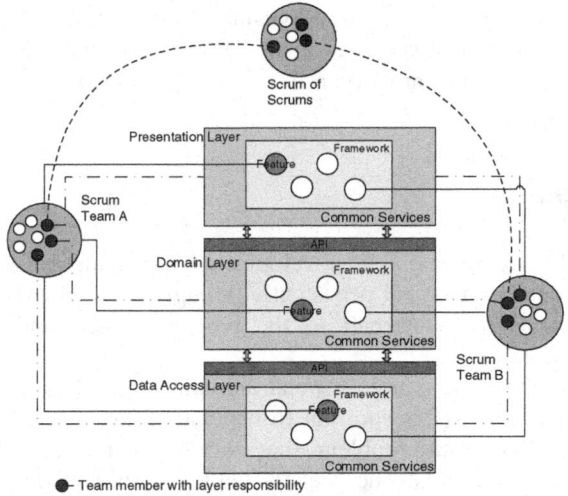

Fig. 6. Different teams assigned to features (vertical alignment), with some team members assigned to keep layers and frameworks consistent

In Fig. 3 we showed the teams organized primarily around the infrastructure. In Fig. 6, the teams have the necessary infrastructure to implement features quickly. Only a few team members, if any, have horizontal responsibilities. Yet every product development has to cope with changing requirements and new technologies.

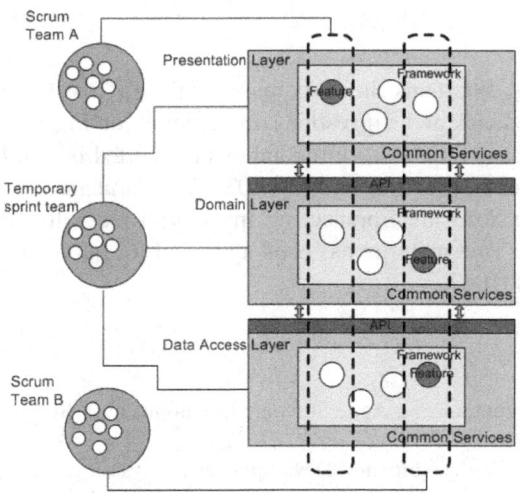

Fig. 7. Different teams assigned to features (vertical alignment), with a temporary team assigned to prepare layers and frameworks for future feature development

In Fig. 7 the teams now have primary responsibility for features. Some team members, including the product architect, look ahead to decide what will be needed in the future. In one or more sprints, they dynamically self-organize into a temporary sprint team to develop the next piece of the runway, and then the team dissolves. Meanwhile, the other teams are organized vertically, developing features for the customer.

7   Conclusion

Architecture enables large-scale agile development. Key elements for success include focusing on architecture early and persistently throughout development, assigning an architecture owner as a counterpart to the product owner, and using the right architecting tools (e.g., tactics).

We contend that the issue is not to tweak individual agile practices to make them work outside of the agile sweet spot but to understand the specific issues of large-scale development, identify the problems that current practices cannot solve, and add architecture practices and tools. The goal for the software-development organization is to be agile at the level of the organization, not only in iteratively refining the architecture of the system under development but also in constantly tuning the development organization and improving the production infrastructure.

In this paper, we give an example of using architectural tactics and aligning architecture, agile development teams, and production infrastructure. A catalog of other tactics mapped to agile development can be collected from successful organizations and literature. Other ongoing and future work includes techniques to make architectural agility visible, identify and analyze architectural dependencies and incorporate dependency management into development, and provide timely feedback to support enhancement agility.

Acknowledgements. We thank the participants of the XP'2014 workshop in Rome on May 26 for their feedback and suggestions, in particular on Fig. 1.

This material is based upon work funded and supported by the Department of Defense under Contract No. FA8721-05-C-0003 with Carnegie Mellon University for the operation of the Software Engineering Institute, a federally funded research and development center. This material has been approved for public release and unlimited distribution. DM-0001067.

References

1. Kruchten, P.: Contextualizing Agile Software Development. J. Softw. Evol. Proc. 25, 351–361 (2013)
2. Highsmith, J.A.: Agile Software Development Ecosystems. Addison-Wesley, Boston (2002)
3. Clements, P., Bachmann, F., Bass, L., Garlan, D., Ivers, J., Little, R., Merson, P., Nord, R., Stafford, J.: Documenting Software Architectures. Addison-Wesley, Upper Saddle River (2011)
4. Perry, D.E., Wolf, A.L.: Foundations for the Study of Software Architecture. ACM SIGSOFT 17(4), 40 (1992)

5. Meyer, B.: Agile! The Good, the Hype, and the Ugly. Springer, Zürich (2014)
6. McConnell, S.: Technical Debt, Software Best Practices (2007), http://blogs.construx.com/blogs/stevemcc/archive/2007/11/01/technical-debt-2.aspx
7. Cockburn, A.: Walking Skeleton (1996), http://alistair.cockburn.us/Walking+skeleton
8. Leffingwell, D.: Agile Software Requirements. Addison-Wesley, Boston (2011)
9. Brown, S.: Software Architecture for Developers. LeanPub., Vancouver (2014)
10. Bellomo, S., Nord, R.L., Ozkaya, I.: A Study of Enabling Factors for Rapid Fielding: Combined Practices to Balance Speed and Stability. In: 35th International Conference on Software Engineering, pp. 982–991. IEEE Press, Piscataway (2013)
11. Nord, R., Ozkaya, I., Sangwan, R.: Making Architecture Visible to Improve Flow Management in Lean Software Development. IEEE Software 29(5), 33–39 (2012)
12. Cataldo, M., Herbsleb, J.D., Carley, K.M.: Socio-Technical Congruence: A Framework for Assessing the Impact of Technical and Work Dependencies on Software Development. In: Second ACM-IEEE International Symposium on Empirical Software Engineering and Measurement, pp. 2–11. ACM, New York (2008)
13. Nord, R.L., Ozkaya, I., Kruchten, P., Gonzalez-Rojas, M.: In Search of a Metric for Managing Architectural Technical Debt. In: Joint Working IEEE/IFIP Conference on Software Architecture and European Conference on Software Architecture, pp. 91–100. IEEE Press, New York (2012)
14. Tamburri, D., Lago, P., Kruchten, P., van Vliet, H.: What Is Social Debt in Software Engineering? In: Sixth International Workshop on Cooperative and Human Aspects of Software Engineering, pp. 93–96. IEEE Press, San Francisco (2013)
15. Desbois, P.: Devops: A Software Revolution in the Making (Special Issue). Cutter IT J. 24, 8 (2011)
16. Shafer, A.C.: Infrastructure Debt: Revisiting the Foundation. Cutter IT J. 23, 36–41 (2010)
17. Bellomo, S., Kruchten, P., Nord, R.L., Ozkaya, I.: How to Agilely Architect an Agile Architecture? Cutter IT J. 27, 12–17 (2014)
18. Bachmann, F., Nord, R.L., Ozkaya, I.: Architectural Tactics to Support Rapid and Agile Stability. CrossTalk 25(3), 21–25 (2012)
19. Conway, M.E.: How Do Committees Invent? Datamation 14(4), 28–31 (1968)
20. Cataldo, M., Herbsleb, J.D.: Factors Leading to Integration Failures in Global Feature-Oriented Development: An Empirical Analysis. In: 33rd International Conference on Software Engineering, pp. 161–170. ACM, New York (2011)
21. Cataldo, M., Herbsleb, J.D.: Coordination Breakdowns and Their Impact on Development Productivity and Software Failures. IEEE T. Software Eng. 39, 343–360 (2013)
22. Leffingwell, D., Martens, R., Zamora, M.: Principles of Agile Architecture (2008), http://scalingsoftwareagilityblog.com/wpcontent/uploads/2008/08/principles_agile_architecture.pdf
23. Bellomo, S., Kazman, R., Ernst, N., Nord, R.: Toward Design Decisions to Enable Deployability: Empirical Study of Three Projects Reaching for the Continuous-Delivery Holy Grail. In: First International Workshop on Dependability and Security of System Operation, pp. 32–37. IEEE Press, New York (2014)

Conventions for Coordinating Large Agile Projects

Jaana Nyfjord[1], Sameer Bathallath[2], and Harald Kjellin[2]

[1] SICS Swedish ICT, Box 1263, 164 29 Kista, Sweden
[2] Stockholm University, DSV, Box 7003, 164 07 Kista, Sweden
jaana@sics.se, {sameer,hk}@dsv.su.se

Abstract. There is no universal way to coordinate Agile teams in large development projects because they have unique challenges. This suggests that the best way to coordinate the teams is to ask them how they want to be managed given a set of constraints. This requires particular communication and negotiation skills in the leadership team, which we discuss in this article. We describe the skills as a set of conventions, founded on the argument that every organization is a complex adaptive system and should therefore be analyzed from multiple system perspectives. We investigate scientific models for managing complexity and evaluate their usefulness through qualitative interviews with 14 managers in large private and public organizations in Saudi Arabia. We conclude that a set of proposed conventions could facilitate coordination by functioning as a supportive context enabling managers to apply various system perspectives simultaneously.

Keywords: Software engineering, Management, Systems thinking, Complexity.

1   Introduction

Many Agile teams operate within larger, complex organizational environments. Their capacity for high performance depends largely on their leaders' ability to manage the various contexts of complexity within and across the teams. Consequently, leaders must be prepared to dynamically and flexibly shift their leadership style to effectively lead the teams and the organization as a whole [29].

There exist many models for how systems thinking can be used to deal with organizational complexity [18]. However, several researchers have described the constraints with using individual systems models disjointedly because they build on different paradigms. For instance, Flood and Romm [15] describe the dangers of adopting one perspective and instead advocate an approach called "Total Systems Intervention" to avoid getting stuck in one perspective of a system that does not cover all aspects of its subsystems. Jackson [18] resonates with this and promotes holistic system thinking as an ability to analyze organizations from different viewpoints by combining system models to ensure that the parts function properly together to serve the needs of the whole. Snowden and Boone [29] also present methods for dealing with the emergent properties of complex social systems, where the setting of system boundaries combined with increasing levels of interaction and communication enable

T. Dingsøyr et al. (Eds.): XP 2014 Workshops, LNBIP 199, pp. 58–72, 2014.

managers to probe and make sense of a variety of complexities and respond accordingly as they emerge.

Today, many researchers have recognized the need for pluralism and advocate the use of a multi-methodology, which implies that several system models are combined when managing large complex organizations such as large software projects consisting of many teams. The problem is how a multi-methodology can be applied effectively in practice. For instance, Brocklesby [7] describes the cognitive difficulties while working across paradigms. We cannot expect managers to be experts in how to combine a number of abstract system models simultaneously. On the contrary, they need to make fast practicable decisions. Speed is particularly important in Agile contexts where the development cycle is continuous. Moreover, we cannot expect managers alone to know all the drivers of complexity involved in coordinating many development teams. It requires collective knowledge [26]. Hence, we draw two conclusions: managers must be (a) familiar with the most relevant theories, opportunities and threats of coordinating complex organizations, and (b) able to create environments where communication can grow and solutions be exploited in interaction with the teams to make faster and more actionable decisions. In practice, this indicates that a useful way to coordinate the teams in large, complex development projects is to ask each team how they want to be managed given a set of constraints. This requires relevant communication and negotiation skills in the leadership team, which we address in this paper. These skills are needed to handle the highly volatile environment of Agile projects that, according to Augustine [4], is completely different from the traditional linear approach to software development.

The overarching purpose of this paper is to argue for the utility of a proposed set of conventions to support increased communication and interaction needed to master the complexity of large Agile projects. The set of conventions aims at the coordination of Agile teams and is based on multi-methodological systems thinking. We investigate scientific models for facilitating coordination in large, complex organizations and evaluate their usefulness through qualitative interviews with 14 managers in public and private organizations in Saudi Arabia. Our goals are to (a) elicit and synthesize a set of high-level conventions providing support for coordinating many Agile development teams, in particular through enhanced communication, and (b) find empirical evidence for their need and usefulness.

The remainder of this paper is: Section 2 describes related research. Section 3 summarizes our research method. Section 4 .presents the candidate conventions and the results of their evaluation. Sections 5 and 6 contain a short discussion of the results, and concluding remarks and suggestions of future research, respectively.

2   Related Research

Agile organizations are complex adaptive systems [4]. There are different approaches for managing organizations as a complex adaptive system, from Learning Organizations [28], Cynefin framework [29] to Human Systems Dynamics [13]. They assume systems thinking to various extents. Systems thinking is the process of understanding how things, regarded as systems, influence one another within a whole [18].

The domain of system thinking is also evolving. Several authors suggest that no single systems method or model alone can solve the problem of complexity [15][18][19]. Generally, different contexts call for different kinds of responses. The more complex, all the more communication and interaction is generally needed to be able to act effectively as a leader [29]. Hence, our conclusion is that a multi-methodological systems approach is needed for coordinating large Agile projects. However, a secondary problem arises as a result of this. As implied by Arell et al. [2], how can managers increase communication and interact more effectively with their teams when they do not have consistent models telling them how to coordinate the dynamics of Agile projects? There seems to be a lack of a common playground or context permitting managers to understand the totality of what is going on in these complex dynamic organizations. Because most management approaches (not based on systems thinking) generally build on conflicting paradigms and reductionist models describing formal routines for fixed systems, they cannot deal with the dynamics and interdependencies in a complex system [18]. Hence, they can be seen as the antithesis of Agility. Instead, the management support models need to be formulated in a way that they can be applied in ever changing dynamic contexts. At the same time, they need to be consistent to provide reliable support. Solutions based on systems thinking often consist of general principles that act as guidelines for dealing with complexity [28]. Yet, general principles may still be perceived as abstract, i.e. relating to or involving general ideas or qualities rather than specific people, objects, or actions. If they are disassociated from any specific instance they will be difficult to understand and implement. Managers need nonabstract guidance to be able to act effectively.

In our research, we have found that a type of generic instructions we call "conventions" can satisfy the requirements on being flexible, dynamic and concrete. A convention is a selection from among two or more alternatives, where the rule then is agreed upon among participants [23]. Conventions can be seen as a stable, but flexible structure in an ever-changing environment supporting the coordination by functioning as a soft or artificial type of guideline aiding the managers with a set of known ways for dealing with the challenges that may arise from complexity.

Leaders must embrace change in Agile organizations. They must be prepared to make fast decisions. They must also secure that the complexity of their production is well coordinated. We assume that the best way to approach a solution is to (a) support the coordination activities by providing flexible guidelines combining multiple system theories, and (b) ensure that these guidelines are harmonized with the development practices used by Agile teams.

3   Research Method

In this section, we describe the research approach and a summary of the steps taken for applying this approach.

3.1   General Research Approach

To develop conventions is such a complex endeavor that it could result in any type of arbitrary solution. To reduce the risk of irrelevant arbitrary solutions and to get a basic scientific foundation, we focused our study on systems thinking models for solving management problems and then extracted candidate conventions that had already been evaluated. We applied a design science approach [32] where we iteratively refined, evaluated and redefined the conventions that were better suited than others to solve the problem of coordinating large Agile projects. Our iteration of steps corresponds to the guidelines for design science as described by Hevner [17].

3.2   Summary of Steps Taken for Applying the Research Approach

Step 1. First, we conducted a literature study of the type of problems that were most frequently described when coordinating large software development projects [11][20] [24][34]. We came across generic statements about well-known problems in software development. After a compilation of a large number of presented problems we concluded that: 1) it is often difficult to get an overview of how changes in one sub-project affects other sub-projects, 2) too many restrictions in the requirement specification makes the whole development process rigid and prevents creative solutions, 3) the larger the project the less flexibility there is, 4) as transaction costs increase with the size of the project, it is necessary to be strict with upholding discipline and thus there is a need for bureaucratic rules that are often not understood.

Step 2. In the second stage we searched for generic solutions to the type of problems that were frequently described as being crucial among the coordination problems. This search was not restricted to software design but rather management principles in general in the areas of system theory, cybernetics, logistics, and chaos theory, e.g. [1][3][6][8][12][18][30]. We will not detail all the variations of coordination problems described in these references. However, in most of these areas a tendency of promoting generic principles for solving complexity problems is found.

Step 3. From a large number of well-documented generic solutions to complexity problems we extracted conventions that we estimated as being plausible candidates for being accepted and applied as conventions for coordinating large Agile projects. We specified six basic quality criteria as a basis for extracting the conventions. The method for specifying these quality criteria was based on an analysis of their applicability with regard to systems thinking. In summary, the criteria were: 1) The convention should be applied as a guideline rather than as a control function since control functions are assumed to become too complex to be useful, which is also advocated by Ackoff [1]. We assumed it to be difficult to implement any convention as a strict rule because we found situations where it was not relevant. 2) The convention should be advisory and not mandatory in order to be supportive without producing any new obstacles in the communication processes. We found that to have mandatory conventions could create bureaucratic obstacles as described by Parkinsson [25]. 3) It should be simple to apply. The whole idea of using conventions is to simplify communication concerning difficult problems. Gudykunst [16] also argues for such simplification of communication. Thus, we assumed that complicated instructions for how it could be applied would increase complexity problems rather than reducing them. 4) It should be possible to explain the convention with simple metaphors that can be easily understood and remembered to overcome the communication difficulties as argued by Brockelsby [7] and Snowden and Boone [29]. Software development is a creative endeavor that needs the sharing of understanding rather than scientific correctness of definitions. 5) The convention should support the Agile values, principles and practices. The argument for this is that we aim at proposing conventions that are aligned with the deeply rooted tradition of Agile software development [22]. 6) It should conform to the principles of game theory. To motivate people to use a convention, it should be possible for its users to understand what they could gain from using them. Game theory concludes that people resist actions that may in any way threaten their personal interests [5].

Step 4. We tested the conventions on various examples of problems as described in Step 1. We found that some seemed to be more useful than others according to our quality criteria and these were selected as the core set of candidate conventions that we present in this paper. Beware that the process of discovering and defining useful conventions can be seen as a never-ending process of continuous refinement of useful support structures in the coordination of many Agile projects. This iterative process can probably not be based on any exact form of science because it is always possible for someone to define a new arbitrary convention that may be intuitively perceived as being more useful. Thus, we have concluded that the only way to validate the usefulness of the conventions is to test them in empirical studies. They can be inspired by generic theories of dealing with complexity and then be validated empirically.

Step 5. Finally, we conducted a pre-study based on semi-structured open-ended interviews to verify the identified research idea and determine future research directions. The objective was to evaluate the usefulness of the candidate conventions. As presented in Table 1, fourteen organizations in Saudi Arabia were chosen based on convenience sampling [27]. Among these, four have multinational presence. The others represent an ERP solution provider and IT-departments within the banking, airline, oil and gas, and public sectors, respectively. The software projects within these organizations either develop software for external customers like the case with the multinational companies and the ERP solution provider, or develop software for their internal corporate users. The size of the organizations ranges from 700 to 70,000 employees, and they are considered leaders in their industries.

Fourteen interviewees, one from each organization, were selected based on three criteria: (1) their job roles and responsibilities (senior managers) (2) years of experience in IT project management (at least 7 years), and (3) an estimation of their adoption and experience of Agile development. All of them were familiar with and had practical experience of the Agile methods.

We created a questionnaire. The questionnaire was open-ended and semi-structured. It focused on finding out (1) whether the conventions were recognized in the industry today, and (2) their status within the organizations studied. To cover the conventions and the evaluation criteria of this study, 50 questions were created. Due to space restrictions, we cannot list them all. However, the questions that were asked followed a somewhat uniform pattern. The pattern was: (1) Do you use this convention? (2) If no, please describe why? (3) If yes, please (a) describe why, (b) describe how, and (c) provide examples. (4) Are there any benefits you find with this convention? (5) Can the convention be improved? If yes/no, please motivate why/how? (6) Are there any additional comments that you would like to add? The questions are also further described in Chapter 4.

Table 1. Organizations studied

	Industry	Employees	Project data	Interviewee
1	Oil & Gas	1,800	Large ERP implementation (SCRUM)	Information technology superintendent
2	Oil & Gas	2,600	Large ERP implementation (SCRUM)	IT Director (CIO)
3	Airline	>30,000	Large ERP implementation (SCRUM)	IT Systems manager
4	Banking & Finance	7000	e-Commerce B2B systems, CRM (Plan-driven and Agile)	Director of project mgmt. office
5	Enterprise software and services	>60,000	CRM, ERP, SCM, etc. (Plan-driven and SCRUM)	Senior project manager
6	Network systems and applications	70,000	MPLS, ATM (Plan-driven and Agile)	Program manager
7	Enterprise software and services	3000	ERP implementation and business process reengineering (SCRUM)	Customer solution manager
8	Real estate, investment, tourism	4000	Large-scale IT security project (Plan-driven and Agile)	Project and IT QA manager
9	Government agency	>2,000	Networking, security, data center and software development (Plan-driven and Agile)	IT infrastructure manager
10	Government agency	>4,000	Web design, security, business intelligent tools etc. (Plan-driven and Agile)	IT program manager
11	Business system integration	>700	Security services, Data centre services, cloud computing etc. (Plan-driven and Agile)	IT project manager
12	Business system integration	>50,000	Large-scale IT transformation (Plan-driven and Agile)	Senior IT consultant and project manager
13	Airline	>1000	Large ERP implementation (Plan-driven and Agile)	IT systems manager
14	Banking & Finance	2,000	e-Commerce B2B systems, CRM (Plan-driven and Agile)	IT services manager

In summary, each convention was briefly described to the interviewee. Then the interviewee was asked if he or she agrees with the convention and whether it is used. If there were signs that the interviewee had experience of the convention, then the discussion kept on going. Otherwise the convention was considered irrelevant and the interviewee was asked to describe why they had not employed any similar approaches as was described in the convention.

4   Candidate Conventions and Results from the Empirical Study

In this section, we describe the eight conventions that were extracted and synthesized from scientific publications, including a summary of the results of their evaluation based on the 14 interviews.

In general, it can be stated that most conventions were aligned with the interviewees' views of how teams should be coordinated. All fourteen interviewees demonstrated that they understood the conventions, also by providing practical examples of their usefulness in terms of both pros and cons in the context of their organizations.

The evaluation of the conventions was carried out by using different evaluation criteria than those that were used to extract candidate conventions. The method to extract the most plausible among the candidate conventions was based on a literature study where we found generic descriptions of types of behavior that was documented to work well in large projects. To evaluate the usefulness of the proposed conventions an entirely different method was used. We assumed that it would not be feasible to interview managers concerning to what extent their behavior could be explained by various systems thinking models. Instead we applied a simple and straightforward method based on the managers' opinions of the applicability of our description of the conventions. In this way, we could collect empirical evidence that would indicate the level of usefulness of the proposed conventions. Asking the following questions to the interviewees accumulated these opinions of the conventions:

- Do you use any approach or combination of approaches that are similar to the described convention?
- If yes:
  - o   Can you provide examples? This was taken as an indication of the usefulness of the convention.
  - o   Can you motivate why it works or not works? The response indicated to what extent the convention could be easily communicated.
- If not, would you be interested in testing the convention? A positive answer was taken as an indication of its potential use. A negative answer was taken as an indication of the conventions as not being useful.
- Can you exemplify possible benefits of using the convention? A positive answer was interpreted as an indication of the convention as being useful. A negative answer was taken an indication of the convention as not being useful.

- Can you exemplify any negative effects of applying the convention? A positive answer was an indication of it not being useful or an understanding of the limitations of the convention. A negative answer was an indication of its usefulness.

When interpreting the answers from the managers we made a clear distinction between what can be considered opinions of the interviewed managers and what can be considered as being based on factual experiences. In all cases where the managers could provide examples, we concluded this data as being more valid than voiced opinions without examples.

Brief descriptions of each of the eight conventions together with a summary of the results of their evaluation are described in the sections 4.1-4.8 below.

4.1   Speak Their Language

Argyris [3] has shown that a major obstacle when dealing with collaboration in complex contexts is the emotional content of various types of communication. Hence, the most effective way to secure that the communication works well when several teams are coordinated is to use their language and also give specific feedback to the teams on how they describe their work, their needs and their progress [3]. At a later stage, communication standards can be developed for how teams should communicate with each other, but if these are prematurely introduced they create more confusion than they solve [16].

Result: Nearly all interviewees shared a similar view that speaking their teams' language implies connecting people to people, and teams to teams not merely a process output to a process input. Ten out of 14 interviewees have explicitly confirmed that continually adjusting the communication will encourage teams' congruence and collaboration. In this regard, it was mentioned: "I spend times with different teams, speak their language, understand how they deliver their work and also try to make them understand how other teams apprehend their work and how they impact other teams when they deliver something." Eight out of 14 interviewees think that the convention would help managers to realize how their teams will deliver as promised. Twelve out of 14 interviewees mentioned that they specifically think that the convention can prevent communication conflicts from escalating. Hence, the convention has a definite acceptance and is likely to be used to secure that the communication works well.

4.2   Create a Culture of Public Benchmarking

One of the most efficient methods for sharing knowledge is by comparing performance between teams. However, if managers do not give feedback, criticism and appreciation in a similar way to various teams it is difficult to create a culture of fair, open communication [8]. In order for teams to adjust descriptions of their work according to how other teams describe their work, it is necessary to develop a continuous dialogue around comparisons between teams. A specific version of this called "Peer Sites" has been successfully tested where one software development site gives a personalized response to another development site [10].

Result: Not all interviewees shared a similar view about the convention's importance. Five out of 14 interviewees think that it is a very sensitive topic, which can easily drive teams to oppose each other. Two reasons were given: due to cultural considerations, four have failed to implement the convention while one believes that the convention is of low priority. The latter indicated that it is inappropriate to compare the teams' presentations because it will be a waste of time and effort to ask other teams to adjust their work accordingly. As he said: "In my view, this could result in an ambition among other teams to re-implement or to add more tasks to comply with the best team… we are talking about an increase in project duration and an increase in cost even if we will get a better quality to some extent." On the contrary, he suggested: "It is better to bring the teams' leaders together, and have them agree on standards and procedures. If the teams follow the same standard and procedures, then they can more easily share knowledge about their results." However, 8 out of 14 interviewees mentioned that benchmarking could help in raising performance standards by enabling knowledge to be shared and reused. Among those it was, for instance, mentioned: "Creating such culture… increases the good competition between the teams, because one team's good performance is an example for the other teams. It enhances the quality of all teams. So, we always raise the standards or the bar higher by showing the great performance of one team as an example for the others and, if there is any great job experience, then we always promote the dissemination of descriptions of this and share all the documents publicly". Hence, the convention has a partial acceptance, as it is less likely to be used to enhance continuous dialogue between teams.

4.3   Motivate from Personal Experience

Managers who cannot argue for their motivation by providing references to practical experience may risk the communication trap of having subordinates not understanding them [33]. This is especially important when there are few fixed routines, which puts a high pressure on people's ability to accept abstract ideas. To provide rational and consistent arguments may also be difficult when several theories or perspectives are discussed. In such cases, using examples will clarify the ideas. Hence, the manager who motivates their arguments combined with real, concrete examples is more likely to be understood than the one who uses abstract theories.

Result: Nearly all interviewees shared a similar view that the use of bundled experiences would help both the managers and teams to overcome communication bottlenecks. However, 9 of out of 14 interviewees indicated that the arguments must be carefully composed to achieve certain needs and to not impose any restraints on the teams' own inspiration. Twelve out of 14 interviewees indicated that the convention could enhance better communication between the managers and teams. Among those it was mentioned: "With the accumulated experience that one has, it will help a lot in discussions, in meetings, in highlighting issues, in reaching to agreements, etc. Especially, when you quote, from your past personal experience, some other companies that did an implementation of the same type of system that you are trying to implement.... this will help others to understand that they can achieve the same things." Another responded: "I believe in managing by examples, so if I have a situation where I am arguing with a team member or a team leader, then clarifying by giving some examples is a good idea to achieve a common understanding... The project managers should also be open to other ideas until there is a consensus about which solution should be taken". Hence, the convention has a definite acceptance, as it is likely to be used to enhance better communication with teams.

4.4   Include Sub-ordinates in Meetings

In all large organizations there are power games [1]. One aspect of power games is that people create territories within the organization impeding effective communication. Hence, to prevent these kinds of situations, representatives from various hierarchical levels should be included in meetings [1]. Meetings between management and team leaders should always include at least one member of the team and it should preferably be a different member at each meeting. This empowers each team member to communicate his/her view of the project and motivates everyone to be part of the decision process. By always trying to include three hierarchical levels in meetings secures that relevant aspects is moving between all levels of the organization. In the proposed system model of "Interactive Planning", Ackoff [1] demonstrates how a similar approach secures that the communication flows more freely among the members of a large project.

Result: All interviewees acknowledged the need of connecting people to people regardless to their positions and responsibilities, which in return would foster their teams' development and learning. In their comments of what benefits they can get, the following motivations were given: "It is a good technique especially to motivate people and to develop people further"; "It is one of the very efficient tools to develop people... and very effective way of decision making"; "You will be surprized how team members can present something that gives you a direction that you did not even think practically about at that time... taking feedback is very important... it will be like a 360 view of any subject"; "[As a developer] listening to how the strategy was brainstormed, how the decisions were made, and how the challenges and conflicts were resolved was like an eye opener for me at that time". Exceptions to that, 5 out of 14 mentioned that managers should be careful when sending subordinates to critical meetings, such as meetings involving financial discussions or some customer executive meetings. Hence, the convention has a definite acceptance among the interviewees, as it is likely to be used to promote communication, team development and learning.

4.5   Combine Various Modeling Methods

Ever since the famous book about Parkinsson's Law of Bureaucracy [25], the dangers of following a specific model too rigidly has been proven over and over again.

The solution is to have a flexible attitude towards models and use them when, and in whatever combination of models, needed and using the models as support tools rather than governing systems [12]. Hence, managers should be skilled in drawing "Rich Pictures" [9] which provide models of the problem that can easily be explained to laymen and make them aware of the various perspectives among stakeholders in a complex project. A manager can apply several different perspectives at the same time and for each perspective make conceptual models. When a number of conceptual models have been presented it is possible to compare all the models with the software development situation and draw conclusions based on more than one perspective.

Result: All interviewees shared a similar view that in complex projects, models are used to address, understand and help solving problems and not merely to describe processes and standards to follow. As one said: "In software development projects, flexibility is essential and very important in managing projects... So, it is advisable to use different models". Another interviewee stated: "Each project has its unique category and level of complexity, so the project manager should be able to employ models that suites the project, in whatever combination he thinks will work well". Ten out of 14 interviewees indicated that the convention could help in building stronger teams that deliver better quality. In the same vein, 5 out of 14 interviewees indicated that the convention could help managing projects in much faster ways due to less formality. Among those it was mentioned: "Combining different models and methods when managing projects will definitely help project managers to accomplish critical goals such as time-to-market". Hence, the convention has a definite acceptance, as it is likely to be used to support project governance by improved communication.

4.6   Use Global Definitions

Using different definitions on various organizational levels will cause confusion. In his works with "Viable System Models", Beer [6] became famous for his introduction of cybernetics. According to his model, the communication processes between all levels of the organization could be recursively described, i.e. the same communication protocols or definitions that are necessary among teams on a lower level are also necessary on higher levels. Hence, by using recursive descriptions support the global communication in large projects because similar communication protocols are used on all levels of the project.

Result: All interviewees shared similar opinion that common definitions across the project organization would provide high synergy among teams and maintain consistency in communication, documentation, and reporting. Generally, their adoption of the convention is primarily to reduce confusion and eliminate potential conflicts that may occur due to misinterpretation especially in complex projects. Nine out of 14 interviewees indicated that using global definitions could be a timesaving and efficient way for project success. In this regard, it was mentioned that: "The convention can bring more advantages including seamless communication, avoid misinterpretation and conflicts, and avoid risk which becomes more important when dealing with offshore teams"; "Having a unified terminology or terms will make everybody understand each other and it plays a critical role for creating environments for clear communication". Hence, the convention has a definite acceptance, as it is likely to be used to support mutual understanding across the project community.

4.7   Accept Chaos as a Driver For Development

Leaders who try to impose order in a complex context will fail [29]. A manager should accept a certain amount of chaos in the development process as long as this does not inflict on the basic goals of the project [30]. To determine an acceptable degree of chaos, managers should be familiar with complexity theory. Stacey [30] claims that in large projects the most highly valued competence of managers is to be able to deal with relationships, dynamism and unpredictability. The managers should not try to control everything but instead use this competence to shift leadership style accordingly.

Result: Nearly all interviewees consider some chaos to be effective in many ways. For instance, a) ten out of 14 interviewees consider it a driver for timely project development and delivery, as it was stated: "Chaos is sometimes important to provide control over the project cycle itself, otherwise many projects might go in no end to be completed" and b) five out of 14 interviewees considered it as an enabler for teams to thrive and assume higher responsibilities. However, three interviewees mentioned that accepting chaos must be accompanied with careful attention, as motivated by one of them: "It should not change the scope of work, it should not change the time frame, it should not affect the budget, and it should not do a drastic change to the project model or to the project standards. I can accept 10-15% percent change here and there whenever it is required." Hence, the convention has a definite acceptance, as it is likely to be used to drive project development forward as a way to gain control over the project cycle and as an enabler for communication and team development.

4.8   Centralize Critical Rules

Using a strict "management by objective" approach in a complex context will likely constrain the productivity of teams [21]. Hence, formalizing goals and constraints as generic rules or principles that can be implemented in whatever ways the teams find appropriate will provide a softer direction enabling team creativity and productivity.

The history of complex systems have many examples of a paradox saying that managers can be free to decentralize decision making if they have been cautious enough to centralize the critical rules. Thomas [31] describes the results from several studies of how productivity rises once there is a sound and stable foundation allowing the employees to design their own work. Another analog example, illustrates how cities can be made to be self-organizing as long as there is an understanding of the critical thresholds of the city [14].

Result: Everyone but two have accepted the convention. The latter two favour "management by objectives" as a support for timely delivery of the project and securing productivity. The other interviewees, on the other hand, share similar views on accepting a critical set of rules instead of strict objectives and systems as a driver of productivity. Among those, one indicated that in complex projects he prefers to give "the minimum set of rules and a lot of flexibility to the teams to decide how they would like to manage their work". He also pointed out that managers must apply certain probes and checks to ensure that teams are independently capable of taking timely decisions. Another interviewee mentioned "I don't agree much with strict management by objectives. I believe that you need to draw the borders for them and let them play or implement the way they want within these borders." Hence, the convention has general acceptance, as it is likely to be used to empower the teams to decide how to best accomplish their tasks and goals, and thereby increase the productivity of the project as a whole.

5   Discussion

In this section, we briefly discuss the results of the evaluation of the conventions. Generally, all of the conventions were considered to be applicable in the interviewees' organizations. We argue that this high level of applicability is due to the correspondence between the conventions and the principles of complex adaptive systems (CAS) as described in [2], where it is shown that the CAS principles self-organization, emergence, interdependence and coevolution also exist in most well functioning Agile organizations. In this regard, as we have also evaluated and ensured that the conventions are aligned with the Agile values, principles and practices, it is also worth noting that our findings also support the findings of Pelrine [26], in his suggestion that complexity science provides a theoretical basis for Agile. Hence, by treating software development as a complex endeavor, rather than a linear, will help managers to master large Agile projects.

Finally, we have often been asked why we restrict the conventions to being suitable for coordinating Agile projects instead of claiming that the conventions are good for coordinating projects in general. Our answer to such questions is that the conventions may very well be applicable to any large project where there is a need for an Agile type of flexibility within a strict framework, but we have intentionally selected an instance of this problem, i.e. large Agile projects, where there is a strong polarity between the need for flexibility on one hand, and a need of strict correctness on the other hand. We have shown how it can be possible to follow a combination of scientific models while at the same time promoting an Agile type of flexibility.

6   Concluding Remarks and Future Research Directions

This research associates systems thinking with the management of large Agile teams. It suggests that the managers' ability to master complexity can be improved if they adopt a set of proposed conventions. The conventions facilitate a multi-methodological system approach to coordinate teams by increasing communication and interaction. A pre-study based on 14 interviews was conducted, the results of which indicated a high degree of usefulness of the proposed conventions. Hence, the results imply that a set of conventions can potentially facilitate coordination by serving as a supportive context enabling managers to apply various system thinking models simultaneously, and thereby help them to focus more on the broad responsibility of leading the project as a whole.

There are different approaches to managing an organization as a complex adaptive system, e.g. "Learning Organizations" [28], Cynefin framework [29] and "Human System Dynamics" [13]. We view each of these approaches as appropriate guides to management of Agile organizations. However, it would be highly valuable to compare the conventions presented here with existing guidelines in these approaches. For instance, a structured analysis of the guidelines defined for the different domains in the Cynefin Framework would contribute to further knowledge about the conventions and their applicability.

This work is still at an early stage, but we aim at continuing our efforts in investigating the potential effects as recognised in the pre-study at a larger scale. The overarching target is to contribute to improving the communication, cohesion, efficiency and performance of large Agile projects. Nevertheless, to reach concrete results, we intend to conduct further empirical investigations, e.g. by case studies. We also assume that there will be continuous modifications of the conventions to ensure they meet the needs of managers of large Agile projects.

References

1. Ackoff, R.L.: Recreating the corporation: A design of organizations for the 21st century. Oxford University Press, New York (1999)
2. Arell, R., et. al.: Characteristics of Agile Organizations. Agile Alliance (2012), http://agilealliance.org/index.php/download_file/view/217/221/
3. Argyris, C.: Knowledge for Action: A Guide to Overcoming Barriers to Organizational Change. Jossey-Bass Inc., Publishers, San Francisco (1993)
4. Augustine, S., Payne, B., Sencindiver, F., Woodcock, S.: Agile Project Management: Steering From the Edges. Communications of the ACM 48, 85–89 (2005)
5. Axelrod, R.: The Complexity of Cooperation: Agent-Based Models of Competition and Collaboration. Princeton University Press (1997)
6. Beer, S.: The Viable System Model: Its Provenance, Development, Methodology and Pathology. The Journal of the Operational Research Society. Palgrave Macmillan Journals 35(1), 7–25 (1984)
7. Brocklesby, J.: Becoming multimethodology literate; An assessment of cognitive difficulties of working across paradigms. In: Multimethodology: The Theory and Practise of Combining Management Science Methodologies, pp. 189–216 (1997)
8. Chan Kim, W., Mauborgne, R.: Fair Process: Managing in the Knowledge Economy. Harward Business Review (1997)
9. Checkland, P.B.: Systems thinking Systems practice. John Wiley & Sons, UK (1999)
10. Clerc, V.: Architectural Knowledge Management Practices in Agile Global Software Development. In: 6th IEEE International Conference on Digital Object identifier (2011)
11. Cockburn, A.: Agile Software Development, The Cooperative Game. Addison-Wesley (2006)

12. Drucker, P.: The Theory of Business. Harvard Business Review (1994)
13. Eoyang, G., Royce, J.: Adaptive Action: Leveraging Uncertainty in Your Organization. Stanford University Press (2013)
14. Felsen, M., Watson, B., Wilensky, U.: Surfacing Urbanisms. Recent Approaches to Metropolitan Design. In: Conference Proceedings, pp. 261–266 (2006)
15. Flood, R.L., Romm, N.R.A.: Diversity Management: Triple Loop Learning. John Wiley & Sons, Chichester (1996)
16. Gudykunst, W.B., Wiseman, R.L.: Toward a theory of effective interpersonal and intergroup communication. In: Koester, J. (ed.) Intercultural Communication Competence. International and Intercultural Communication Annual, vol. XVII, pp. 33–71. Sage Publications, CA (1993)
17. Hevner, A.R., March, S.T., Park, J., Ram, S.: Design Science in Information Systems Research. MIS Quarterly 28, 75–105 (2004)
18. Jackson, M.C.: Creative Holism for Managers. John Wiley & Sons, Chichester (2003)
19. Johnson, N.F.: Two's Company, Three is Complexity: A Simple Guide to the Science of All Sciences. Oneworld Publ., Oxford (2007)
20. Kraut, R.E., Streeter, L.A.: Coordination in Software Development. Communications of the ACM 38(3), 69–81 (1995)
21. Levinsson, H.: Management by Whose Objectives 81(1), 107–116 (2003)
22. Manifesto for Agile Software Development (2001), http://agilemanifesto.org/ (accessed January 2014)
23. Merriam-Webster Online Dictionary (2014), http://www.merriam-webster.com
24. Paasivaara, M., Lassenius, C.: Communities of practice in a large distributed agile software development organization case Ericsson. Information and Software Technology, http://www.sciencedirect.com/science/article/pii/S0950584914001475
25. Parkinsson, C.N.: Parkinssons Law. The Riverside Press, Cambridge (1957)
26. Pelrine, J.: On Understanding Software Agility - A Social Complexity Point of View. E:CO 13(1-2), 26–37 (2011)
27. Robson, C.: Real World Research. Blackwell Publishing (2002)
28. Senge, P.M.: The Fifth Discipline: The Art and Practice of the Learning Organization. Doubleday (1992)
29. Snowden, D., Boone, M.E.: A Leader's Framework for Decision Making. Harvard Business Review 85(11), 68–76 (2007)
30. Stacey, R.D.: Strategic Management and Organizational Dynamics - The Challenge of Complexity. Prentice Hall (2007)
31. Thomas, K.W.: Intrinsic Motivation at Work: What Really Drives Employee Engagement. Berrett Koehler Publishers, Inc., San Francisco (2009)
32. Van Aken, J.E.: Management research based on the paradigm of the design sciences: The quest for field-tested and grounded technological Rules. Journal of Management Studies 41(2), 219–246 (2004)
33. Wood, R., Bandura, A.: Social Cognitive Theory of Organizational Management. The Academy of Management Review 14(3), 361–384 (1989)
34. Zmud, R.W.: Management of Large Software Development Efforts. MIS Quarterly 4(2), 45–55 (1980)

Supporting a Large-Scale Lean and Agile Transformation by Defining Common Values

Maria Paasivaara[1], Outi Väättänen[2],
Minna Hallikainen[2], and Casper Lassenius[1]

[1] Department of Computer Science
Aalto University, FIN-00076 Aalto, Finland
{firstname.lastname}@aalto.fi
[2] Ericsson R&D Center Finland
Jorvas, Finland
{firstname.lastname}@ericsson.com

Abstract. This paper describes how a rapidly growing distributed product development organization at Ericsson used "Value Workshops" to align the different sites and teams when adopting agile and lean software development. The workshops were held at two main sites, and involved people from four sites. During the workshops, the teams worked on common values: their interpretation and behavioral implications, using a tree metaphor. The workshops were viewed as very valuable in creating a common organizational identity, and it was considered important to continue the work and reinforce the values to make them drive behavior in daily work.

Keywords: agile software development, large-scale agile, value workshop.

1 Introduction

Agile adoption in large, distributed organizations is difficult for many different reasons [1]. In this paper, we discuss the problem of integrating and aligning the goals and values in a large, globally distributed software development organization at Ericsson.

The case organization develops a XaaS [2] platform and a set of services, which we will refer to as the "product". Ericsson acquired the product in 2011. Currently the product is in its early life-cycle with tens of customers, the number of which is expected to grow rapidly, and is considered to have a vast market potential. As part of the acquisition, around ten people from the previous development organization moved to Ericsson and formed the core team.

The development organization has grown rapidly since: from two teams in 2011 to 15 agile teams, and altogether 200 people in the spring of 2014. Currently the development organization is distributed to five sites located in three countries. Four of the sites are in Europe and one is in Asia, see Figure 1.

T. Dingsøyr et al. (Eds.): XP 2014 Workshops, LNBIP 199, pp. 73–82, 2014.

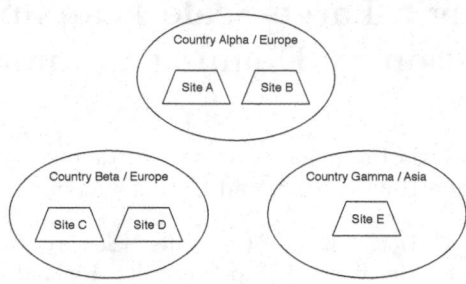

Fig. 1. Sites and Countries in the Case Project

The product has been built on several different sites, leading to challenges in end-to-end development, as all sites might not have all the different functional competencies needed in feature development.

Ericsson has traditionally used a plan-driven software process, but is currently undertaking a global adoption of lean and agile software development. Thus, in our case organization the reasons to transition to lean and agile were twofold: 1) The Ericsson wide lean and agile adoption was successfully progressing in many projects even at the same development sites as our case organization; thus lean and agile were natural choices for improving the way of working. 2) The aim of the case organization was to shorten the lead-time for features and to move from the current eight week release cycle to continuous deployment, which would mean being able to release a new feature instantly when it is ready. Agile feature teams that would be able to develop a new feature very fast without extra handovers, from end-to-end, i.e., from requirement until it is part of the product, seemed like a perfect fit for this need.

The transition in the case organization has been particularly challenging, as the organizational growth has been extremely rapid. The transition steps, the major challenges that the organization faced and the mitigating actions taken are described in our previous article [3]. In this current paper we concentrate on one of the major steps of this transformation: how the highly distributed and rapidly growing organization aimed to find a common ground and common direction through common values and joint value workshops.

The paper is structured as follows: Section 2 describes the research goals and methods, Section 3 presents our results, and finally Section 4 concludes the paper.

2   Research method

2.1   Research Goals and Questions

This is a case study [4] of one Ericsson product development organization. The broader goal of our research has been to study the large-scale agile and lean adoption in this organization. In this paper we report the initial results of one of the major steps the organization took: finding a common direction by defining and working with common values.

In this paper we address the following research questions:

RQ1: Why did the organization choose common values and value workshops as one of the major steps of its lean and agile journey?
RQ2: How were the value workshops organized?
RQ3: How did the participants perceive the value workshops?

2.2 Data Collection and Analysis

The main data collection methods were semi-structured interviews and observations during the winter 2013/2014. Regarding the whole transformation journey, we interviewed 32 people from four sites and in different roles ranging from team members to Product Owners, coaches and managers. The goal was to have as broad representation of the organization as possible. Each interview lasted 1-2 hours, with two researchers participating, one being the main interviewer, and the other taking notes. We used an interview guide approach with predetermined themes. The goal of these interviews was to understand the transformation from waterfall to lean and agile. In these interviews, we were told that the organization had started to define common values, and would be working further with the values in workshops.

We had the possibility to participate in and observe two 2-day workshops arranged at sites A and D during winter 2013/2014. The fist workshop was observed by two researchers and the second by one researcher. Detailed notes were taken during the workshops both on what happened, as well as on what was discussed in the workshops.

After the second workshop, we interviewed 12 participants from three different sites on their experiences and opinions regarding the workshops. The interviewees in these short, 15-30 min interviews, ranged from team members to managers. These semi-structured interviews were conducted by a single researcher. Counting both of the interview rounds, we interviewed a total of 44 subjects. The roles and sites of the interviewees are shown in Table 1.

In addition to interviews and observations, we received documents from our interviewees to support their stories, e.g., presentation slides of the process, product and organization structure, as well as the "Showcase", a story created by the agile coaches together with the management team to describe a fictional story of how this organization would look like in two years.

All the interviews were recorded and then transcribed by a professional transcription company. The transcribed interviews were analyzed by a qualitative data analysis software Atlas.ti. We used inductive analysis to discover themes and to categorize the qualitative data.

2.3 Limitations and Validation

Unfortunately, for cost reasons, we were able to visit and interview project participants only at the four European sites, but not at the Asian site. The European

Table 1. Interviewees and their roles (transformation interviews + value interviews)

Role	Site A	Site B	Site C	Site D	Site E	Total
Team members	3+2	1	1+5	1		13
Product owners	2	1	1			4
Architects			1	1+2		4
Coaches	2	1	3	3		9
Subsystem responsibles	1			3		4
Line managers	2+2		1			5
Other managers			6	1+1		8
Total	**14**	**3**	**18**	**12**	**0**	**47**

Note: The sum exceeds the total number of interviews, as some people had several roles.

sites were Ericsson internal sites, but the Asian site was a hired consulting company. Thus, it would would have been extremely interesting to visit and interview people from that site as well. However, we were able to interview one visiting engineer from that company, a team member currently located at site D.

After the data collection and analysis we validated our findings by giving a feedback session to the case organization based on all data collected. The feedback session took place in a team area at the site A, from where we had a videoconference connection to all the other European sites. The whole organization was invited to this feedback session and around thirty people participated actively in the session. We received positive feedback: the organization had already started to implement some of the suggested improvements and would take into account our findings when planning the next improvement steps. No corrections to our findings were presented. Moreover, the two authors of this paper coming from Ericsson have together with the researchers checked the correctness of this paper.

3   Results

The results section is divided into three parts, each providing answers to one of the three research questions.

3.1   Motivation for Value Workshops

In this subsection we focus on the first research question, "Why did the organization choose common values and value workshops as one of the major steps of its lean and agile journey?"

The first phase of the lean and agile transformation included forming a pilot team and after a couple sprints rolling out agile to the whole organization. In this organization-wide roll-out cross-functional and cross-component agile teams were formed. Even though the goal was to form mainly site-specific teams, due to the knowledge differences between the sites, approximately half of the teams were cross-site teams. The organization was not immediately satisfied with this initial organization structure, but after a few trials the structure started to gain acceptance.

Even though the agile teams were now formed and working, the organization was highly distributed both regarding geography and previous organizational boundaries, as project project personnel came from several Ericsson sites and organizations, as well as from the acquired company and a hired consulting company. Thus, besides geographical barriers, there were national and organizational culture barriers, language barriers, as well as time-zone differences in place. Most of the people had not met each other face-to-face. Some of our interviewees, even mentioned site politics, or competition between the sites, as one of the problems, as the following quotation illustrates.

I see site politics as one of the problems. It's difficult to communicate between the sites. So we build up some kind of, "us and them" feelings. That hinders our way of working. We don't have a perfect flow in the system. Because we don't really trust each other. And that's a problem.   — A Coach

Moreover, management saw that the organization did not have a common direction. Many of our interviewees mentioned this problem. They felt that a common direction was missing both regarding the future direction of the product, as well as regarding the common way of working. Thus, management and coaches thought that the next step in the transformation journey would be to define a common direction for this new and highly distributed organization and build a "we" spirit in which people identified with one single organization rather than with different competing sites.

Why we have started with values, [...] is that we would have a common baseline to continue further, [...] a baseline on which we build this common understanding and common direction. That we have something common to discuss together. I have seen as a problem in this whole project that different sites and different people have taken a bit different direction.   — A Manager

To achieve these goals the work started by doing a "Futurospective", a workshop where the agile coaches and a few managers created a vision of where the organization would be in a couple of years. Based on the results of the Futurospective the coaches wrote a "Showcase" —a fictional story of what the organization would look like and how it would work in two years time, when they had collaborated and together created a success story. Based on the showcase, the five core values were created in collaboration between the coaches and the management team: one organization, step-by-step, customer collaboration, passion to win and fun. To share the values within the whole organization a series of value workshops were organized. Besides sharing the values, the aim of these workshops was to find out whether these are the best possible values for this organization, as well as to work on what these values could mean and where they could lead to as concrete behaviors.

3.2   Organizing the Value Workshops

In this subsection we answer the second research question, "How were the value workshops organized?"

The value workshops were organized during the winter 2013–2014. The goals were twofold:

1. To create a common vision for the whole organization in the form of common values
2. To create contacts and collaboration between the sites, and building a "we" spirit across the sites to really create a one project

The workshops were arranged at the biggest sites, A and D, with around 20 people traveling from the three other European sites. The ones traveling were the whole management team and coaches, as well as a few team members. All sites participated. However, from site E (the consultancy firm) there were only a few participants who, at the time of the workshops, worked as visiting engineers at the European sites. The idea was that all team members from sites A, B, C and D would be able to participate in one of the workshops, as well as meet all the managers and coaches from all sites face-to-face.

The coaches and managers initially held joint workshops, in which they wrote a "showcase", a vision of how the organization would look like and work in two years when the whole organization had collaborated and together created a highly successful product. The aim of the showcase was to answer the question: "What made this product such a huge success?" The values were then created based on this showcase.

The idea of the 2-day value workshops called "Value Harvesting Fairs" or "Value Bootcamps" was to discuss and elaborate the values together with the whole personnel by using different approaches and ways of working. The metaphor of a cherry tree [5] was chosen as a common theme, see Figure 2. The roots of the tree were the common values, the leaves were the behaviors, e.g., what a team could do to realize the values, and the fruits were the end results. This tree metaphor was used though the workshops in all the activities.

The workshops started by tree hugging and continued by "planting the seeds" in the form of instructions how the teams could "grow" their own trees. Then the teams worked with sticky notes to build their trees and presented them to the others. At the end of the workshops, real trees were planted together: A cherry tree outside the windows of the team areas at site A. At site D, as it was winter already, two trees were planted inside for sites C and D. The coaches from different sites planned and facilitated these workshops as a collective effort.

The workshops included different kind of group activities and exercises regarding values done in varying groups: both within the whole group, within own cross-functional teams, as well as in highly mixed teams with people from different roles and from different sites. Next, we will elaborate some of the major activities.

In the beginning of both value workshops the showcase was presented by the managers and coaches. They presented it in the format of an "interview" by a

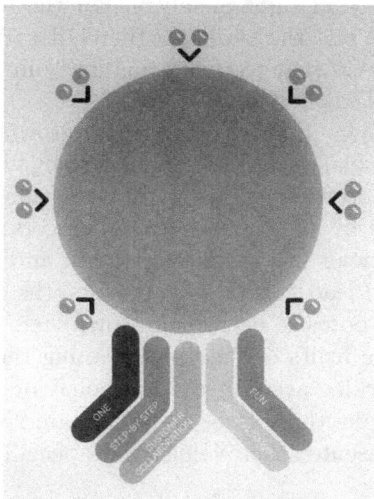

Fig. 2. Value Tree

journalist who was studying, two years in the future, why this organization and the product it had built, had been so successful. The interviewer, an organizational coach, playing the role of a journalist, asked the managers to explain their views behind the success story. Each manager "played" their role by answering the questions of this journalist, each from one specific point of view on why and how this product had been a success story, e.g., regarding organizational culture, product quality and customer collaboration.

The next step during the first Value Workshop was an interactive Value Orienteering, during which each value and what it could mean, was discussed in small groups. The teams orienteered in the office building and stopped at control points, each located under some inside tree, following the tree metaphor. At each control point a pair of coaches or managers presented one of the values to the team by very interactive means: video, drawing, discussion, sticky notes etc. The participants could discuss, ask questions, and share their own interpretations, e.g., by adding sticky notes to the drawings or flip-charts so that the next teams arriving to that control pout could see them as well. The goal of this activity was to discuss the interpretations of each value together, so that everybody would at least have an idea of what that value could mean. At the second value workshop, arranged at site D, the office spaces were different, thus a "Gallery Walk" was chosen as the approach for this activity, instead. However, the contents stayed the same. At each of the rooms along the Gallery Walk, the managers and coaches took the role of "artists" and made drawings together with the participants while presenting and discussing the value of that Gallery room.

The teams for the Value Orienteering and for the next group activity, "growing the tree", were formed in the first Value Workshop mainly based on the existing agile teams of around eight members. For the second workshop, a different approach was taken and the teams for the Gallery Walk and "growing the tree" were predetermined so that the participants from all four sites and from different roles were mixed in the teams.

The second group activity in both workshops, growing an own tree for the team, was to discuss and elaborate the values in teams based on this question: "What kind of behaviors do we see when we live our values?". The discussion in each team was facilitated by the coaches and managers. The teams considered what each value would mean in practice for them, and what kind of concrete behavior each value could lead to. These behaviors, the leaves of the tree, were added written on post-it notes to each team's own tree. Finally, the teams discussed what would be the fruits of the tree, meaning the end results when following the values and working according to the behaviors. The teams of the first Value Workshop would take these trees to their team space after the event. In both events each team presented their value tree, especially a few most important behaviors, to everybody.

In the end of the second value workshop each participant also worked with their own value tree: They were asked to write to that tree a few concrete actions that they would do in the future, so that the tree would grow. These actions were then shared and discussed with a pair during a pair walk. The idea was that each participant would take that tree to their own workplace as a reminder on what he or she was planning to do or change in the future.

3.3   Participants' Perception of the Value Workshops

This section discusses our third research question, "How did the participants perceive the value workshops?"

The first impression of the value workshops was highly positive. In particular, participants felt that the organization took a huge step closer to the goal of being one organization building a common product. Especially meeting with people from the other sites and talking face-to-face was a benefit that several of the interviewed participants mentioned.

One of the value this event brings that I see is that we are no longer just names and faces behind the screen. You see real people and talk to real people.
— A Team member

Regarding the values, most of the participants in the workshops seemed to feel that the chosen values were good. Our interviewees confirmed that:

I completely agree with these values. [...] [the values are] not so easy as before to forget, or ignore in the daily work, I think that's the main benefit of the workshop.
— A Team member

Actually, some of our interviewees were surprised at how well the workshop participants, coming from different sites and teams, all agreed both regarding the values, but also regarding the planned behaviors the teams presented to each other. Even though some felt that the presentations of each team's own value trees were a bit boring, they felt that these presentations actually showed that they all agreed on what should be done, which they saw as a great achievement.

[the best part was] the conclusion that we all agree on the same things. [...] we said almost the same things as the other teams. [...] So it was agreed from many posts, from the whole organization, basically.   — An Architect

Several of our interviewees agreed that they were aiming to personally act differently after these events and that the events had made the values more clear and meaningful to them.

I will probably do a lot of things differently. [...] I'm gonna try to collaborate more, between the teams. Because I think that's one of the biggest flaws we have right now.   — A Team member

I feel more commitment. [...] after this value bootcamp, or what ever you call it, I'm more committed to act. [...] . For example, for [my team] we should get the roles more clear and we should work together with the [organization at the other site] and have a bootcamp there, have a kick-off together for example and set the roles.   — An Architect

I think it's good when you go to every individual, I think one of the tasks was to write down, what you can do, the coming days or weeks and continue doing, to live after what we have discussed now. Those sort of exercises are probably good I think, because then, all of a sudden it means something to you.   — A Team member

Some participants were slightly worried about what would happen after the events, if the values would just be forgotten, expressing that good intentions formed during the workshops are not enough to implement the values in the normal working environment.

I believe that I'm sincere in these kind of happenings and want to change, and act according to what we have planned. But when you return to your daily life and you face the same problems as before, then it is not so easy to change your ways of working, or even remember them. That's why I think there should be somebody who kicks you...   — A Team member

The plan to tackle this was to have the coaches help the teams to work towards the common values and exhibit the behaviors they had planned. Many of our interviewees also suggested that some kind of a common follow up for these events would be needed after half a year or so.

I would say a follow-up in maybe six months or something like that, just to have a recap of what has changed, what has happened, what I have done. Just a kind of retrospective, just to see what is happening and what kind of next steps we can take. [...] All sites should be involved with that follow-up, [...] because we should fight for this one [name of the product].   — A Team member

I think we could follow-up. [...] if it's improved or if we are living by these values or not. [...] It would be nice if we can have some kind of session in half a year and then conclude was it good, are we going to this direction or what is happening. [...] Maybe we don't have to have this really big group, that we have today. But maybe within a team or within a site. — An Architect

Even though overall the values were seen as good and the workshops as beneficial by all of the interviewed participants, some were still hoping to have even more concrete vision than what the values and the showcase could provide them. Especially a concrete vision or a roadmap for the product was what a few of our interviewees were hoping to receive.

4   Conclusions

The use of value workshops seems to be a mechanism for starting the alignment of different sites and teams in a globally distributed organization. This is particularly important in agile development, as teams can have significant degrees of freedom in deciding how they work. Defining and communicating joint values can guide the teams and their actions when back in their normal environments, and can help create a common project identity.

We plan to continue studying this ongoing transformation, e.g., by interviewing people on value adoption in the teams and following how the next steps of the journey will take place.

References

1. Paasivaara, M., Lassenius, C., Heikkila, V.T., Dikert, K., Engblom, C.: Integrating global sites into the lean and agile transformation at ericsson. In: 2013 IEEE 8th International Conference on Global Software Engineering (ICGSE), pp. 134–143 (2013)
2. Banerjee, P., Friedrich, R., Bash, C., Goldsack, P., Huberman, B., Manley, J., Patel, C., Ranganathan, P., Veitch, A.: Everything as a service: Powering the new information economy. Computer 44(3), 36–43 (2011)
3. Paasivaara, M., Behm, B., Lassenius, C., Hallikainen, M.: Towards rapid releases in large-scale xaas development at ericsson: A case study. In: Proceedings of the 9th International Conference on Global Software Engineering. IEEE Computer Society Press (2014)
4. Yin, R.K.: Case Study Research: Design and Methods, 4th edn. SAGE Publications, Thousand Oaks (2009)
5. Adkins, L.: Coaching Agile Teams: A Companion for ScrumMasters, Agile Coaches, and Project Managers in Transition. Addison-Wesley (2010)

A Model for Understanding When Scaling Agile Is Appropriate in Large Organizations

Ken Power

Cisco Systems
Ireland
ken.power@gmail.com

Abstract. The term "agile at scale" is used frequently in relation to agile approaches in large organizations, but the meaning of "scale" is not always clear. Without a proper understanding of meaning and context, inappropriate methods are applied. It is important to understand when "scaling agile" is the solution to the problem at hand, and when its not. There is a difference between agile approaches used by a team in a large organization, agile approaches used on a large development effort, and organization agility. The distinction is important. This paper explores that distinction using Human Systems Dynamics as a lens through which to understand and articulate which of the three contexts an organization is dealing with. By analyzing a system through the HSD lens it becomes possible to predict and influence the impact on the flow of work through the system, and in particular, it is possible to understand what types of impediments might impact the flow of work. This helps organizations to understand appropriate approaches to agility that better suit their context.

Keywords: agile, scale, large-scale, complexity, human systems dynamics, coordination cost, communication, flow, impediments.

1   Introduction

A team working inside a large organization does not necessarily need a scaled approach to agile. There is a difference between (1) agile approaches used in a large organization, (2) agile approaches used on a large development effort, and (3) organization agility. This paper draws from research on impediments to flow in teams and organizations [1], and explores the distinction between these three categories from the perspective of Human Systems Dynamics (HSD). This research uses HSD to understand and articulate each of the three contexts. This helps organizations to understand appropriate approaches to agility that better suit their context.

2   Human Systems Dynamics

Teams and organizations are complex adaptive human systems. Human Systems Dynamics (HSD) provides a useful lens through which to understand teams and

T. Dingsøyr et al. (Eds.): XP 2014 Workshops, LNBIP 199, pp. 83–92, 2014.

organizations [2]. Self-organization is a key property of complex adaptive systems and agile [3]. Research in complex adaptive systems show that three factors shape patterns in self-organization: containers, significant differences, and transforming exchanges" [4]. These three elements form the CDE model in Human Systems Dynamics, and are the conditions for self-organization in human systems. A **container** sets the boundary for self-organizing systems [2]. The container's purpose is *"to hold the system together, so relationships between and among agents can be established"* [2]. A system may be contained by an external boundary, by some central attracting force, or by one-to-one forces between agents in the system – what Eoyang refers to as a *fence*, *magnet* or *affinity container*, respectively [2]. Eoyang notes that any human system can contain multiple containers simultaneously, and the agents in the system can be part of multiple containers simultaneously [2]. A **difference** is something that represents the potential for change in a container, and is a necessary condition for self-organization to occur [2]. Differences determine the patterns that emerge in self-organizing systems. Examples of significant differences include power, levels of expertise, quality, cost, gender, race and educational background [4]. A **transforming exchange** is the interdependence between agents in a complex adaptive system, and is critical to the ability of the agents to self-organize [2]. Examples of transforming exchanges include synchronization meetings that keep the work of two or more teams coordinated, and other communications that provide constructive interaction across container boundaries.

3   Research Approach

3.1   Research Objective

The objective of this research is to understand when scaling approaches are appropriate in a large organization. The research offers the following hypotheses:

1. That scaling approaches are not always applicable in a large organization.
2. That an analysis of the organization based on the conditions for self organization will help to understand the contexts in which scaling approaches are appropriate.

3.2   Research Method

This research uses a qualitative approach [8, 9], and employs a case study of a large company. Yin recommends to define the unit of analysis when using case study research [10, 11]. The units of analysis in this study are teams, organizations within the company, and the company itself.

The primary analysis tool is a CDE analysis of a large company. The researcher examined the structure of multiple teams, projects, programs, business units and organizations in the company. This was cross-correlated with available literature on large-scale agility. A coding analysis was performed on the available data [12]. The coding analysis helped to identify containers, differences and exchanges.

4 Case Study of a Large Company

The case study is based on a large, globally distributed company, which we will refer to as Company X. Many teams and organizations within the company have been adopting an agile approach to their work since 2008. The company delivers products, solutions and services to a diverse range of markets. Table 1 in section 4.1 below provides additional data about the company. One of the organizations within Company X can itself be considered "large". We will refer to this organization as Organization Y.

4.1 What Does "Large" Mean?

To put the term "large" in context, it is helpful to first define what we mean by "small: and "medium", and use those as a basis for relative comparison. The European Union, for example, has an official definition for small and medium sized enterprises [13]. According to EU law, the main attributes that define whether a company is a small-medium sized enterprise (SME) are number of employees and either turnover or balance sheet total [14]. SMEs are enterprises that employ *"fewer than 250 persons and which have an annual turnover not exceeding 50 million euro, and/or an annual balance sheet total not exceeding 43 million euro"* [14]. The company in this case study can be defined as "large" based on a simple comparison against the attributes defined for micro, small and medium SMEs. The data in Table 1 includes a comparison with Small-Medium Enterprises (SMEs).

Table 1. Attributes that define what "large" means

Factor	Company X	Organization Y	Micro	Small	Medium
# of employees	80,000	8000	<10	<50	< 250
Turnover	$48.6bn in FY 2013	Confidential, but is a subset of Company X turn over	≤€2m	≤€10m	≤€50m
# of people on a "large" project	100s	100+ people.			N/A

5 A CDE Analysis of the Organization

The diagram in Fig. 1 shows a large organization represented as a set of containers.

The container labeled "Organization" represents the organization as a whole, i.e., the company. Containers T1-T10 represent different teams. BU1-BU4 represent business units. C1-C2 represent customers, P1-P2 represents partners, and S1-S2 represent suppliers. The arrows between containers represent exchanges, and show the degree of coupling that exists between containers.

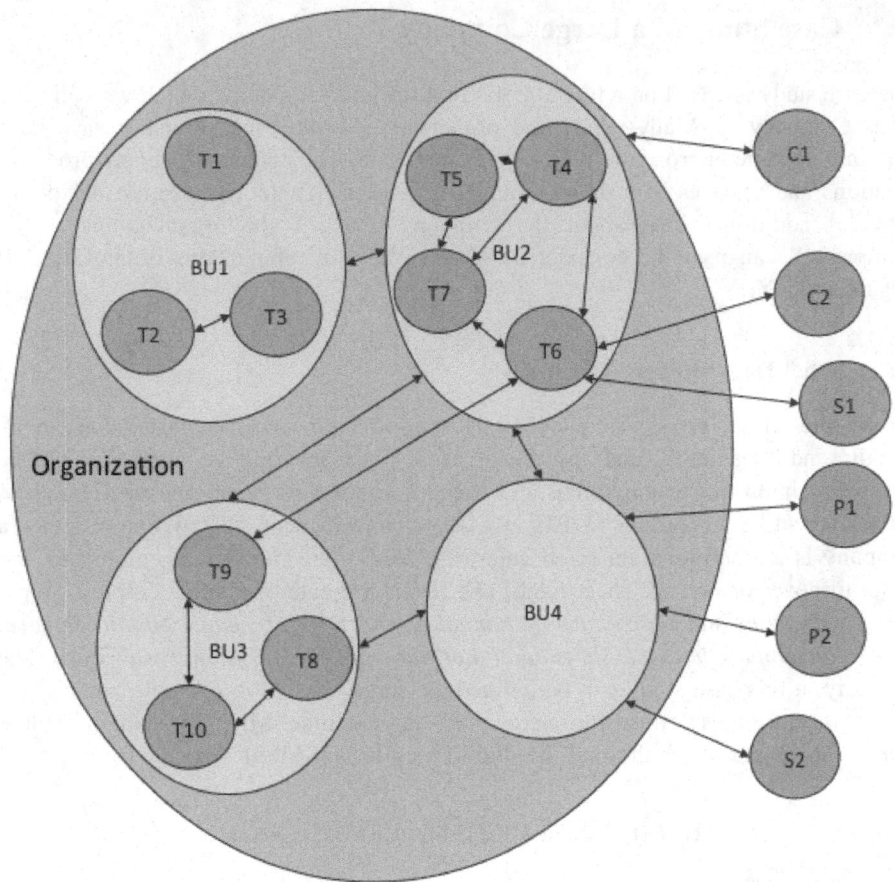

Fig. 1. Understanding the context for agility by visualizing containers and exchanges

To consider the difference within a container, we can look at any set of distinguishing attributes. For example we could examine gender, power, status, age, ethnic diversity, education history, or musical preferences. It is important to choose a difference or set of differences that are directly relevant to the research question(s). Although many of these examples could be relevant to this study, this research considers the example of skillsets within a team as being one significant difference that influences agility. Fig. 2 shows an example of two teams. The team on the left has a high degree of difference; the team on the right has a low degree of difference. The team on the left could represent a typical cross-functional team with a mix of skills including development, test, user experience design and automation. The team on the right more closely resembles a team where everyone has the same, or similar, skills. This is often seen in a testing team, a user experience design team, or a technical documentation team, for example. Teams with a higher degree of difference have a much greater chance of being agile, and capable of delivering customer value as a team. In complexity terms, the team on the left has better conditions for self-organization than the team on the right.

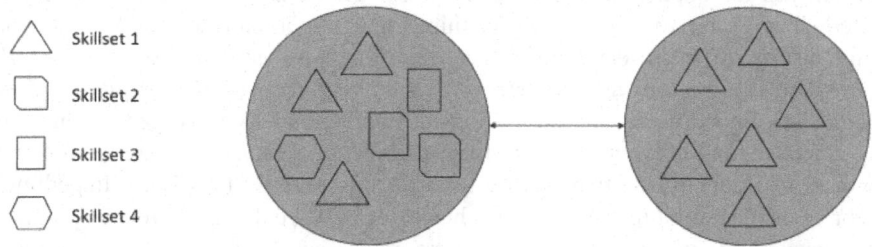

Fig. 2. Understanding the context for agility by visualizing differences within a container

Methods such as Scrum [15, 16] and XP [17], and frameworks like SAFe [18] talk about the importance of teams. They place an emphasis on the importance of cross-functional teams and having the right mix of skills on the team to allow the team to be successful. In CDE terms, this means having a high degree of difference within the container. They also talk about the importance of communicating effectively within and outside the team. In CDE terms, this means having a high quality exchanges within the container, and across containers.

Teams are not a homogenous entity. A team of all testers or all user experience designers will have comparatively low internal difference when compared to a cross-functional Scrum team. A co-located team sharing the same physical workspace will have a higher quantity of exchanges, and because of the face-to-face interactions these exchanges will be of a higher quality than distributed or dispersed teams.

6   Determining Factors

It is useful to consider the factors that impact work in large organizations. This research considers three dimensions that help to illustrate which context is appropriate in large organizations: coordination cost, communication cost and overall impact on the flow of work through the system.

6.1   Coordination Cost

Coordination cost relates to the cost incurred in coordinating the people and systems that perform the work. It can be measured in time and money. The coordination cost increases as the number of containers increases.

6.2   Communication Cost

Communication cost relates to the cost incurred in communicating within the team and outside the team. It can be measured in time and money. The communication cost increases as the number of exchanges within and between containers increases.

6.3   Impact on the Flow of Work

Establishing a smooth flow of work through the system is a goal for agile teams and lean organizations. The context within which products are developed, or services provided, has an impact on the flow of work. To determine how flow might be affected, it is useful to consider those things that might impede the flow of work through a system. This research defines an impediment as *"anything that obstructs the smooth flow of work through the system and/or interferes with the system achieving its goals"* [1]. Impediments are those things that prevent teams and organizations from being effective, and prevent the work from flowing smoothly. There are a number of categories of impediments that can be used for this purpose [1]. These impediment categories include extra features, delays, handovers, failure demand, work in progress, context switching, unnecessary motion, extra processes, and unmet human potential. From a HSD perspective, the number of containers, and the quality and quantity of exchanges, influence the likely occurrence of these types of impediments. Differences within and between containers also influence the likely occurrence of impediments.

Table 2 below shows the results of preliminary analysis of impediment categories from this research, and correlates the likelihood of impediments with characteristics of containers, differences and exchanges.

Table 2. Summary of Impediment Categories and how Impediments to Flow are influenced by Containers, Differences and Exchanges

Impediment Category	Containers	Differences	Exchanges
Extra Features	Considering the product as a container, extra features result in a larger container that needs to be maintained and managed	Can occur if the differences within a container are too high, and it is hard to reach alignment on core product vision, or if differences are too low and the product is the result of group think	Low quality exchanges between customers and teams can result in adding features customers do not want or need
Delays	Can increase as the number of containers increases		Can increase as the number of exchanges within and between containers increases
Handovers	Can increase as the number of containers increases	Can occur where differences lead to hard specialization in skills	Can increase as the number of exchanges within and between containers increases
Failure Demand			Can occur if the exchanges are low quality, which can result for example in errors, poor design or the team building the wrong thing
Work In Progress			Too few exchanges can mean collaboration is low within a team, which can lead to a high amount of work in progress

Table 2. (*Continued*)

Context Switching			Can occur if the number of exchanges is too high, and especially of the exchanges are not relevant to the work in progress.
Unnecessary Motion	Can occur where containers are physically dispersed, e.g., across a building or campus, or around the world		
Extra Processes	The higher the number of containers, the greater the coordination and communication cost, potentially requiring extra processes to manage		The higher the number of exchanges, the greater the coordination and communication cost, potentially requiring extra processes to manage
Unmet Human Potential	Unmet human potential is correlated more with the system as a whole than specifically with the containers, differences or exchanges. For example the system needs to actively support team members in meeting their potential. This can be a factor of how differences are developed over time, or can be influenced by the quality and quantity of exchanges.		

7 Discussion: Three Contexts for Agility and Scale

From the perspective of this paper, and the author's experience working with large organizations using agile, there are a number of factors that apply. It is important to distinguish between agile used in a large organization, agile used in a large development effort in a large organization, and the agility of the organization itself.

7.1 Being Agile in a Team Inside A Large Organization

In this context, "large" refers to the size of the company, and is largely influenced by the number of employees in the overall organization. An organization of 70000 people is large in terms of number of employees, number of products, number of customers, number of target markets, etc. The container marked "Organization" in Fig. 1 above represents the organization. The diagram shows other containers representing the market, customers, and other entities. However, there can be cases where a single agile team is developing something in that large organization, and they have no other dependencies on any other team. They are completely self-contained. container "Team 1" represents this agile team in Fig. 1. This is agile in a large organization, but is clearly not large-scale agile. There could be a thousand such teams in a large organization, each working on different, unrelated things. It is true that at some level the organization's management needs to understand what is going on in the organization, but this is not a question of agility; they need to know this regardless.

Taking this a step further, two agile teams working on a common product in the same organization, and are completely self-contained. Containers "Team 2" and

"Team 3" represent these agile teams in Fig. 1 above. Having two teams instead of one introduces some necessary overhead in terms of communication and coordination costs, ensuring consistency of the product architecture, having a common Definition of Done, etc. The two teams are working in a larger container that is the organization of 80000 people, yet this is still not large-scale agile. It is simply two teams working together inside a large organization. At some point, however, adding more people and teams changes the scope of the problem. That is the focus of the next section.

7.2   Using Agile Approaches in a Large Development Effort inside a Large Organization

In this context, "large" refers to the size of the organization, and is largely influenced by the number of employees in the overall development effort. Additional factors include the number of people and teams involved in the development effort. At large scale it becomes increasingly important to be aware of Conway's Law, and understand that the structure of the system mirrors the structure of the organization that creates it [19]. It becomes increasingly important to consider system architecture at this scale. In HSD terms, the architecture can be considered a container. This is the sweet spot where scaled agile approaches can add value to the organization.

7.3   Organization Agility: The Large Organization Itself is Agile

In this context, "large" refers to the size of the organization, and is largely influenced by the number of employees in the overall organization. Container "Organization" in Fig. 1 above represents the organization. Agility in this context can be inferred by the number of differences within this container and the exchanges (both quality and quantity) with other containers. An organization is likely to be more agile if it has a balance of containers, with the right balance of high-quality exchanges between them.

8   Conclusions and Future Work

Agility in a large organization comes in at least three contexts. Understanding your context helps you choose the right approach for improving the agility of your team and organization.

1. If the container is small and relatively decoupled, even within a much larger container, and there are a low number of exchanges with other containers, then the concept of "large-scale agile" likely does not apply.
2. If there are a high number of containers, with a high degree of transforming exchanges between them, the organization itself could be agile. Whether approaches to scaling agile apply depends on the third scenario.
3. If you have multiple containers that have a high degree of transforming exchanges between them, and the agents in those containers are working toward a shared outcome, then once the number of containers and exchanges goes above a certain threshold, there is benefit in applying principles of large-scale agility.

8.1   Future Work

The researcher is continuing with further work in the area of large-scale agility, and understanding the nature of product development in large teams and organizations. First, the research includes further use of the CDE model to analyze large teams and organizations, and using the CDE model to understand the properties of self-organization in large teams and organizations. Second, in research that expands on the work described in section 6.3 above, the researcher is exploring how to better understand the flow of work in teams and organizations, and impediment removal in large-scale teams and organizations [1].

References

[1] Power, K., Conboy, K.: Impediments to Flow: Rethinking the Lean Concept of 'Waste' in Modern Software Development. In: Cantone, G., Marchesi, M. (eds.) XP 2014. LNBIP, vol. 179, pp. 203–217. Springer, Heidelberg (2014)

[2] Eoyang, G.H.: Conditions for Self-Organizing in Human Systems. Doctor of Philosophy PhD Thesis for Doctor of Philosophy in Human Systems Dynamics. The Union Institute and University (2001)

[3] Power, K.: Social contracts, simple rules and self-organization: A perspective on agile development. In: Cantone, G., Marchesi, M. (eds.) XP 2014. LNBIP, vol. 179, pp. 277–284. Springer, Heidelberg (2014)

[4] Olson, E.E., Eoyang, G.H.: Facilitating Organization Change: Lessons from Complexity Science. Jossey-Bass/Pfeiffer, A Wiley Company, San Francisco (2001)

[5] Larman, C., Vodde, B.: Scaling lean & agile development: Thinking and organizational tools for large-scale Scrum. Addison-Wesley, Upper Saddle River (2009)

[6] Larman, C., Vodde, B.: Practices for scaling lean & agile development: large, multisite, and offshore product development with large-scale Scrum. Addison-Wesley, Upper Saddle River (2010)

[7] Cockburn, A.: Crystal clear: A human-powered methodology for small teams. Addison-Wesley, Boston (2005)

[8] Bailey, C.A.: A Guide to Qualitative Field Research, 2nd edn. Pine Forge Press, Thousand Oaks (2007)

[9] Yin, R.K.: Qualitative Research from Start to Finish. The Guildford Press, New York (2012)

[10] Yin, R.K.: Applications of case study research, 2nd edn. Sage Publications, London (2003)

[11] Yin, R.K.: Case Study Research: Design and Methods. SAGE, Inc., Thousand Oaks (2009)

[12] Saldaña, J.: The Coding Manual for Qualitative Researchers, 2nd edn. SAGE Publications Ltd., London (2013)

[13] European_Commission, Commission Recommendation 2003/361/EC. Official Journal of the European Union L 124, 36, (May 20, 2003)

[14] EU recommendation 2003/361, European_Commission (2003)

[15] Cohn, M.: Succeeding with Agile: Software Development Using Scrum. Addison-Wesley, Upper Saddle River (2010)

[16] J. Sutherland and K. Schwaber: The Scrum Guide. The Definitive Guide to Scrum: The Rules of the Game (October 2013), http://Scrum.org

[17] Beck, K., Andres, C.: Extreme Programming Explained: Embrace Change, 2nd edn. Addison-Wesley, Boston (2005)

[18] Leffingwell, D.: Scaled Agile Framework (December 1, 2013), http://www.scaledagileframework.com/

[19] Conway, M.: How do Committees Invent? Datamation 14, 28–31 (1968)

Control in Software Project Portfolios:
A Complex Adaptive Systems Approach

Roger Sweetman, Orla O'Dwyer, and Kieran Conboy

Discipline of Business Information Systems, National University of Ireland, Galway
{roger.sweetman,orla.odwyer,kieran.conboy}@nuigalway.ie

Abstract. Effective project portfolio management (PPM) can both help reverse the prevailing trend of software failure and act as a key driver of business value. Despite the importance of PPM and its success in other disciplines such as finance and new product development, it has not been studied widely in information systems with little research examining PPM in an agile context. This study proposes to address this gap by using complex adaptive systems theory as a lens to study the enactment and effectiveness of four known modes of control (behavior, outcome, clan and self) in agile software project portfolios. It proposes an interpretivist approach using exploratory case studies to investigate portfolio control in its natural context. This study will contribute to the advancement of control theory and provide new insights for theory and practice by integrating the study of PPM and control in an agile environment.

Keywords: large-scale agile software development, project portfolio management, complex adaptive systems, control, agile methods.

1 Introduction

Increasing numbers of software development teams are embracing agile principles [1, 2] to overcome the serious problem of information systems development (ISD) project failure [3, 4]. While questions about the scalability of agile methods to large scale projects and portfolios are being addressed [5, 6] considerable work remains. A workshop at XP2013 identified inter team co-ordination and large project and portfolio management as two of the most important topics for research [7]. This is supported by research that shows portfolio and program failure is almost as widespread as project failure. For example, between 40 and 60% of IT programs fail to meet budget, time and expectations and are in many cases are very much under-utilized when implemented, if implemented at all [8-10].

Modern organizations are using project portfolio management (PPM) as a means to govern a set of projects that may be related by having a common objective, common client, shared resources or other interdependencies [11, 12]. PPM differs from project management in that it is about doing the right projects as opposed to doing projects right [13]. It has been estimated that 90% by value of all projects are carried out in a multi-project context [14], yet, research has focused almost solely on the management of single projects with PPM and even more specifically agile PPM remaining poorly understood.

T. Dingsøyr et al. (Eds.): XP 2014 Workshops, LNBIP 199, pp. 93–104, 2014.
© Springer International Publishing Switzerland 2014

Difficulties with PPM are greater in organizations practicing agile methods [15]. These methods have been considered as constrained to small co-located projects carried out by individual teams [16] with the transition from the agile project to the agile portfolio proving difficult. For example, problems have been reported in scaling scrum [17, 18]. While agile project management literature has increased in recent years e.g. [19], there are only a handful of empirical studies that have addressed the issues of scaling agile to the portfolio [e.g 15, 17]. Little research exists on how IS PPM can be enacted in a way consistent with agile principles [17]. The most notable exceptions are studies by [15, 20] who examine current agile portfolio management practices.

2   Background and Motivation

Portfolio theory is well studied in disciplines such as financial portfolio management, research and development and new product development [21]. It is surprising that it is so rarely applied in IS given its maturity and effectiveness in other fields. Similar to financial portfolios the success of an individual project does not lead to portfolio success, Also a portfolio of software projects can fail despite some successes at the underlying project level [3, 22]. Consequently, the view that a good project management control framework applied across a portfolio of projects inevitably leads to a successful portfolio does not always hold true. Portfolios take a long term view while agile projects are dynamic and subsequent to rapid changes, which introduces new challenges for management.

Traditionally PPM has taken a linear approach to the completion of individual projects. This is an extension of the "lonely project" perspective where a portfolio consists of a set of projects executed in isolation from each other and the changing environment. Lycett et al. [23] outline how current PPM frameworks assume that highly structured and prescriptive approaches will be equally effective regardless of context. However, in agile this is not valid as projects are flexible, embracing change even towards the end of the project [24]. Agile projects are organic and there can be many interdependencies between projects within the portfolio. Delays or changes requested by clients on a single project may affect the portfolio as a whole. The difference between the idealized vision of a project portfolio and the reality of an agile portfolio where projects start, stop, and change direction as they progress is illustrated in Figure 1.

Project portfolio literature tends to assume a top down construction of the portfolio. An example of this is the over-emphasis on the project selection phase of PPM, assuming that a range of projects are available for selection and that the decision to proceed resides with the controlling body. On the other hand, contemporary project management methods such as Scrum [25] embrace bottom-up customer-driven requirements change. Consequently, there can be an inconsistency or tension between the centralized control approach of project portfolio management and the self-organizing principles of agile. This dichotomy is central to the problem of scaling agile methods from small projects to enterprise wide portfolios. Control frameworks need to incorporate both approaches. However, control research has not yet been extended to either PPM or agile PPM.

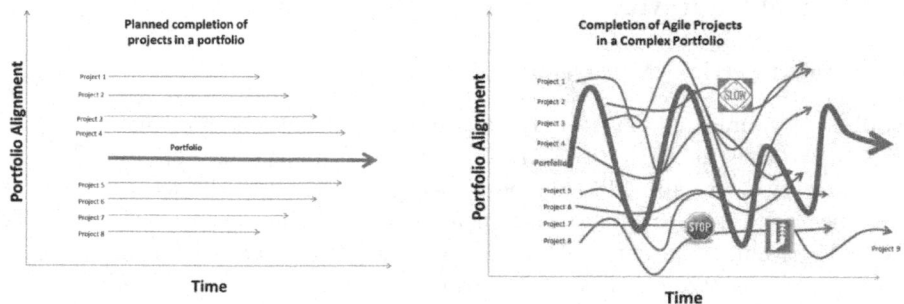

Fig. 1. An idealized project portfolio compared with the reality of agile portfolios

Further, there is a mismatch between research and practitioner needs. PPM research has in general focused on selection as opposed to ongoing management and control of the portfolio with many of the selection methods proposed highly mathematical as opposed to being derived from practical demands [26]. While there has been some progress, such as the identification of success factors and the development of maturity models [11, 27-30], significant research is still required especially to create a better understanding how agile project management methods can be applied to IT portfolios.

Finally, while some studies help to explain how PPM is carried out in organizations, they fail to provide an overarching theory to explain agile PPM. It has been suggested that techniques without an underlying theory end up reduced to a series of steps executed by rote [31]. Agile project portfolios can be complex. They often have goals that are ill defined, ambiguous or are subject to change as they seek to maintain alignment with organizational strategy which is responsive to changes e.g. the environment. This indicates that a portfolio is not an entity whose behavior can be predicted by an analysis of its components but rather a complex system capable of adapting its own behavior and makeup. Such systems are common in the sciences (e.g. ecosystems, the immune system) and are known as complex adaptive systems (CAS). Investigations into the behavior of complex systems are revealing new insights from which project management can learn [32]. An important feature of CAS is the lack of a single point of control. This means that behaviors can be unpredictable and direct control is difficult with a reliance on influence [33]. Seeing a portfolio as a CAS has significant implications for research. It is no longer valid to attempt to understand complex portfolios by breaking them into components, studying them and integrating the results [34].

Arising from this, our study seeks to use complex adaptive systems theory as a lens to:

1) Identify the mix of controls (behavior, outcome self & clan) used in agile software project portfolios
2) Study how these controls are enacted in agile software project portfolios
3) Develop a set of criteria to evaluate the effectiveness of the controls used in agile software project portfolios

3   Literature Review

3.1   Project Portfolio Management

Portfolio theory emerged in the field of investment [35] and was subsequently applied to fields like construction [36], R&D [37, 38], new product development [39] and information systems [40]. PPM is about managing a group of projects carried out under the sponsorship and/or management of a particular organization [41]. The Project Management Institute [42] defines PPM as *"the centralized management of one or more portfolios, which includes identifying, prioritizing, authorizing, managing, and controlling project, programs, and other related work to achieve specific strategic business objectives"*.

Effective IS PPM has a number of advantages for organisations. It ensures that risk is balanced across a portfolio [40], projects are aligned to organisational strategy [11] and is critical to achieving value from software development [43]. This requires immense coordination and control of budgets, resources, time and projects across the entire portfolio [44, 45], especially in large portfolios with complex interdependencies between projects [46, 47]. Portfolio managers must not only select projects but also be able to pause or remove projects that are not contributing to overall portfolio goals [11] and reallocate resources when required [12]. This is even more difficult when agile is adopted at enterprise level with organisations facing challenges such as how to manage frequent releases, customer integration and architecture across the portfolio. To date the PPM literature has not examined how agile project portfolios (i.e. portfolios built upon agile principles and managed dynamically (Krebs, 2004)), once established, are controlled, which this study aims to address.

While the iterative nature of agile practices is not necessarily compliant with established portfolio management practices, there have been some attempts to describe agile practices in portfolio management [48-50]. For example, the Scaled Agile Framework (SAFe) describes practices to implement agile at organizational level. However, SAFe assumes that there only about 5-10 agile teams executing projects [51]. Vähäniitty [50] limits his description of agile PPM to small software organizations whereas Krebs [49] proposes a portfolio approach based on agile principles and splits portfolio management into project, resource and asset management. He further highlights the need for a project management office and transparency as key to agile portfolio management. However, there is little empirical evidence to support these frameworks [15] with many challenges identified around areas such as strategic alignment [52], resource allocation and governance [17, 53] thus, justifying the need for further research into the exercise of control in portfolios.

3.2   Control

Control can be defined in a number of ways. In this study it refers to an attempt by organisations to influence people to take actions and make decisions, which are consistent with the goals and objectives the organisation [54-57]. Organizations typically use a broad range of control modes and mechanisms to control the behavior of their employees [58]. These control modes are divided into formal (behaviour and outcome) and informal control (clan and self-control) [55-57]. A detailed explanation of the characteristics of each control mode is available in Kirsch [59]. Formal control is typically documented and specifies rules that require particular behaviors to achieve desired outcomes, which are then monitored and evaluated resulting in rewards or sanctions [54, 55] e.g. project plans, budgets. Informal controls are unwritten rules. They can be social or people-based and focus on the role that individuals or groups play in the exercise of control [55, 56, 60] e.g. peer pressure, culture. Many organizations tend to focus on formal controls [61] even though it is recognized that informal controls have an equally important role [62, 63]. PPM involves the control of multiple projects and therefore multiple controllers by one controller, which brings its own distinct set of challenges for organisations and potentially increases the complexity of the controller-controllee relationship and the interactions between them. The importance of informal controls such as culture (clan) and self-organization (self-control) in agile methods as well as the need for accountability at the portfolio level suggest that a broad mix of formal and informal controls is necessary in agile IS PPM. The interaction of these controls is likely to result in complex outcomes.

3.3   Complex Adaptive Systems

Complexity theories have arisen from attempts in the natural sciences to model natural phenomenon [64]. They are concerned with the emergence of higher level order in dynamic non-linear systems where the laws of cause and effect do not appear to apply [65]. Complexity theories differ from mechanistic theories in that rather than assuming a centrally controlled governing structure, order emerges from the interaction between the different components within the system. The three main branches of complexity theory are chaos [66], dissipative structures theory [67] and complex adaptive systems (CAS) [68]. CAS is the most appropriate of these theories to act as lens to study project portfolios. This is because it is the only one that does not take a macro approach to modelling systems. Instead, it models the phenomena at the micro level using the agents[1] that make up the system. It does not attempt to formulate rules for the whole system, but instead formulates rules of interaction for the individual agents in the system. The software portfolio can be studied by focusing on the individual teams and projects and the interactions between them.

While CAS is defined in a number of different ways, most definitions of CAS involve *agents interacting* in *self-organizing* ways with each other and the *environment* [e.g. 69, 70]. For example, Benbya and McKelvey [71] define a complex adaptive system as a system poised between order and chaos, that not only self organizes, but directs its activity towards its own optimization. Vessey and Ward [72] define a complex adaptive system as "any system featuring a large number of interacting components that exhibits self-organization and emergence under a certain

---

[1] An *agent* is a general term to describe the parts of a complex adaptive system such as atoms molecules, processes, people and teams. In this study the agents in a complex portfolio are individuals, teams, projects portfolios and programs.

level of tension, and whose aggregate activity is non-linear" e.g. biological habitats, cities and the internet. However, the definition used for this study is the most all-encompassing one where Holland [70, 73] defines a CAS as a system composed of interacting agents, which undergo constant change, both autonomously and in interaction with their environment to produce complex and adaptive behaviours and patterns. These patterns are aggregate behaviours and structures that are not predictable from an analysis of the component parts of the system. Rather self-organization emerges as agents interact through sometimes simple rules which can change and adapt as experience accumulates and environmental conditions change. [73, 74]. Feedback is the driving force of complex systems adaption [71]with interrelated parts feeding back to each other driving or damping change [75]. A system is not considered a complex adaptive system if its elements lack agency [76, 77]. To summarise, the main concepts in CAS are *agents*, *interactions*, *environment*, and *feedback loops*, all of which combine to result in the *emergence* of *self-organization*.

While CAS is no longer considered a new theory in organization studies [74], its application to IS is more recent. CAS has been applied to IT enabled organizational learning [78], IT supported team processes [79], improving IS alignment [80], the role of IT in the development of bureaucracy [81], and the impact of IT on organizational culture [82] and further examples of CAS in IS research include processes for technology use [69], IS project management [83] and agile software development [84, 85]. This increasing prevalence of CAS in information systems research led to Merali [86] describing it as the "emergent domain" in management research. There has been a greater emphasis on the theoretical aspects of CAS rather than empirical studies. Vidgen and Wang [87] attribute this to the difficulty in making the abstract principles of CAS suitable concrete for case study research.

The suitability of CAS as a lens to study agile software development is supported by Highsmith and Cockburn [88]. They argued that organizations are complex adaptive systems, where independent people interact in self-organizing ways, guided by rules to create innovative results. Furthermore, Kent Beck suggested that CAS is "the only way to make sense of the world" [89]. CAS allows researchers capture interactions and relationships between entities and their environment and study their effect on observable phenomena [69]. The absence of a single point of control [71] makes it an ideal lens to study control in a portfolio where there are multiple controllers and controllees. CAS has already been used to study control in supply chains [76], however, to our knowledge, it has not been used to study control in agile software project portfolios.

4   Research Method

A qualitative approach is proposed for this study [90]. While modelling is often deemed an appropriate method for gaining insights into complex systems, Cilliers [91] warns that models by necessity, have to reduce the complexity of a system. Therefore, a model of complex system is flawed by default. Worse still because a complex adaptive system is nonlinear, we cannot know what the flaw is as we cannot predict the importance of what we leave out. This, combined with a lack of existing research on control in agile software project portfolios through the lens of CAS justifies a qualitative approach [90]. This approach will provide us with a rich insight into agile software portfolios. As the study is exploratory in nature we will use multiple case studies, which is appropriate when a research phenomenon is investigated in its natural setting [92]. This will broaden empirical evidence and allow for comparison and cross-case analysis. The intention is to conduct a number of case studies across the public and private sector using a purposeful case selection strategy to select cases that are information–rich [93]. Selection will be on the basis that at organisations are using an agile methodology, that at least one portfolio of projects exists and that the organisation has scaled agile practices to portfolio level or is in the process of doing so. Data collection will continue until saturation is reached [94].

A traceable 'audit trail' of the research process will be followed to improve the reliability and repeatability of the research. An interview protocol will be prepared using primarily open-ended questions. It will identify (i) how the four control modes (behaviour, outcome, clan and self) are used in agile IS project portfolios and (ii) use the main principles of CAS (*agents, interactions, environment, feedback loops, emergence* and *self-organization*) to determine how the control mechanisms identified are enacted in agile software project portfolios. It will also address how project and portfolio managers evaluate project and portfolio controls and the effect of controls on feedback and interactions both within the portfolio and between the portfolio and its environment. Initially, a pilot study will be conducted with one project manager and a portfolio manager to test and refine the interview protocol. Subsequently, a number of organisations and personnel within those organisations will be identified to participate in data collection. Interview data collected will first demonstrate the mix of controls used in agile software projects and portfolios across a number of organisations. This will inform the development of a set of criteria to evaluate the effectiveness of controls used in agile software project portfolios. Interview data will be corroborated with other sources of evidence e.g. documentation and observation.

Data will be analyzed using Corbin & Strauss's [94] open coding and axial coding techniques. To answer the first research question interview transcripts will be reviewed with text describing specific control mechanisms coded as a behaviour, outcome clan or self-control. Where control mechanisms (e.g. project plan, budget) faciliate more than one control mode they will be classified under both. The codes and categories for the second and third research questions will arise from a more in-depth review of the literature and provide a list of 'intellectual bins' or 'seed categories' [90] to structure the data collection and the coding stage of data analysis.

5   Conclusion and Next Steps

This study is motivated by the increasing complexity of software portfolios within organisations. Despite the importance of PPM to the creation of business value and its identification as a key research objective, there has been a significant dearth of academic research on the topic, especially that which addresses control in agile project portfolios. From a research perspective this study will advance current understanding of agile PPM by using the theory of complex adaptive systems as a lens to study the enactment of control in agile portfolios and to develop a set of criteria to evaluate the effectiveness of the different control modes (behaviour, outcome, clan and self) in agile project portfolios. This is important as it will show the range of controls portfolio managers use to manage agile portfolios, which is currently unknown and it will develop a set of criteria to evaluate the effectiveness of such controls. This will make a contribution by helping organizations determine the most appropriate portfolio controls for their needs and evaluate their effectiveness, which may result in the removal of existing controls and the addition of new or modification of existing portfolio controls. Finally, this study will provide guidance for future researchers who wish to study control in agile project portfolios.

In terms of next steps we will first conduct a pilot study to compile an initial list of agile portfolio controls (behaviour, outcome, clan and self) and understand how such controls are enacted. We are currently in the process of identifying a pilot organisation and personnel within that organisation to participate in the pilot study. Following analysis of the pilot data we will then be in a position to identify a number of organisations to participate in the second phase of data collection.

There are a number of interesting possibilities for future research. Firstly, a complexity perspective on agile software portfolios will inform future research on the effective governance of agile software portfolios using self-organization. CAS is an appropriate lens to study self-management and self-organization in agile portfolios. Some work has already looked at barriers to self-management in agile teams [95]. This work could be extended to develop a framework to enable self-organization in agile portfolios. Secondly, the operationalization of CAS will enable future empirical research into a number of areas relevant to agile PPM such as ambidextrous portfolios, the emergence of culture and the role of feedback in portfolios. Finally, once the key controls in agile software portfolios have been identified, it will be possible to model agile portfolios as complex adaptive systems using agent based modelling.

Acknowledgements. This work was supported, in part, by Science Foundation Ireland grant 10/CE/I1855 to Lero - the Irish Software Engineering Research Centre (www.lero.ie). The authors would also like to thank the anonymous reviewers for their help in developing this article.

References

1. Abrahamsson, P., Conboy, K., Wang, X.: 'Lots done, more to do': The current state of agile systems development research. European Journal of Information Systems 18(4), 281–284 (2009)
2. Dybå, T., Dingsøyr, T.: Empirical studies of agile software development: A systematic review. Information and Software Technology 50(9-10), 833–859 (2008)
3. Conboy, K.: Project failure en masse: a study of loose budgetary control in ISD projects. European Journal of Information Systems 19(3), 273–287 (2010)

4. The Standish Group, CHAOS Manifesto The Laws of CHAOS and the CHAOS 100 Best PM Practices (2010)
5. Lindvall, M., et al.: Agile software development in large organizations. Computer 37(12), 26–34 (2004)
6. Boehm, B.: Get ready for agile methods, with care. Computer 35(1), 64–69 (2002)
7. Dingsøyr, T., Moe, N.B.: Research challenges in large-scale agile software development. ACM SIGSOFT Software Engineering Notes 38(5), 38–39 (2013)
8. Whittaker, B.: What went wrong? Unsuccessful information technology projects. Information Management and Computer Security 7(1), 23–29 (1999)
9. Keil, M., Mann, J., Rai, A.: Why software projects escalate: An empirical analysis and test of four theoretical models 1, 2. Mis Quarterly 24(4), 631–664 (2000)
10. Bartis, E., Mitev, N.: A multiple narrative approach to information systems failure: A successful system that failed. European Journal of Information Systems 17(2), 112–124 (2008)
11. de Reyck, B., et al.: The impact of project portfolio management on information technology projects. International Journal of Project Management 23(7), 524–537 (2005)
12. Blichfeldt, B.S., Eskerod, P.: Project portfolio management - There's more to it than what management enacts. International Journal of Project Management 26(4), 357–365 (2008)
13. Petit, Y.: Project portfolios in dynamic environments: Organizing for uncertainty. International Journal of Project Management 30(5), 539–553 (2012)
14. Payne, J.H.: Management of multiple simultaneous projects: a state-of-the-art review. International Journal of Project Management 13(3), 163–168 (1995)
15. Stettina, C.J., Hörz, J.: Agile portfolio management: An empirical perspective on the practice in use. International Journal of Project Management (2014)
16. Hoda, R., Kruchten, P., Noble, J., Marshall, S.: Agility in context. In: ACM Sigplan Notices. ACM (2010)
17. Rautiainen, K., Von Schantz, J., Vähäniitty, J.: Supporting scaling agile with portfolio management: Case Paf.com (2011)
18. Kalliney, M.: Transitioning from agile development to enterprise product management agility. In: Agile Conference, AGILE 2009. IEEE (2009)
19. Fernandez, D.J., Fernandez, J.D.: Agile project management - Agilism versus traditional approaches. Journal of Computer Information Systems 49(2), 10–17 (2008)
20. Lagerberg, L., Skude, T., Emanuelsson, P., Sandahl, K., Stahl, D.: The Impact of Agile Principles and Practices on Large-Scale Software Development Projects: A Multiple-Case Study of Two Projects at Ericsson. In: 2013 ACM / IEEE International Symposium on Empirical Software Engineering and Measurement (2013)
21. Kumar, R., Ajjan, H., Niu, Y.: Information Technology Portfolio Management: Literature review, framework, and research issues. Information Resources Management Journal 21(3), 64–87 (2008)
22. Billows, D.: Managing Complex Projects, 8th edn. The Hampton Group (2001)
23. Lycett, M., Rassau, A., Danson, J.: Programme management: A critical review. International Journal of Project Management 22(4), 289–299 (2004)
24. Fowler, M., Highsmith, J.: The Agile Manifesto. Software Development, 28–32 (August 2001)
25. Schwaber, K., Beedle, M.: Agile Software Development with Scrum. Prentice Hall, Upper Saddle River (2002)
26. Frey, T., Buxmann, P.: IT project portfolio management - a structured literature review. In: ECIS 2012 (2012)

27. Jeffery, M., Leliveld, I.: Best practices in IT portfolio management. Mit Sloan Management Review 45(3), 41–49 (2004)
28. Martinsuo, M., Lehtonen, P.: Role of single-project management in achieving portfolio management efficiency. International Journal of Project Management 25(1), 56–65 (2007)
29. Meskendahl, S.: The influence of business strategy on project portfolio management and its success — A conceptual framework. International Journal of Project Management 28(8), 807–817 (2010)
30. Pennypacker, J.: Project Portfolio Management Maturity Model. Centre for Business Practice (2005)
31. Highsmith, J.: Adaptive software development: A collaborative approach to managing complex systems. Addison-Wesley (2013)
32. Cooke-Davies, T., Cicmil, S., Crawford, L., Richardson, K.: We're Not in Kansas Anymore, Toto: Mapping the Strange Landscape of Complexity Theory, and Its Relationship to Project Mangement. IEEE Engineering Management Review 36(2), 5–21 (2008)
33. Rouse, W.B.: Managing Complexity. Information, Knowledge, Systems Management 2(2), 143–165 (2000)
34. Rouse, W.B.: Health care as a complex adaptive system: implications for design and management. Bridge-Washington-National Academy of Engineering- 38(1), 17 (2008)
35. Markowitz, H.: Portfolio Selection. The Journal of Finance 7(1), 77–91 (1952)
36. Blomquist, T., Müller, R.: Practices, roles, and responsibilities of middle managers in program and portfolio management. Project Management Journal 37(1), 52–66 (2006)
37. Dahlgren, J., Söderlund, J.: Modes and mechanisms of control in multi-project organisations: The R&D case. International Journal of Technology Management 50(1), 1–22 (2010)
38. Mikkola, J.H.: Portfolio management of R&D projects: Implications for innovation management. Technovation 21(7), 423–435 (2001)
39. Cooper, R.G., Edgett, S., Kleinschmidt, E.: New Product Portfolio Management: Practices and Performances. Journal of Product Innovation Management 16(4), 333–351 (1999)
40. McFarlan, F.W.: Portfolio approach to information systems. Harvard Business Review 59(5), 142–150 (1981)
41. Archer, N.P., Ghasemzadeh, F.: An integrated framework for project portfolio selection. International Journal of Project Management 17(4), 207 (1999)
42. PMI, The Standard for Portfolio Management, 2nd edn. The Project Management Institute, Newtown Square (2009)
43. Li, Z., Yanfei, X., Chaosheng, C.: Understanding the value of project management from a stakeholder's perspective: Case study of mega-project management. Project Management Journal 40(1), 99–109 (2009)
44. Teller, J., Unger, B.N., Kock, A., Gemünden, H.G.: Formalization of project portfolio management: The moderating role of project portfolio complexity. International Journal of Project Management 30(5), 596–607 (2012)
45. Phillips, B.: A Theoretical Framework for Information Systems Portfolio Management. In: AMCIS 2007 Proceedings (2007)
46. Bardhan, I., Bagchi, S., Sougstad, R.: Prioritizing a Portfolio of Information Technology Investment Projects. Journal of Management Information Systems 21(2), 33–60 (2004)
47. Rungi, M.: Interdependency management in project portfolio management: How to implement required procedures. In: PICMET 2010 - Portland International Center for Management of Engineering and Technology, Proceedings - Technology Management for Global Economic Growth, Phuket (2010)

48. Leffingwell, D.: Scaling Software Agility: Best Practices for Large Enterprises. Addison-Wesley, USA (2007)
49. Krebs, J.: Agile Portfolio Management. Microsoft Press (2008)
50. Vähäniitty, J.: Towards agile product and portfolio management (2012)
51. Leffingwell, D.: Agile software requirements: lean requirements practices for teams, programs, and the enterprise. Addison-Wesley Professional (2010)
52. Hodgkins, P., Hohmann, L.: Agile program management: Lessons learned from the verisign managed security services team. In: Agile Conference (AGILE). IEEE (2007)
53. Thomas, J.C., Baker, S.W.: Establishing an agile portfolio to align IT investments with business needs. In: Proceedings of Agile 2008, Toronto (2008)
54. Das, T.K., Teng, B.-S.: Between Trust and Control: Developing Confidence in Partner Cooperation in Alliances. The Academy of Management Review 23(3), 491–512 (1998)
55. Eisenhardt, K.M.: Control: Organizational and Economic Approaches. Management Science 31(2), 134–149 (1985)
56. Jaworski, B.J.: Toward a Theory of Marketing Control: Environmental Context, Control Types, and Consequences. Journal of Marketing 52(3), 23–39 (1988)
57. Ouchi, W.G.: A Conceptual Framework for the Design of Organizational Control Mechanisms. Management Science 25(9), 833–848 (1979)
58. Kirsch, L.J.: Portfolios of Control Modes and IS Project Management. Information Systems Research 8(3), 215 (1997)
59. Kirsch, L.J.: The Management of Complex Tasks in Organizations: Controlling the Systems Development Process. Organization Science 7(1), 1–21 (1996)
60. Ouchi, W.G.: Markets, Bureaucracies, and Clans. Administrative Science Quarterly 25(1), 129–141 (1980)
61. Anthony, R.: Management controls in industrial research organizations. Bailey & Swinfen (1952)
62. Jaworski, B.J., Stathakopoulos, V., Krishnan, H.S.: Control Combinations in Marketing: Conceptual Framework and Empirical Evidence. Journal of Marketing 57(1), 57–69 (1993)
63. van der Meer-Kooistra, J., Scapens, R.W.: The governance of lateral relations between and within organisations. Management Accounting Research 19(4), 365–384 (2008)
64. Gleick, J.: Chaos: Making a new science. Random House (1997)
65. Beeson, I., Davis, C.: Emergence and accomplishment in organizational change. Journal of Organizational Change Management 13(2), 178–189 (2000)
66. Bechtold, B.L.: Chaos theory as a model for strategy development. Empowerment in Organizations 5(4), 193–201 (1997)
67. Prigogine, I., Stengers, I., Pagels, H.R.: Order out of Chaos. Physics Today 38, 97 (1985)
68. Goodwin, B.C.: How the leopard changed its spots: The evolution of complexity. Princeton University Press (1994)
69. Nan, N.: Capturing bottom-up information technology use processes: A complex adaptive systems model. MIS Quarterly 35(2) (2011)
70. Holland, J.H.: Complex adaptive systems, pp. 17–30. Daedalus (1992)
71. Benbya, H., McKelvey, B.: Toward a complexity theory of information systems development. Information Technology & People 19(1), 12–34 (2006)
72. Vessey, I., Ward, K.: The Dynamics of Sustainable IS Alignment: The Case for IS Adaptivity. Journal of the Association for Information Systems 14(6), 283–311 (2013)
73. Holland, J.H.: Hidden order: How adaptation builds complexity. Basic Books (1995)
74. Anderson, P.: Complexity theory and organization science. Organization Science 10(3), 216–232 (1999)

75. Mitleton-Kelly, E.: Complex systems and evolutionary perspectives on organisations: The application of complexity theory to organisations. Elsevier Science Ltd. (2003)
76. Choi, T.Y., Dooley, K.J., Rungtusanatham, M.: Supply networks and complex adaptive systems: Control versus emergence. Journal of Operations Management 19(3), 351–366 (2001)
77. Kauffman, S.A.: The origins of order: Self-organization and selection in evolution. Oxford university press (1993)
78. Kane, G.C., Alavi, M.: Information technology and organizational learning: An investigation of exploration and exploitation processes. Organization Science 18(5), 796–812 (2007)
79. Curşeu, P.L.: Emergent states in virtual teams: a complex adaptive systems perspective. Journal of Information Technology 21(4), 249–261 (2006)
80. Benbya, H., McKelvey, B.: Using coevolutionary and complexity theories to improve IS alignment: A multi-level approach. Journal of Information Technology 21(4), 284–298 (2006)
81. Boisot, M.: Moving to the edge of chaos: bureaucracy, IT and the challenge of complexity. Journal of Information Technology 21(4), 239–248 (2006)
82. Canessa, E., Riolo, R.L.: An agent-based model of the impact of computer-mediated communication on organizational culture and performance: an example of the application of complex systems analysis tools to the study of CIS. Journal of Information Technology 21(4), 272–283 (2006)
83. Xia, W., Lee, G.: Grasping the complexity of IS development projects. Communications of the ACM 47(5), 68–74 (2004)
84. Vidgen, R., Wang, X.: Organizing for agility: A complex adaptive systems perspective on agile software development process. In: 14th European Conference on Information Systems, Goteborg (2006)
85. Jain, R., Meso, P.: Theory of complex adaptive systems and Agile software development (2004)
86. Merali, Y.: Complexity and information systems: The emergent domain. Journal of Information Technology 21(4), 216–228 (2006)
87. Vidgen, R., Wang, X.: Coevolving systems and the organization of agile software development. Information Systems Research 20(3), 355–376 (2009)
88. Highsmith, J., Cockburn, A.: Agile software development: The business of innovation. Computer 34(9), 120–127 (2001)
89. Highsmith, J.: What is agile development? The Journal of Defense Software Development 15(10) (2002)
90. Miles, M., Huberman, M.A.: Qualitative Data Analysis: An Expanded Sourcebook, 2nd edn. Sage Publications, Thousand Oaks (1994)
91. Cilliers, P.: Boundaries, hierarchies and networks in complex systems. International Journal of Innovation Management 5(02), 135–147 (2001)
92. Yin, R.K.: Case study research: Design and methods, vol. 5. Sage (2009)
93. Patton, M.: Qualitative evaluation and research methods. Sage, Beverly Hills (1990)
94. Corbin, J., Strauss, A.: Basics of Qualitative Research, 3rd edn. Sage Publications, London (2008)
95. Moe, N.B., Dingsoyr, T., Dyba, T.: Overcoming barriers to self-management in software teams. IEEE Software 26(6), 20–26 (2009)

A Measure of the Modularisation of Sequential Software Versions Using Random Graph Theory

Mahir Arzoky[1], Stephen Swift[1], Steve Counsell[1], and James Cain[2]

[1] Brunel University, Middlesex, UK
{mahir.arzoky,stephen.swift,steve.counsell}@brunel.ac.uk
[2] Quantel Limited, Newbury, UK
james.cain@quantel.com

Abstract. Software module clustering is the problem of automatically partitioning the structure of a software system using low-level dependencies in the source code to understand and improve the system's architecture. Munch, a clustering tool based on search-based software engineering techniques, was used to modularise a unique dataset of sequential source code software versions. This paper investigates whether the dataset used for the modularisation resembles a random graph by computing the probabilities of observing certain connectivity. Modularisation will not be possible with data that resembles random graphs. Thus, this paper demonstrates that our real world time-series dataset does not resemble a random graph except for small sections where there were large maintenance activities. Furthermore, the random graph metric can be used as a tool to indicate areas of interest in the dataset, without the need to run the modularisation.

Keywords: software module clustering, modularisation, SBSE, random graph, time-series, fitness function.

1 Introduction

Large software systems tend to have complex structures that are often difficult to comprehend due to the large number of modules (classes) and inter-relationships that exist between them. As the modular structure of a software system tends to decay over time, it is important to modularise. Modularisation is the process of partitioning the structure of software system into subsystems. It makes the problem at hand easier to understand, as it reduces the amount of data needed by developers [7]. Subsystems group together related source-level components to assist with system's understandability. Subsystems can be organised hierarchically to allow developers to navigate through the system at various levels of details, they include resources such as modules, classes and other subsystems [7].

Graphs can be used to make the software structure of complex systems more comprehensible [17]. They can be described as language-independent, whereby components such as classes or subroutines of a system are represented as nodes and the inter-relationships between the components are represented as edges. Such graphs are

T. Dingsøyr et al. (Eds.): XP 2014 Workshops, LNBIP 199, pp. 105–120, 2014.

referred to as Module Dependency Graph (MDG). Creating an MDG of the system does not always make it easy to understand the system's structure; graphs could be partitioned to make them more accessible and easier to comprehend. Mancoridis et al [14] were the first to use MDG as a representation of the software module clustering problem. There have been a large number of studies [8] [11] [12] [18] using the search-based software engineering approach to solve the software module-clustering problem. In previous studies, techniques that treat clustering as an optimisation problem were introduced. A number of various heuristic search techniques, including Hill Climbing were used to explore the large solution space of all possible partitions of an MDG.

Refactoring is defined as the change made to software system which improves the internal structure of the code while maintaining its external behaviour [8]. Refactoring is one of the most common techniques used to transform software in order to improve its internal quality attributes [19] [20]. If applied correctly, refactoring can improve maintainability, enhance performance and simplify the structure of the code. Hence, within the development of large software systems, there is significant value in being able to predict when refactoring occurs. Nonetheless, both managers and developers can be hesitant when it comes to using refactoring due to the amount of effort needed to make even a slight change in the code and also the risk of introducing new bugs.

This paper performs modularisation on source code check-ins (commits), taking advantage of the fact that the dataset is a time-series. The nearer the source codes in time, the more similar they are expected to be. The aim is to use code structure and sequence to obtain more effective modularisation and also to locate the possible occurrence of major changes, in particular refactorings. We look to verify the quality of the results of the modularisation by finding out whether the time-series dataset resembles a random graph. There are currently few studies [4] [16] [21] that use random graph theories for source code analysis. For this paper, we aim to calculate the probabilities of the graphs (software versions) resembling a random graph for the whole dataset. We look to investigate whether the probabilities increase as the maintenance increases and whether the architecture resembles more randomness throughout the life of the project.

The paper is organised as follows: Section 2 describes the clustering algorithms and fitness functions. Section 3 describes the creation and pre-processing of the source data and the experiment. Section 4 discusses the results and Section 5 draws conclusions and outlines future work.

2   Experimental Methods

2.1   Clustering Algorithm

This work extends that of Arzoky et al [2] [3] and, follows Mancoridis et al and Mitchell [14] [17], who first introduced search-based approach to software modularisation. The clustering algorithm was re-implemented from available literature on Bunch's clustering algorithm [18] to form a tool called Munch. Munch is a prototype implemented to carry out experimentations of different heuristic search approaches and fitness functions. Munch uses an MDG as an input and produces a hierarchical decomposition of the system structure as an output. Closely related modules are grouped into clusters that are loosely connected to other clusters. A cluster is a set of the modules in each partition of the clustering.

The clustering algorithm uses a simple random mutation Hill Climbing approach to guide the search. The pseudo-code of the algorithm is shown in Algorithm 1. It is a simple, easy to implement technique that has proven to be useful and robust in terms of modularisation [18]. The aim is to produce a graph partition that minimises coupling between clusters and maximises cohesion within each cluster. Coupling is defined as the degree of dependence between different modules or classes in a system, whereas cohesion is the internal strength of a module or class [7].

```
Algorithm 1. MUNCH(ITER,M)
Input: ITER- the number of iterations (runs), M - An MDG
  1) Let C be a random (or specified - for seeded) clustering
     arrangement
  2) Let F = Fitness Function (See Section 2.2)
  3) For i = 1 to ITER (number of iterations)
  4)    Choose two random clusters X and Y (X≠Y)
  5)    Move a random variable from cluster X to Y
  6)    Let F'= Fitness Function
  7)    If F' is worse than F Then
  8)       Undo move
  9)    Else
 10)       Let F = F'
 11)    End If
 12) End For
Output: C - a modularisation of M
```

2.2   Fitness Function

A fitness function is used to measure the relative quality of the decomposed structure of system into subsystems (clusters). Previously, we experimented with several fitness functions: the Modularisation Quality (MQ) metric of Mancoridis et al [14], and the EValuation Metric (EVM) of Tucker et al [22].

EVM rewards maximising the cohesiveness of the clusters, clustering with a high number of intra-module relationships, but it does not directly penalise inter-clustering coupling. It searches for all possible relationships within a cluster and rewards those that exist within the MDG and penalises those that does not exist within the MDG [14]. For the following formal definition of EVM, a clustering arrangement C of n items is defined as a set of sets $\{c_1, \ldots, c_m\}$, where each set (cluster) $c_i \subseteq \{1,...,n\}$ such that $c_i \neq \phi$ and $c_i \cap c_j = \phi$ for all $i \neq j$. Note that $1 \leq m \leq n$ and $n > 0$. Note also that $\bigcup_{i=1}^{m} c_i = \{1,...,n\}$. Let MDG M be an n by n matrix, where a '1' at row i and column j (M_{ij}) indicates a relationship between variable i and j, and '0' indicates that there is no relationship. Let c_{ij} refer to the jth element of the ith cluster of C. The score for cluster c_i is defined in Equation 2.

$$EVM(C,M) = \sum_{i=1}^{m} h(c_i, M)$$
(1)

$$h(c_i, M) = \begin{cases} \sum_{a=1}^{|c_i|-1} \sum_{b=a+1}^{|c_i|} L(c_{ia}, c_{ib}) & ,\text{if } |c_i| > 1 \\ 0 & ,\text{Otherwise} \end{cases}$$
(2)

$$L(v_1, v_2, M) = \begin{cases} 0 & ,v_1 = v_2 \\ +1 & ,M_{v_1 v_2} + M_{v_2 v_1} > 0 \\ -1 & ,\text{Otherwise} \end{cases}$$
(3)

To speed up the process of the modularisation, we introduced EValuation Metric Difference (EVMD), a faster version of the EVM function. EVMD was selected as the fitness function for the modularisations as it is more robust than MQ and faster than EVM [2]. It utilises an update formula on the assumption that one small change is being made between clusters. It is a faster way of evaluating EVM, where the previous fitness is known and the current fitness is calculated, without having to do the move. It produces the same results as EVM, but effectively reduces the computational operations from $O(n\sqrt{n})$ to $O(\sqrt{n})$.

For the formal definition of EVMD, let f_{old} be the EVM fitness function. Also, let x be the *from* cluster, y be the *to* cluster and z be the *index*. Function G, defined in Equation 5, determines the relationship (from MDG M) that exists between variable v and cluster k. Equation 3 simply checks whether it is a positive or negative influence (i.e. does a relationship exist?).

$$EVMD(f_{old}, C, x, y, z, M) = f_{old} - G(C_x, C_{xz}, M) + G(C_y, C_{xz}, M)$$
(4)

$$G(C_k, v, M) = \sum_{i=1}^{|C_k|} L(c_{ki}, v, M)$$
(5)

From this point forward EVM will be used when referring to the EVMD metric.

2.3   HS Metric

Homogeneity and Separation (HS) is an external coupling metric defined in [1] to measure the quality of the modularisation. HS is based on the Coupling Between

Objects (CBO) metric, first introduced by Chidamber and Kemerer [6]. CBO (for a class) is defined as the count of the number of other classes to which it is coupled [6].

HS is a simple coupling metric that calculates the ratio of the proportion of internal and external edges. As shown in Equation 6, HS is calculated by subtracting the number of links within clusters from the number of links that are between clusters, and then dividing the answer by the total number of links (to normalise it). It searches through all the links within the MDG, finding all the pairs that are not equal to 0. If the two variables are in the same cluster, H is incremented, and if they are in different clusters, S is incremented. The more links between the clusters the worse the modularisation, as only internal links are modularised. A value of +1 is returned if all the links are within the modules, a value of −1 is returned if all links are external coupling, and 0 is produced if there is an equal number.

For the formal mathematical definition of the HS metric, we define a function $P(v,C)$ which returns the cluster number within C that variable (class) v resides.

$$HS(C,M) = \frac{H(C,M) - S(C,M)}{H(C,M) + S(C,M)} \tag{6}$$

$$H(C,M) = \sum_{i=1}^{n-1} \sum_{j=i+1}^{n} (1 - \delta(M_{ij},0))\delta(P(i,M),P(j,M)) \tag{7}$$

$$S(C,M) = \sum_{i=1}^{n-1} \sum_{j=i+1}^{n} (1 - \delta(M_{ij},0))(1 - \delta(P(i,M),P(j,M))) \tag{8}$$

We use Kronecher's Delta function $\delta(i,j)$, which is defined as follows:

$$\delta(i,j) = \begin{cases} 1, & i = j \\ 0, & i \neq j \end{cases} \tag{9}$$

2.4   Weighted-Kappa

Weighted-Kappa (WK) [1] is a simple statistical metric for the comparative assessment of two or more components. For this paper it is used for the comparison of two clustering arrangements. It rates the agreement between the classification decisions made by two or more observers (clustering methods). It not only measures similarity but also takes into account the degree of disagreements. The WK value ranges from −1.0 (no concordance) to 1.0 (complete concordance). A high WK value suggests that the two clustering arrangements are similar, whereas a low value suggests that they are dissimilar. A value of approximately 0 is normally observed for two random clusters. An interpretation table of the WK values is shown in Table 1.

Table 1. Agreement strength of Weighted-Kappa

Weighted-Kappa (WK)	Agreement Strength
$-1 \leq WK \leq 0.0$	Very Poor
$0.0 < WK \leq 0.2$	Poor
$0.2 < WK \leq 0.4$	Fair
$0.4 < WK \leq 0.6$	Moderate
$0.6 < WK \leq 0.8$	Good
$0.8 < WK \leq 1.0$	Very Good

3   Experiment

The creation and pre-processing of the source data is described in this section. It explains a simple metric for calculating the similarity between subsequent graphs and describes the experiments conducted for this paper.

3.1   Data Creation

The large dataset used for this paper is from the processed source code of an award winning product line architecture library, provided by Quantel Limited. The dataset consists of information on different versions of a software system over time. The dataset comprises of over 0.5 million lines of C++ code collected over the period 17/10/2000 to 03/02/2005, with 503 versions (check-ins) in total. There are roughly 2-3 days' gap between each check-in (corresponding to a graph), giving a total time span of 4 years and 4 months for the dataset [5].

A total of 6120 classes exist in the system, however, not all classes exist at the same time slice; there are between 434 and 2272 of classes that exist at a particular point in time, referred to as "active" classes. Classes generally "appear" and "disappear" at various time points through the dataset. One reason for these occurrences is that when a class is renamed, it will appear in the dataset as a new class with a new identifier. The dataset consists of five time-series of un-weighted graphs. For this paper, graphs of the five types of relationship were merged together to form the 'whole system' for particular time slices. Table 2 describes how each graph represents a relationship between classes.

Table 2. Class Relation Types

Class relationship	Description
Attributes	Data members in a class
Bases	Immediate base classes
Inners	Any type declared inside the scope of a class
Parameters	Parameters to member functions of a class
Returns	Return from member functions of a class

Also, for this paper, the MDGs were significantly reduced; all modules that were not produced by Quantel and are not active at the time slice were removed. Classes not produced by Quantel include the Standard Template Library (STL), the Windows COM Interface classes and components from a third-party library. This required a re-write of the Munch tool which has reduced the runtime of the modularisation process considerably. There are now between 202 and 1193 active classes at any one point. Fig 1 shows all of the active classes at each software check-in (graph), all of the graphs are ordered in time.

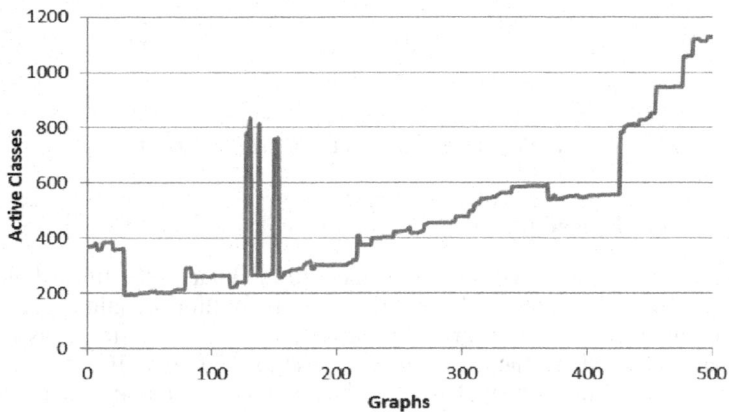

Fig. 1. Quantel's active classes at each software check-in

3.2   Absolute Value Difference (AVD)

Our previous work [2] [3] showed that there were few significant changes to the source code between two successive software versions. We produced a set of results showing the similarity between the graphs by subtracting every two successive binary matrices from each other's. Equation 10 shows how the AVD is calculated for each graph, where X and Y are two n by n binary matrices (MDGs). An AVD value of 0 indicates that two matrices are identical, whereas a large positive value indicates that they are different. A value between 0 and a large number gives a degree of similarity.

$$AVD(X,Y) = \sum_{i=1}^{n}\sum_{j=1}^{n}\left|X_{ij} - Y_{ij}\right| \tag{10}$$

Fig. 2 shows the AVDs of the full dataset of 503 graphs. The majority of the graphs have very low AVD, as there were only a few days of development between each check-in. In fact, 46 per cent of the graphs have an AVD of 0. However, sudden peaks and drops can be observed from the plot, which could indicate where major changes or refactoring activities occurred.

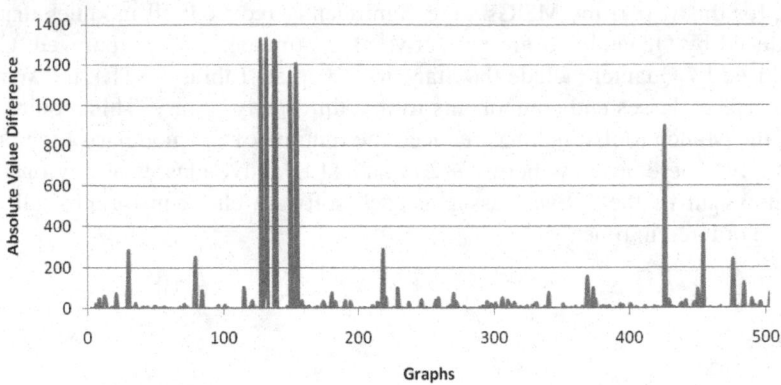

Fig. 2. Plot showing the AVDs of the full dataset

3.3   Experiment Procedure

For this paper, we have devised one experiment to modularise the full dataset of 503 graphs. The runtime for each modularisation was 10 million iterations. The starting clustering arrangement consisted of every variable in its own cluster. It assumes that all classes are independent; there are no relationships. The experiment was repeated 25 times as Hill Climbing is a stochastic method and there is a risk of the search only reaching a local maximum.

3.4   Random Graph

A random graph can be modelled with a set of n nodes, adding edges between them at random. One of the most commonly studied random graph models is the one introduced by Erdős–Rényi [9] and Gilbert [10], denoted $G(n,p)$. An edge can occur independently with probability $0 < p < 1$. Edges are chosen randomly for a fixed set of n nodes and each edge is chosen to be added or removed from the graph with probability p. Thus, the expected number of edges can be calculated as in Equation 11, however, the number of edges can change randomly and all graphs have $p \neq 0$ of being selected.

$$E = p\frac{n(n-1)}{2} \tag{11}$$

We generated the expected distribution of edges based on the Erdős–Rényi random graph model. Subsequently, we created the observed distribution from each MDG. We used the binomial distribution to compute the probability of observing $1...n-1$ connectivity. p is calculated from the density and the density is calculated from the MDG. The density is simply calculated by dividing the number of edges by the total number of edges that there could have been. Lastly, we use the Kolmogorov-Smirnov test (K-S) [15], which determines if two datasets differ significantly. It allows us to find out if the probability of the two distributions is equivalent i.e. whether it is a random graph or not.

4   Results and Discussion

For each graph in the dataset we recorded the frequency of the number of edges. There will be no nodes that have 0 edges as everything is connected to each other. For this paper, all of the modules that are not produced by Quantel and all of the non-active classes were removed. For example, for Graph 1, there are 85 classes that are connected to only 1 class and there are 66 classes that are connected to 2 classes. Fig 3 shows the connectivity of Graph 105 for both the observed and the expected number of edges. It can be observed from the plot that there is a noticeable similarity between observed and expected edges; this is due to the high probability value (0.0343) of this graph resembling a random graph i.e. the chances of these two being the same distribution is reasonably high. Conversely, we would expect a graph with a lower probability to be immensely different as the chances of it becoming from the same probability is very unlikely.

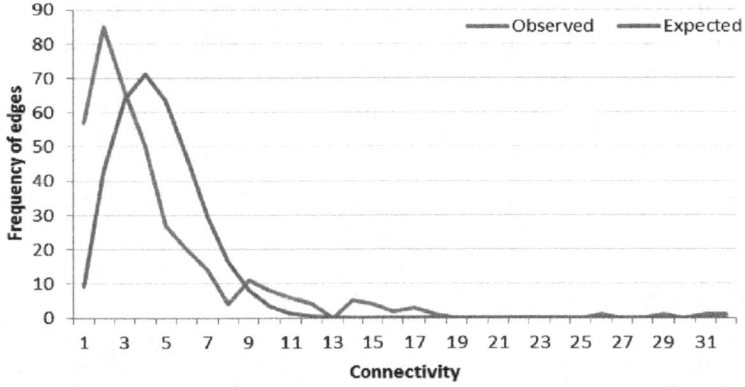

Fig. 3. Connectivity against the frequency of edges for Graph 105 from the dataset

Fig 4 displays the probability values of whether a graph resembles a random graph for the full dataset. From the plot it can be seen that the majority of the probabilities have extremely small values that range from 1.3086E-05 to 2.2806E-52. The lower the probability values the less the graph resembles a random graph, which suggests that the majority of the graphs are not random. However, few of the graphs have probability values of up to 0.034 which indicate that there is a 3.4 per cent chance of these graphs resembling a random graph. These values are reasonably high and it shows that there is an area of randomness in the way the software is structured at these points. Modularisation is not possible with data that resembles random graphs.

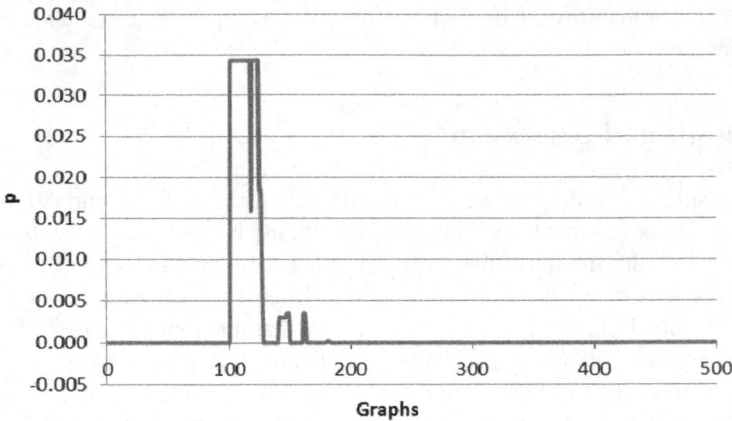

Fig. 4. Probability values representing the randomness of the graph

Due to the extremely small probability values produced we have computed the natural logarithm of these probabilities. Fig 5 shows the natural logarithm of the probability values ($\ln(p)$), the higher the value the more the graph resembles a random graph. From the plot it can be observed that graphs 100-180 have higher $\ln(p)$ values which indicates that at these points the graphs more resemble random graphs.

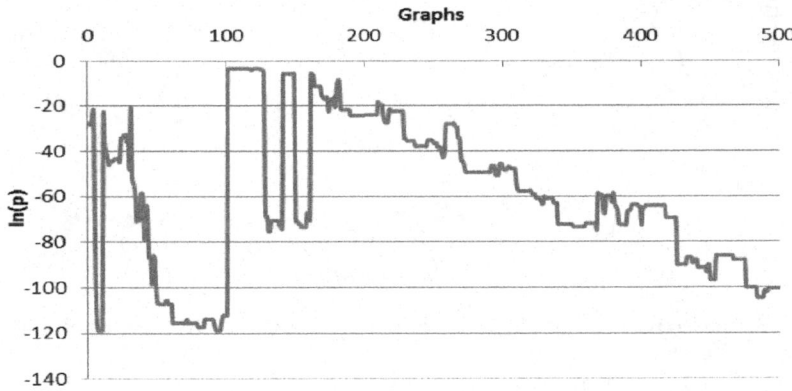

Fig. 5. The natural logarithm of the probability values for the whole dataset

Fig 6 shows a plot of the $\ln(p)$ against active classes for the whole dataset. A general relationship can be observed from the plot, which shows that as the number of active classes increases $\ln(p)$ decreases, apart from the large peaks and drops between graphs 100-200. A value of -0.372 is produced when correlating $\ln(p)$ against active classes. This still indicates a high correlation as there are over 500 pairs of observations; the 1 per cent significance level is at 0.115.

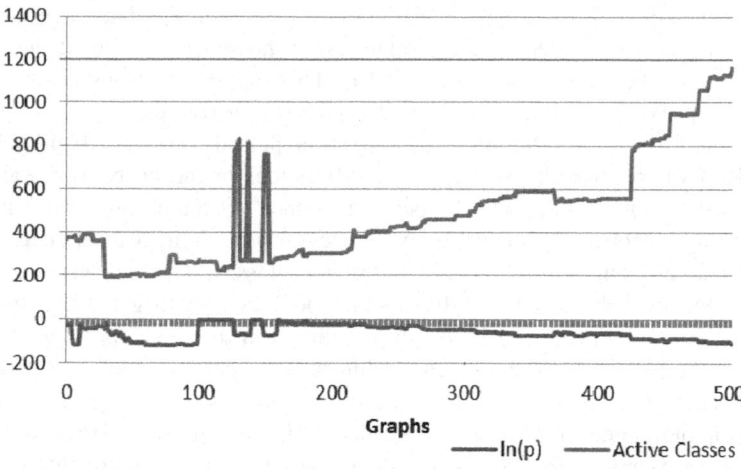

Fig. 6. The natural logarithm of the probability values against active classes

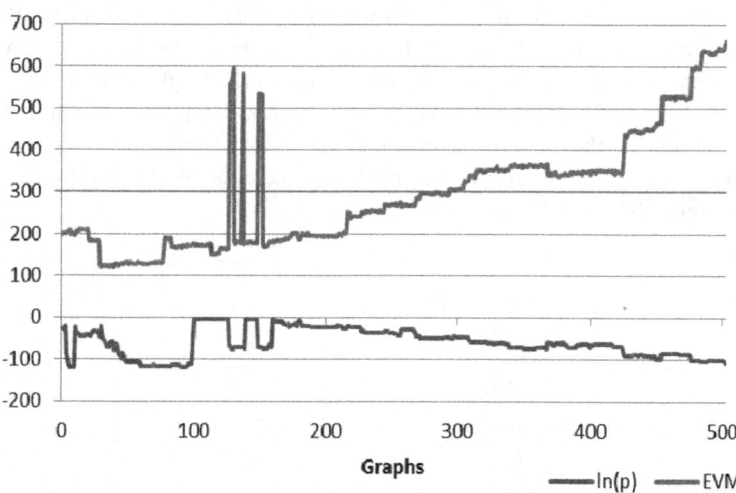

Fig. 7. The natural logarithm of the probability values against EVM

Fig 7 shows the relationship between $\ln(p)$ and EVM. It can be observed that as EVM increases, $\ln(p)$ decreases. To find out how strong is this relationship we correlated the two values for the whole dataset and for graphs 100-200 only. A value of 0.266 is produced for the whole dataset and −0.513 is produced for graphs 100-200. These values indicate a strong correlation. In addition, correlating the $\ln(p)$ against the HS metric produced −0.403 over the whole dataset, which also indicates a very high correlation. These relationships demonstrate that the modularisation works well for the majority of the dataset (apart from the small activities between graph 100-200). It also suggests that the random graph metric can be used to quickly measure how effective the search is going to be and to indicate areas (software check-ins) of interest in the software, such as locating major changes and refactoring activities.

Fig 8 shows a plot of the ln(p) against AVD. Correlating the dataset results of the two values together produced no clear relationship, however, looking at the 100-200 graphs section of the dataset, produced −0.407. This suggests a strong negative correlation for this period, mainly due to the large number of activities.

In addition, Fig 8 shows that there are three time periods (graphs 101-127, 141-149 and 161-163) where there were very large differences in the probability values, revealing that these graph had up to 3.4 per cent chance of resembling a random graph. It is interesting to notice that these large changes in probability values occur just before the sizeable changes in the AVD and active classes. This suggested to us that during this period there was instability in the code. We investigated this further by correlating the results produced with information from the developers; we have had feedback on the results from the senior architect at Quantel, and were provided with all of the check-in comments for the dataset currently being analysed. During this period, the implementation of a new library caused some of the libraries to be unstable and to have unpredictable behaviour, developers were in a state of flux on how to use the libraries. There were a few months of implementation that included coding the interface and trying out the libraries in different ways and then a roll back to the previous code. The roll back did not only include the library classes but also their own code. Thus, there were sizable shifts in the number of classes as they went through the different library models. It finally stabilises as they worked out the appropriate model to use. During this period there was evidence to suggest early product implementation with many issues in the code. We consider these large changes to be refactoring events and not new functionalities as internal structures of the code was changed without changing the functionality of the software.

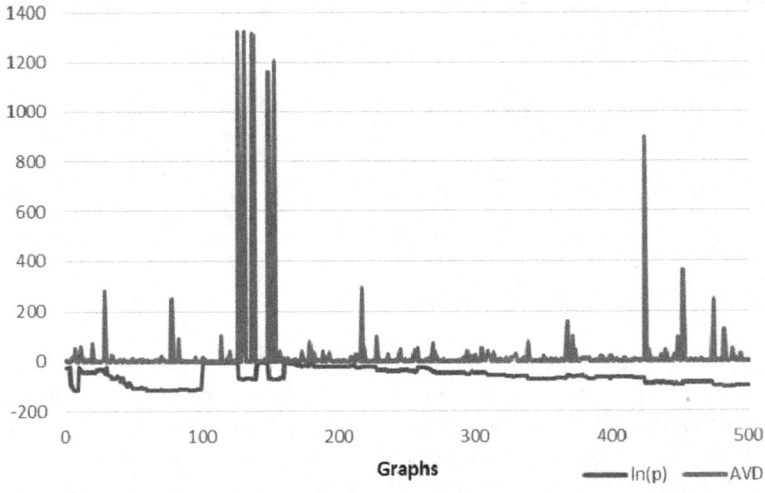

Fig. 8. The natural logarithm of the probability values against AVD

WK values for the clustering results of the 1st graph and the ith clustering results for the full modularisation were produced. There is a decreasing trend of the WK values which suggests that the original structure of the system deteriorates over time. Correlating $\ln(p)$ and WK did not produce a high correlation (0.159), however a relationship can still be observed. We look to investigate this further as part of future work.

One of the aims of our project is to be able to identify areas of major change, from the source code. These changes can either be new functionality or refactoring. We did not have the data to distinguish between the two, but being able to identify areas of interest is useful, as it allows us to indicate the potential locations of refactoring in the code. We suspected that refactoring is occurring and not simply other development because we were informed by Quantel that they refactor 'mercilessly' and that this is a practice they encourage all staff to strive towards. Quantel has now provided us with more detailed classifications for each of the classes in the dataset. We were also provided with the check-in comments of the whole dataset. Now we look to map results of the modularisations back to the architecture. We have had discussions about the results with the senior architect at Quantel and were provided with comments and feedback for each high value change in the number of classes from the dataset. Table 3 provides a summary of the domain expert comments for these check-ins. Three main categories were defined for these check-ins, they are; feature change i.e. new functionality, library change (involves sizeable refactoring activities) and roll back error (regression).

Table 3. Domain expert comments on the dataset

Check-in No (Time slice)	AVD	Comments
30	283	Roll back error
79	250	Library change
115	104	Library change
128	1325	Library change
132	1327	Feature change
138	1317	Library change
139	1309	Library change
150	1164	Library change
154	1203	Roll back error
218	290	Feature change
369	157	Feature change
426	894	Library change
454	363	Feature change
476	243	Feature change
484	123	Feature change

From the table above, several feature change can be noticed. These are due to the impact of merges, when a branch is committed into the main trunk. The dataset under analysis is only the main trunk. Developers were working on branches for a number of weeks or months and then checking in the code all at once. From the table it can also be noticed that library changes have a large impact on the number of classes. It involves inheriting a number of classes and subsequently refactoring the code to work with the new library. It does not involve new feature development but at the same time it is not pure refactoring activities, it almost falls into a third category.

5   Conclusions and Future Work

In this paper we have demonstrated that our time-series system does not resemble a random graph except for very small sections of the datasets where there were large activities i.e. major roll backs. Thus, from the results it can be seen that the random graph metric can be used as a tool to focus on and indicate areas of interest in the dataset (without running the modularisation), such as where the system is starting to decay, if the link between classes is random or strongly resemble a random graph then the software is decaying. In addition, from results of this research we have found out that as the software grows, the architecture of the software gets more eroded and less coherence. These results were backed up by the senior software architect at Quantel.

By looking at the source code check-ins, we look to use random graphs, observing when a certain percentage of randomness occurs, to indicate whether/when refactoring should be performed. The random graph test may also be used to indicate areas where a higher running time of the modularisation is needed. We look to investigate these relationships further as part of future work.

We believe that this project can have an impact on practitioners. The possibility of furthering their understanding of the evolution of large program source code is of high importance to Quantel, since bespoke software product development is one of their core business activities. Also, being able to predict future changes would greatly enhance their ability to allocate resources, and hence give them a more competitive and adaptable edge. For future work, we look to develop the approach aforementioned in this paper in order to predict when the system will be in needs of refactoring. We look to find out whether it can be useful for project team leaders to predict in advance when maintenance or refactoring session should be planned in the future.

Our current dataset is over 4 years and the architecture of the system itself has taken around 3 years to build. We currently have over 9 years of data. For future research we look to investigate the rate of change of the classes and whether they would slow as the code gets into maintenance mode. We look to investigate whether the complexity and the structure of the code stabilises over time and look to explore whether that could be used as a feedback mechanism to justify to management that a particular way of developing the code actually works.

The development process at Quantel involves subsystems or classes being owned by individual(s) developers. Thus, modularisation of the dataset represents how people work together. We believe that there is a relationship between the modularisation and how people are grouped into teams. A software architecture that keeps developers as de-coupled as possible is needed in order for them to not impede on each other. The more coupled the software become the less the programmer's productivity, and as programmers' comprehension gets worse things such as the impact of changes in classes emerges and bugs will re-appear because of merge errors. As part of future work, we look to investigate the impact of these measures changing on programmer productivity.

There are a number of random graph models; however, for this paper we only used the Erdős–Rényi model which calculates the probability of a node being connected to another node. Other models which include the degree of the number of edges that are connected to a node as opposed to the connectivity of the node will also be investigated.

Acknowledgment. The authors would like thank Quantel Ltd for providing us with their unique dataset and for their valuable feedback and comments on the dataset.

References

1. Altman, D.G.: Practical Statistics for Medical research. Chapman and Hall (1997)
2. Arzoky, M., Swift, S., Tucker, A., Cain, J.: Munch: An Efficient Modularisation Strategy to Assess the Degree of Refactoring on Sequential Source Code Checkings. In: IEEE Fourth International Conference on Software Testing, Verification and Validation Workshops, pp. 422–429 (2011)
3. Arzoky, M., Swift, S., Tucker, A., Cain, J.: A Seeded Search for the Modularisation of Sequential Software Versions. Journal of Object Technology 11(2), 6:1-27 (2012)
4. Barabási, A.L., Albert, R., Jeong, H.: Scale-free characteristics of random networks: The topology of the world-wide web. Physica A: Statistical Mechanics and its Applications 281(1), 69–77 (2000)
5. Cain, J., Counsell, S., Swift, S., Tucker, A.: An Application of Intelligent Data Analysis Techniques to a Large Software Engineering Dataset. In: Adams, N.M., Robardet, C., Siebes, A., Boulicaut, J.-F. (eds.) IDA 2009. LNCS, vol. 5772, pp. 261–272. Springer, Heidelberg (2009)
6. Chidamber, S.R., Kemerer, C.F.: A metrics suite for object oriented design. IEEE Trans. Software Eng. 20(6), 476–493 (1994)
7. Constantine, L.L., Yourdon, E.: Structured Design. Prentice Hall (1979)
8. Doval, D., Mancoridis, S., Mitchell, B.S.: Automatic clustering of software systems using a genetic algorithm. In: Software Technology and Engineering Practice. IEEE Proceedings STEP 1999, pp. 73–81 (1999)
9. Erdős, P., Rényi, A.: On the evolution of random graphs. Magyar Tud. Akad, Mat. Kutató Int. Közl. 5, 17–61 (1960)
10. Gilbert, E.N.: Random graphs. The Annals of Mathematical Statistics, 1141–1144 (1959)
11. Harman, M., Hierons, R., Proctor, M.: A new representation and crossover operator for search based optimization of software modularization. In: Proc. Genetic and Evolutionary Computation Conference, pp. 1351–1358. Morgan Kaufmann Publishers (2002)
12. Harman, M., Mansouri, S.A., Zhang, Y.: Search-based software engineering: Trends, techniques and applications. ACM Computing Surveys 45(1), 11 (2012)
13. Harman, M., Swift, S., Mahdavi, K.: An empirical study of the robustness of two module clustering fitness functions. In: Genetic and Evolutionary Computation Conference, Washington, DC, pp. 1029–1036 (2005)
14. Mancoridis, S., Mitchell, B.S., Rorres, C., Chen, Y., Gansner, E.R.: Using automatic clustering to produce high-level system organizations of source code. In: International Workshop on Program Comprehension (IWPC 1998), pp. 45–53. IEEE Computer Society Press, Los Alamitos (1998)

15. Massey, F.J.: The Kolmogorov-Smirnov Test for Goodness of Fit. Journal of the American Statistical Association 46(253), 68–78 (1951)
16. Mislove, A., Marcon, M., Gummadi, K.P., Druschel, P., Bhattacharjee, B.: Measurement and analysis of online social networks. In: Proceedings of the 7th ACM SIGCOMM Conference on Internet Measurement, pp. 29–42 (2007)
17. Mitchell, B.S.: A Heuristic Search Approach to Solving the Software Clustering Problem. PhD Thesis, Drexel University, Philadelphia, PA (2002)
18. Praditwong, K., Harman, M., Yao, X.: Software Module Clustering as a Multi–Objective Search Problem. IEEE Transactions on Software Engineering 37(2), 264–282 (2011)
19. Sommerville, I.: Software Engineering, 5th edn. Addison-Wesley (1995)
20. Stroggylos, K., Spinellis, D.: Refactoring does it improve software quality? In: WoSQ 2007: Proceedings of the 5th International Workshop on Software Quality. IEEE Computer Society, Washington, DC (2007)
21. Roth, C., Kang, S.M., Batty, M., Barthelemy, M.: A long-time limit for world subway networks. Journal of The Royal Society Interface 9(75), 2540–2550 (2012)
22. Tucker, A., Swift, S., Liu, X.: Variable Grouping in multivariate time series via correlation. IEEE Transactions on Systems, Man, and Cybernetics, Part B: Cybernetics 31(2), 235–245 (2001)

Refactoring Clustering
in Java Software Networks

Giulio Concas, C. Monni, M. Orrù, M. Ortu, and Roberto Tonelli

DIEE - Department of Electrical and Electronic Engineering
P.zza D'Armi, Cagliari, Italy
{concas,cristina.monni,matteo.orru,marco.ortu}@diee.unica.it,
roberto.tonelli@dsf.unica.it
http://www.diee.unica.it

Abstract. We present a study on the refactoring activities performed during the evolution of 7 popular Java open source software systems, using a complex network approach. We find that classes affected by refactorings are more likely to be interlinked than others, forming connected subgraphs. Our results show that in a software network, classes linked to refactored classes are likely to be refactored themselves. This result is meaningful because knowing how refactored classes are arranged inside a network could be useful to support developers in maintenance and refactoring activities.

Keywords: Refactoring, Clustering, Software Networks.

1 Introduction

Software systems evolve to meet new needs and often new features are added over time. It could happen that after several months and new versions, the code needs to be rewritten or abandoned or, eventually, if nothing is done on it, it will go through code decay. Software maintenance has the purpose of avoiding this by performing activities such as the addition of functionalities, but it requires lots of efforts and time. With good design and advance planning, refactoring can help in software maintenance. According to Fowler's definition [1], refactoring consists in rearranging the internal structure of a piece of software without altering its external behavior, in order to improve code functionality and readability. It has the advantage of requiring short-term time and low work costs and allows to get long-term benefits. Refactoring is different from other activities such as rewriting or debugging code, or adding features or bug fixing. It is aimed at improving software design by making it more extensible, flexible, understandable, and at improving performance.

Built-in tools can be used to retrieve refactoring operations. The most known and widely used is RefFinder [2], which compares two different versions of the same code (e.g. a class) and uses a template model based on the work of Kim and Prete [2,3,4] to detect the specific refactorings. Since refactoring can be applied to classes which are strongly connected with each other, its impact can extend

T. Dingsøyr et al. (Eds.): XP 2014 Workshops, LNBIP 199, pp. 121–135, 2014.
© Springer International Publishing Switzerland 2014

over the single class to involve other related classes. This phenomenon is studied in this work using a software network approach [5,6,7,8,9], where classes are represented by network nodes and relationships among classes (such as inheritance, composition, etc.) are represented by network links. Object Oriented software systems show indeed complex network properties such as a modular structure with interconnections among modules, and also a large number of modules, so they can be conveniently studied as complex networks [8]. Our goal is to perform a software network analysis of refactorings to understand if they are related to the network structure, in order to retrieve information which can be useful when planning more refactoring, or to make predictions on future refactorings. To our knowledge, how and to which extent the impact of refactoring can spread over the associated software network has not been thoroughly studied so far.

In this work we built the software networks of 7 different Java projects, namely Ant, Azureus, Jedit, Jena, Jtopen, Tomcat and Xalan, in order to understand whether refactoring operations are applied randomly on the nodes of the software network or if they mostly involve classes that are linked together. We are specifically interested to figure out if developers apply refactoring taking into account just the class properties, not considering their dependency from other classes, or if they accidentally or explicitly evaluate the impact of the performed refactoring on the neighboring classes, namely on the network topology. In the first case, refactoring operations should look like random interventions on the nodes corresponding to classes, whereas in the second one we expect to find connections among the different refactored classes, that we are referring to as clustering. For every system we retrieved the associated software network by parsing the source code, then we used RefFinder to recover all the refactorings related to these systems, and associated them to the corresponding nodes in the software network. To gain information about clustering properties of refactored classes, we compared sets of refactored nodes to randomly chosen nodes. To understand if refactoring activities spread among connected classes, we analyzed the neighbors of refactored classes in the software networks, looking for other refactorings, and then performed again a comparison with classes randomly selected.

Our results show that refactored classes tend to be more connected than randomly selected classes, and the analysis on the first neighbors indicates that devising the topological structure of the software network can be of help in identifying which classes need to be refactored. The reported results are purely empirical and, at the present stage we have not yet found a specific cause or explanation for these findings. Nevertheless, we consider them quite interesting because they appear counterintuitive. In fact, according to the definition of refactoring, it is mandatory that the changes performed on source code do not alter software external behaviour. Thus refactored classes should have on average the same connection density as other classes. On the contrary, we found that refactored classes are more tightly connected than average.

This paper is organized as follows. In Section 2 we will introduce some background information about software network analysis and the literature about refactoring. In Section 3 we present the analyzed systems and perform an outline of our experimental setting, explaining how we checked the connections among refactorings. Finally we present and discuss our results in Section 4, threats to validity in Section 5 and end with our conclusions in Section 6.

2   Background

Refactoring was first formally described by William Opdyke in his Ph.D. dissertation [10] but it started gaining popularity in 1999, after Fowler defined his catalog containing information on when and how to do refactoring [1]. After being introduced by Fowler, the code smells were also made recognizable in a book by Wake [11], while Simon et al. presented a generic approach for visualizing which classes need to be refactored [12]. Usually developers decide to apply refactoring by examining or changing the software code while they are performing other operations [13], such as bug fixing, addition of functionalities, or other code changes. For this reason, refactoring represents an important part of the software development cycle. In this work we address the issue of the impact of refactoring on the connections among classes in a Java system to understand if there are some relationships among these activities and the topological structure of a software network. To pursue this task, we built the software networks associated to every release of our software projects and then studied the connections between classes before and after refactoring as represented on the software graph. We will make use of the knowledge of previous works on software network systems [9,8,5,14,15].

Previous studies claim that refactoring improves the quality of software [1], but they do not provide quantitative evidence. However, in the literature there are some works showing some effects of refactoring on external software quality attributes, such as changeability, maintainability and modifiability [16,17] or on internal attributes, by exploiting the relationships between internal and external attributes. The relationship between refactorings and software metrics, such as internal quality metrics, has been studied in different works [18,19,20,21]. Other works [20,22,23] propose coupling and cohesion metrics to evaluate and measure the effect of refactoring on maintainability or reusability. More recent works [24,25] analyzed refactorings in the context of software networks, presenting a relationship between refactorings and node degree, but they did not address the issue of clustering.

To our knowledge, our work represents a first attempt to analyze clustering properties of refactored classes in software networks, and follows our previous work [26], which was a preliminary analysis.

3   Experimental Setting and Methodology

Our dataset is composed by 7 popular Object Oriented Open Source Java software: Ant, Azureus, Jedit, Jena, Jtopen, Tomcat and Xalan, for a total of 66 releases studied. The source code can be found in the Java Qualitas Corpus [27,28], release version 20101126e. We analyzed the refactoring activities that took place along the evolution of these systems. We first parsed the source code and retrieved the software network associated to each system at the class level. In order to build the software graph we focused our attention on the relationships between classes (inheritance, composition, aggregation, collaboration, etc). This means that we consider two classes as connected if one of them extends the other or if one of them contains a field of the same type of the other or when it happens that a method signature included in the first class includes the second one as a parameter – or the other way around. Thus the nodes of the associated network represent classes and the edges represent the reciprocal relationships among classes. We performed our analyses on the maximal connected component (MCC), namely the largest connected graph.

To retrieve information about refactoring activities we relied on the state-of-the-art software tool in the field, RefFinder [2]. Based on the work of Kim and Prete [29], RefFinder is an Eclipse plugin that analyzes the differences between two sections of source code, looking for refactoring operations. The software is able to detect 65 out of the 72 refactorings reported in Fowler's catalog, representing the most exhaustive coverage of all existing techniques. Although RefFinder had some limitations, it is able to provide valuable information about code changes introduced between two releases that can be considered as refactoring operations [3].

We performed several tests on some kind of toy classes that we built from scratch in order to figure out if RefFinder is able to properly detect refactoring operations and to associate them to the right classes. In particular, we checked if RefFinder retrieves refactoring in the correct way, avoiding side effects on connected classes. In fact, an error in associating the refactorings to the proper classes would introduce a bias on the analysis of the connectivity of the classes. Consider, for example, the case of "rename method" refactoring. When this refactoring is performed on a class, the renamed method is called also in the connected classes. However, the refactoring was performed on the first class and not on the connected ones. We would like to check whether RefFinder associated this specific refactoring to the classes where it was performed and not to its connected classes which call the renamed method. These connected classes would undergo code changes which should not be retrieved as refactorings. RefFinder could have introduced a bias, since in the successive analysis we label the classes as refactored according to the output that it provides. In order to check this out, we build a simple network of connected classes, and perform a "rename method" refactoring on some of them. As a result, we found that this refactoring is properly associated to the classes where it was performed, namely the classes to which the method belongs to, as it should be, and not to their connected classes.

After retrieving the refactorings on a class, we associate them to the corresponding node in the software network and looked at the links among refactored classes in the software network, with specific regards to the clustering phenomenon. With the term "clustering" we mean the tendency of refactored classes to form subnetworks composed by connected nodes. The most general definition of cluster we devised is the following: we consider a set of n nodes as belonging to the same cluster if there is a path of length d connecting each pair of nodes inside the set. In this work we limit our study to the case of $d = 1$, so we consider clusters as connected subnetworks.

We analyze the clusters formed by classes involved in different refactorings and perform a comparison with clusters formed by randomly chosen classes. Our hypothesis is that when a refactoring is applied, the involved classes have a higher probability of being connected with each other. To verify the hypothesis we selected in the software network the classes affected by a specific refactoring and denoted with n their number. Inside this set of size n we computed the number c of independent clusters. The number of clusters c varies from 1, when all classes are connected into one single cluster, to n when all the selected classes are isolated. We compared c with the corresponding number of clusters c_{rand} obtained examining a number n of classes selected at random in the entire software network. In this last case we performed 100 samplings and computed the average number of clusters. If classes involved in the same refactoring are on average more connected, the number of clusters they form must be lower than the corresponding number obtained for randomly selected classes, on average.

Afterwards, we tried to understand if the knowledge of network nodes corresponding to refactored classes may be used to infer which other classes may be in need of refactoring. To check this conjecture we selected a random subsample of all refactored classes to start from, about 10% of the total, and looked for refactored classes that were close to the starting set. To get a measure of closeness, we selected their first neighbors, namely the classes at distance $d = 1$ from the refactored ones. Then we computed how many classes among the set of first neighbors had also been refactored. We finally compared the number of refactored neighbors with the number of first neighbors of an equivalent set of classes selected at random.

Our work thus aims at answering to the following research questions:

- RQ1: *Do refactored classes tend to be more interconnected than not refactored ones for a given type of refactoring?*
- RQ2: *Is it possible to identify refactoring-prone classes from the knowledge of other refactored classes?*

In Section 4 we illustrate our results.

4   Results

In Fig. 1 we report a few examples of clusters for different refactorings in various systems.

In order to check whether refactored classes tend to be more interconnected than average and to form clusters we computed the ratio among the number of clusters formed by refactored classes and the number of clusters formed by randomly chosen classes. While computing this ratio, in order to reduce any fluctuation due to statistical noise, we considered only the clusters with size

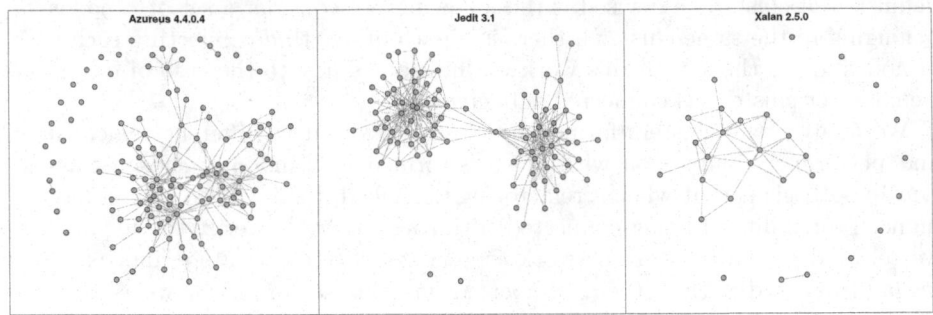

Fig. 1. Three examples of networks composed only of classes involved in refactoring operations for Azureus 4.4.0.4 (left), JEdit (centre), Xalan 2.5.0 (right)

larger than (or equal to) 10 which we set arbitrarily - any other number could work. This choice is a trade-off between two extreme situations. In the first, considering fewer than 10 refactored classes, the chance to find a similar number of clusters from randomly chosen classes is high. In fact, in the hypothesis that random classes are generally disconnected, they tend to form n clusters. Since refactored classes are not completely connected into a single cluster, with n low the two numbers will be very similar. In the second, considering only clusters with many more than 10 classes, this would optimize the ratio between the number of clusters formed by refactored classes and the number of clusters formed by randomly chosen classes, but the statistics will be drastically reduced, since the number of refactored classes per system is not very high (e.g. 45 for Ant 1.5 as reported in Tab. 4). Therefore the chosen value would provide a fair ratio with the mean square error (MSE) that increases according to $\sqrt{n}$ along with the number n of the samples. Tab. 1 reports these ratios for one release for each analyzed project. Ratios are systematically lower than one for all refactorings suggesting that also one specific kind of refactoring involves classes which are more interconnected than average.

Table 1. Ratio between the number of clusters formed by different types of refactoring and the number of clusters formed by randomly selected classes

	Ant 1.8.0	Azureus 4.4.0.4	JEdit 3.2	Jena 2.1	Jtopen 5.0	Tomcat 5.5.3.1	Xalan 2.5.0
Add Parameter	-	-	-	-	0.206	-	-
Cons. Cond. Expression	-	-	-	-	0.091	-	-
Cons. Dup. Cond. Fragments	-	0.215	0.126	0.142	-	-	-
Extract Interface	0.5	0.037	-	-	-	-	-
Introduce Local Extension	-	-	-	-	-	0.503	-
Introduce Null Object	-	-	-	-	-	0.405	-
Inline Temp.	0.503	-	0.021	-	-	-	-
Move Fields	-	0.056	0.168	-	-	-	0.119
Remove Ass. to Param.	-	-	0.084	-	-	-	-
Remove Control Flag	-	-	-	-	-	-	0.079
Rep.Magic N. with Const.	-	-	0.021	0.142	0.251	-	-

Results in Tab. 1 provide a positive answer to RQ1: refactored classes tend to form interconnected clusters more than other classes on average.

We now show the results of the analysis on the classes directly connected to refactored classes. We select at random a subset of refactored classes, S_{ref}, of size $n_{S_{ref}}$, which is about 10% of all refactored classes, and examine the set of classes directly connected to this subset. We denote the set of "first neighbor" classes with SN_{ref}. We repeat the procedure selecting at random subsets of classes regardless of refactoring, namely randomly chosen, of the same size $n_{S_{ref}}$, and examine the corresponding set of "first neighbor" classes, SN_{rand}. For both neighbor sets, SN_{ref} and SN_{rand}, we compute the fraction of classes affected by refactoring operations, F_{ref} and F_{rand} respectively, and compare the two results. These fractions represent the probability of finding a class in need to be refactored when starting from a set of refactored classes or starting from a set of random classes respectively. We averaged these fractions over 1000 cases where the set of refactored classes and that of random classes were repeatedly selected at random. Tables 2 and 3 report these results. Tab. 2 shows the fractions F_{ref} and F_{rand} mediated over the releases for each of the 7 projects, giving a general overview of the results, while in Tab. 3 we report some selected examples for both releases "Source" and "Target", where the Source is the release before refactoring and the Target is the release after the application of refactorings.

The interpretation of this result is straightforward. F_{ref} provides the empirical probability of finding a class in need to be refactored when picking up classes among the neighbors of a small set of refactored classes. F_{rand} provides instead the same probability when choosing the classes at random inside the entire set. Thus, when looking for classes in need to be refactored, it is more convenient to examine first a set of classes directly linked to already refactored classes in the software network. This provides developers with an empirical practice to use when checking for classes to refactor. The ratio among the two fractions can be considered as an empirical index related to the "convenience" of looking in the first neighbors of a refactored set.

Table 2. Average values the fractions of refactored classes in the first neighbors network and the corresponding mean values computed for randomly selected classes, for each analyzed system

System	F_{ref} Sources	F_{ref} Targets	F_{rand} Sources	F_{rand} Targets
Ant	0.218	0.196	0.062	0.057
Azureus	0.151	0.163	0.052	0.053
Jedit	0.458	0.448	0.281	0.271
Jena	0.094	0.085	0.024	0.024
Jtopen	0.107	0.11	0.038	0.04
Tomcat	0.25	0.249	0.166	0.163
Xalan	0.293	0.294	0.032	0.034

In Tab. 4 we present some representative cases taken from our dataset (one release for each system) that show the clusters formed by refactored classes

Table 3. Fractions of refactored classes in the first neighbors network and the corresponding values for randomly selected classes. The values refer both to "Source" and "Target" releases, of two releases of each system.

Source Release	Target Release	F_{ref} Source	F_{ref} Target	F_{rand} Source	F_{rand} Target
Ant 1.5	Ant 1.6.0	0.137	0.111	0.072	0.063
Ant 1.6.0	Ant 1.7.0	0.106	0.105	0.069	0.065
Ant 1.7.0	Ant 1.8.0	0.130	0.130	0.062	0.063
Azureus 4.0.0.0	Azureus 4.1.0.2	0.175	0.195	0.084	0.085
Azureus 4.1.0.2	Azureus 4.2.0.2	0.048	0.054	0.019	0.019
Jedit 3.0	Jedit 3.1	0.419	0.400	0.218	0.213
Jedit 3.1	Jedit 3.2	0.481	0.493	0.347	0.357
Jena 2.0	Jena 2.1	0.124	0.163	0.014	0.015
Jena 2.1	Jena 2.2	0.092	0.146	0.028	0,030
Jtopen 3.3	Jtopen 4.0	0.254	0.303	0.074	0.091
Jtopen 4.0	Jtopen 4.1	0.204	0.217	0.121	0.129
Tomcat 4.1.4.0	Tomcat 5.0.0	0.154	0.14	0.052	0.046
Tomcat 5.0.0	Tomcat 6.0.0	0.206	0.205	0.067	0.059
Xalan 2.5.0	Xalan 2.6.0	0.331	0.334	0.034	0.038
Xalan 2.6.0	Xalan 2.7.0	0.175	0.21	0.037	0.04

(up to 7, due to space constraints), together with their size, the size of the set of first neighbors relative to each cluster, indicated by n_i, and the size of the set of first neighbor classes relative to the entire set of refactored classes, indicated by n_{all}. This analysis confirms the convenience of examining refactored first neighbor classes when looking for possible classes in need to be rafactored. In fact the more common situation is the presence of a large cluster of refactored classes (which we name cluster C from now on) along with a set of smaller clusters, many of them containing just one class. Considering the largest cluster C, and observing the set of its first neighbor classes, its size n_C is close to the size n_{all} of all refactored classes and the number n_{ref} of all refactored classes.

Consider now a developer with a set of already refactored classes and in search for more classes to refactor, adopting the strategy of examining linked classes.

1. The probability that among the set of classes already refactored there will be at least one belonging to the larger cluster is very high.
2. Examining neighbor classes the entire cluster will be explored.
3. Examining all neighbor classes, there is an upper limit to the number of classes to check, given by c_{all}, which is a small fraction of system's size.
4. This upper limit will almost be reached starting from classes into cluster C, and thus the probability of reaching it is very high.
5. If all the classes selected at first belong to isolated refactorings, most of the classes in need to be refactored will not be reached, but at the same time the effort is minimal, since $\sum_i n_i$ for $i \neq C$ is small.

At the same time one can work jointly with other strategies devised for detecting classes to refactor, like code smells detection, [30,12] in order to reduce the

Table 4. Values of the number of neighbors and the clusters size n_i for the first 7 clusters of 7 software releases, in a decreasing order by cluster size. n_{ref} is the total number of classes involved in refactoring operations affecting the corresponding release

System Name	n_{ref}	n_{all}	Clus. 1		Clus. 2		Clus. 3		Clus. 4		Clus. 5		Clus. 6		Clus. 7	
			size	n_1	size	n_2	size	n_3	size	n_4	size	n_5	size	n_6	size	n_7
Apache Ant 1.5	45	401	24	357	6	14	2	60	2	2	1	1	1	3	1	1
Azureus 4.2.0.2	216	1603	191	1551	7	52	1	28	1	22	1	21	1	16	1	13
JEdit 4.1	141	338	138	331	2	2	1	12	-	-	-	-	-	-	-	-
Jena 2.3	5	268	1	249	1	11	1	5	1	2	1	1	-	-	-	-
Jtopen 4.1	46	632	43	629	1	3	1	3	1	2	-	-	-	-	-	-
Tomcat 6.0.0	157	530	134	447	2	28	2	19	4	12	1	8	1	7	1	6
Xalan 2.4.0	14	146	8	126	2	17	2	8	1	14	1	1	-	-	-	-

number of neighbor classes to examine. Since the fraction of refactored classes is usually not too high, a fixed number of classes to refactor can be programmed in advance, and once this number is reached, the search among the first neighbors can stop and the classes in need to be refactored eventually missing will be very few.

Next we discuss as an example the case of Jedit 1.4. We are going to suggest how our empirical results can be used, together with other methodologies, to find refactor-prone classes. Fig. 2 reports the network of refactored classes for this case study. In this specific case the above mentioned strategy could be applied starting from one of these classes, and proceeding by inspecting the neighboring classes looking for refactoring opportunities. JEdit 1.4 is characterized by a total of 974 refactorings distributed over 46 classes, that represents the 7% of the entire system and they mainly belong to a cluster whose dimension are close to the totality of the refactored classes, as reported in Tab. 4. Refactored classes are reported in decreasing order of number of refactoring into Tab. 5. We consider one of the most refactored classes, namely `org.gjt.sp.jedit.textarea.JEditTextArea`.

In Fig. 3 the network of first neighbors for this class is represented. Tab. 5 reports, along with the number of refactorings per class, also the ratio between the neighboring classes affected by refactorings and the total number of neighbors. As reported in Tab. 5 for this specific class, the fraction of neighboring classes that, among all the neighboring classes, are also involved in refactoring activities is 0.5 if they are connected by in-links (In-Ratio) and 0.71 if they are connected by out-links (Out-Ratio). It is worth to report that some neighbors are connected with both in-links and out-links. So we consider now the scenario of a developer that is carrying out some refactoring operations and is working on `JEditTextArea`. We already know that, according to RefFinder, the neighboring classes were involved in refactoring operations. If he is looking for refactoring opportunities, even selecting at a random a class belonging to the set of neighboring classes, he has from 50% to 71% of chance to find a refactor-prone class, depending on which kind of connection he is looking at - in-links or out-links.

Jedit 4.1

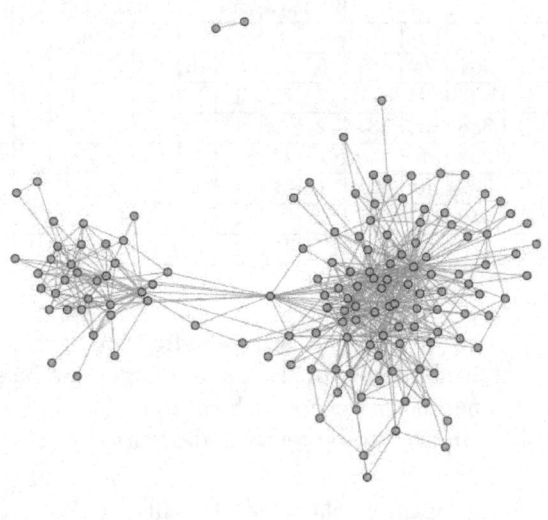

Fig. 2. Jedit refactored classes network

Table 5. Number of refactorings per classes affected by more than 13 refactorings. In-Ratio and Out-Ratio columns report for, respectively, in-links and out-links, the fraction of neighboring classes that, among all the neighboring classes, are also involved in refactoring activities and the total number of neighbors.

Class Name	N. Ref.	In-Ratio	Out-Ratio
bsh.ParserTokenManager	83	1	0.25
org.gjt.sp.jedit.syntax.ParserRule	72	1	0.6
org.gjt.sp.jedit.textarea.JEditTextArea	40	0.5	0.71
bsh.Parser	35	1	0.45
org.gjt.sp.jedit.Buffer	29	0.4	0.64
org.gjt.sp.jedit.jEdit	27	0.39	0.69
org.gjt.sp.jedit.browser.VFSBrowser	26	0.3	0.72
bsh.NameSpace	25	0.65	0.6
bsh.Interpreter	21	0.84	0.75
org.gjt.sp.jedit.syntax.DisplayTokenHandler	19	1	0.6
org.gjt.sp.jedit.browser.BrowserView	15	0.22	0.75
org.gjt.sp.jedit.gui.DockableWindowManager	15	0.26	0.55
bsh.Reflect	14	0.75	0.62
org.gjt.sp.jedit.search.SearchAndReplace	14	0.45	0.79

The mean value of the fraction of refactored classes reported in Tab. 5 is 0.63 and 0.62 for neighboring classes connected respectively with in and out-links. Fig. 4 and 5 report a series of box plots representing in-links and out-links distributions and statistics for each analyzed release, showing that often the ratio is higher than 0.5. It is worth to underline that the suggested strategy is not expected to work alone and in any circumstance, but it could be useful when the software network present a specific topology. For this reason our proposal is not to use clustering information alone, but in cooperation with other topological analysis and integrated by other strategies as those described in [31].

**Neighbors network of
org.gjt.sp.jedit.textarea.JEditTextArea**

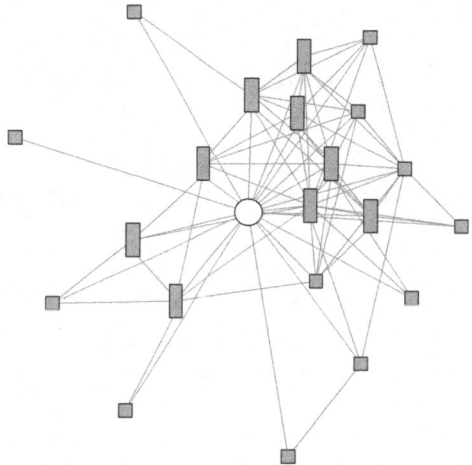

Fig. 3. Neighboring classes for `org.gjt.sp.jedit.textarea.JEditTextArea`. The white circle represents the vertex corresponding to `JEditTextArea` class, whereas the rectangle-shaped and the squared-shaped vertices, represent the neighbors connected to `JEditTextArea` by respectively in-link and both in and out-link.

5   Threats to Validity

The present study is affected by some threats to validity. All these threats are to be taken into account while replicating the study. In this section we present them according to the usual division in threats to the internal, external and construction validity.

Internal Validity. We empirically found a significant relationship between classes involved in refactoring activity and network topology. However, the tendency of refactored classes to be more connected than others could be due to some undetected factors that we did not yet thoroughly investigate.

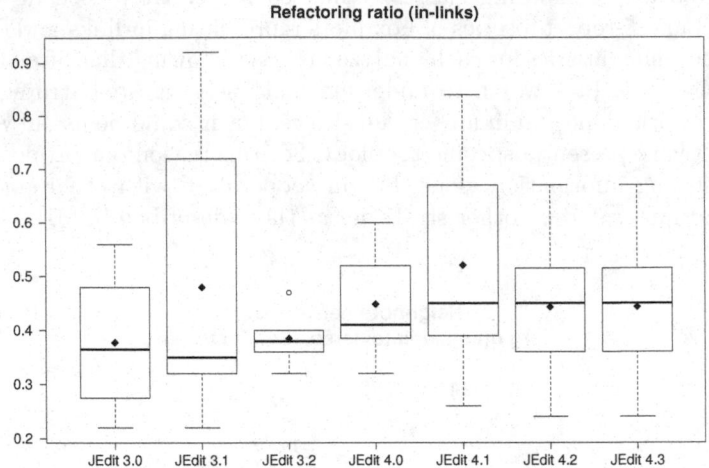

Fig. 4. Average values of the fraction of the refactored neighboring classes linked by in-links for all the JEdit analyzed releseas. Diamond-shaped point represents the mean value.

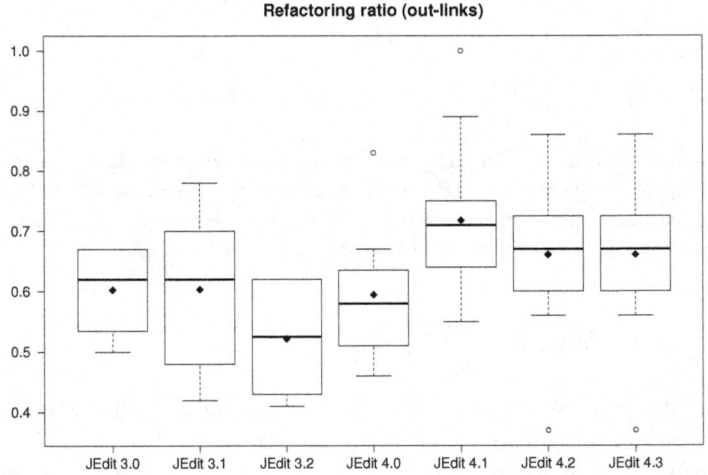

Fig. 5. Average values of the fraction of the refactored neighboring classes linked by out-links for all the JEdit analyzed releseas. Diamond-shaped point represents the mean value.

For example we did not consider class complexity, and the fact that refactored classes could belong to the same package. Moreover, we studied refactoring activities without making distinctions among different refactorings. Our empirical results could be determined only by part of them. We considered all refactorings together in order to enhance our statistics and we did not have enough data for investigating each single refactoring separately.

External Validity. We considered a certain number of software systems belonging to different categories, and performed different tasks. We made this choice in order to analyze a representative set of Java software system, that encompasses different kind of software, in order to avoid any influence of the specific domain on the results. Nevertheless, our sample is certainly limited. We analyzed only open source software, since it gave us the opportunity to freely parse the source code. We can not exclude the fact that different dynamics taking place in proprietary development environment could influence refactored classes topology. Additionally, all the analyzed software is written in Java (RefFinder parse only Java code) and all the software is written using the object oriented paradigm. Refactoring activities carried out on different languages, or in software designed according to different programming approaches, could lead to different results.   .

Construction Validity. Refactorings retrieved using RefFinder depend on the reliability of this software. Despite being an acknowledged software for this kind of task, RefFinder cannot always retrieve all the refactorings. In addition, it cannot retrieve all the refactorings in the original Fowlers catalog and it is possible that results might change while studying these not covered refactorings.

6   Conclusions

In this work we presented a study on the clustering of the classes interested by refactoring activities performed during software evolution. We analyzed several Open Source Object Oriented Java software systems using a complex network approach. We firstly retrieved the networks associated to the software systems at the class level. Then we studied the class networks, addressing our attention specifically to the relationships among the classes and their tendency to form clusters, namely groups of connected nodes. Our results seem to support the initial hypothesis that refactored classes tend to form clusters. In order to deepen our understanding on the relationship between refactoring activities and node connectivity, we studied the subnetworks composed by the first neighbors of refactored clusters. In this work we reported that not only the refactored classes form clusters according to the provided definition, but also a significant fraction of their first neighbors are interested by refactoring activities, providing a comparison with a null model represented by randomly sampled classes. This result suggests some practical applications in the field of software engineering, since it could allow developers to find out other classes to refactor while carrying out refactoring activities.

Acknowledgments. This research is supported by Regione Autonoma della Sardegna (RAS), Regional Law No. 7-2007, project CRP-17938 "LEAN 2.0".

References

1. Fowler, M.: Refactoring: Improving the design of existing code. Addison-Wesley Longman Publishing Co., Inc., Boston (1999)
2. RefFinder, https://webspace.utexas.edu/kp9746/www/reffinder/
3. Prete, K., Rachatasumrit, N., Sudan, N., Kim, M.: Template-based reconstruction of complex refactorings. In: Proceedings of the 2010 IEEE International Conference on Software Maintenance, ICSM 2010, pp. 1–10. IEEE Computer Society, Washington, DC (2010)
4. Kim, M., Gee, M., Loh, A., Rachatasumrit, N.: Ref-finder: A refactoring reconstruction tool based on logic query templates. In: Proceedings of the Eighteenth ACM SIGSOFT International Symposium on Foundations of Software Engineering, FSE 2010, pp. 371–372. ACM, New York (2010)
5. Kohring, G.A.: Complex dependencies in large software systems. Advances in Complex Systems (ACS) 12(06), 565–581 (2009)
6. Wen, L., Kirk, D., Dromey, R.G.: Software systems as complex networks. In: Proceedings of the 6th IEEE International Conference on Cognitive Informatics, COGINF 2007, pp. 106–115. IEEE Computer Society, Washington, DC (2007)
7. Li, D., Han, Y., Hu, J.: Complex network thinking in software engineering. In: Proceedings of the 2008 International Conference on Computer Science and Software Engineering, CSSE 2008, vol. 01, pp. 264–268. IEEE Computer Society, Washington, DC (2008)
8. Myers, C.R.: Software systems as complex networks: Structure, function, and evolvability of software collaboration graphs. Phys. Rev. E 68(4), 46116 (2003)
9. Valverde, S., Cancho, R., Sole, V.: Scale free networks from optimal design. Europhysics Letters 60 (2002)
10. Opdyke, W.F.: Refactoring object-oriented frameworks. Technical report (1992)
11. Wake, W.C.: Refactoring Workbook, 1st edn. Addison-Wesley Longman Publishing Co., Inc., Boston (2003)
12. Simon, F., Steinbrückner, F., Lewerentz, C.: Metrics based refactoring. In: Proc. 5th European Conference on Software Maintenance and Reengineering, pp. 30–38 (2001)
13. Murphy-Hill, E., Parnin, C., Black, A.P.: How we refactor, and how we know it. IEEE Transactions on Software Engineering 38(1), 5–18 (2012)
14. Šubelj, L., Bajec, M.: Community structure of complex software systems: Analysis and applications. Physica A Statistical Mechanics and its Applications 390, 2968–2975 (2011)
15. Turnu, I., Marchesi, M., Tonelli, R.: Entropy of the degree distribution and object-oriented software quality. In: Proceedings of the 2012 ICSE Workshop on Emerging Trends in Software Metrics, WETSoM 2012, pp. 77–82 (2012)
16. Geppert, B., Mockus, A., Rößler, F.: Refactoring for changeability: A way to go? In: IEEE METRICS, p. 13. IEEE Computer Society (2005)

17. Wilking, D., Kahn, U.F., Kowalewski, S.: An empirical evaluation of refactoring. e-Informatica 1(1), 27–42 (2007)
18. Chidamber, S., Kemerer, C.: A metrics suite for object-oriented design. IEEE Trans. Software Eng. 20(6), 476–493 (1994)
19. Gyimothy, T., Ferenc, R., Siket, I.: Empirical validation of object-oriented metrics on open source software for fault prediction. IEEE Transactions on Software Engineering 31(10), 897–910 (2005)
20. Bois, B.D., Mens, T.: Describing the impact of refactoring on internal program quality, pp. 37–48. Vrije Universiteit Brussel (2003)
21. Stroggylos, K., Spinellis, D.: Refactoring–does it improve software quality? In: Proceedings of the 5th International Workshop on Software Quality, WoSQ 2007, p. 10. IEEE Computer Society, Washington, DC (2007)
22. Kataoka, Y., Imai, T., Andou, H., Fukaya, T.: A quantitative evaluation of maintainability enhancement by refactoring. In: Proceedings of the International Conference on Software Maintenance, pp. 576–585 (2002)
23. Moser, R., Sillitti, A., Abrahamsson, P., Succi, G.: Does refactoring improve reusability? In: Morisio, M. (ed.) ICSR 2006. LNCS, vol. 4039, pp. 287–297. Springer, Heidelberg (2006)
24. Murgia, A., Marchesi, M., Concas, G., Tonelli, R., Counsell, S.: Parameter-based refactoring and the relationship with fan-in/fan-out coupling. In: Proceedings of the 2011 IEEE Fourth International Conference on Software Testing, Verification and Validation Workshops, ICSTW 2011, pp. 430–436. IEEE Computer Society, Washington, DC (2011)
25. Murgia, A., Tonelli, R., Marchesi, M., Concas, G., Counsell, S., McFall, J., Swift, S.: Refactoring and its relationship with fan-in and fan-out: An empirical study. In: 2012 16th European Conference on Proceedings of Software Maintenance and Reengineering, CSMR 2012, pp. 63–72 (2012)
26. Concas, G., Monni, C., Orrù, M., Tonelli, R.: Are refactoring practices related to clusters in java software? In: Cantone, G., Marchesi, M. (eds.) XP 2014. LNBIP, vol. 179, pp. 269–276. Springer, Heidelberg (2014)
27. Java Qualitas Corpus, http://qualitascorpus.com/
28. Tempero, E., Anslow, C., Dietrich, J., Han, T., Li, J., Lumpe, M., Melton, H., Noble, J.: Qualitas corpus: A curated collection of java code for empirical studies. In: 2010 Asia Pacific Software Engineering Conference (APSEC 2010), pp. 336–345 (December 2010)
29. Kyle Prete, N.R., Kim, M.: Catalogue of template refactoring rules. Technical Report (August 15, 2010)
30. Hamza, H., Counsell, S., Hall, T., Loizou, G.: Code smell eradication and associated refactoring. In: Proceedings of the 2nd Conference on European Computing Conference, ECC 2008, pp. 102–107. World Scientific and Engineering Academy and Society (WSEAS), Stevens Point (2008)
31. Moha, N., Gueheneuc, Y.G., Duchien, L., Le Meur, A.F.: Decor: A method for the specification and detection of code and design smells. IEEE Trans. Softw. Eng. 36(1), 20–36 (2010)

Are Some Refactorings Attached to Fault-Prone Classes and Others to Fault-Free Classes?

Steve Counsell[1], Stephen Swift[1], Alessandro Murgia[2], Roberto Tonelli[3], Michele Marchesi[3], and Giulio Concas[3]

[1] Dept. of Computer Science, Brunel University, Uxbridge, UK
[2] Dept. of Informatics, University of Antwerp, Belgium
[3] DIEE, University of Cagliari, Cagliari, Italy
steve.counsell@brunel.ac.uk

Abstract. A topical and relevant issue in the area of refactoring is the nature and characteristics of classes to which refactorings are applied. In particular, if we scrutinise the total set of refactorings applied to the classes of a system over different releases, which refactorings are applied to fault-prone classes and which to fault-free classes? In this paper, we explore that facet of refactoring. Refactorings applied between six releases of three Eclipse packages are used as a basis of the study and the *Ref-Finder* tool used to extract up to sixty-five different refactorings. Interestingly, results showed that refactorings applied to highly fault-prone classes differed significantly from those applied to fault-free classes, in particular related to the 'rename method' refactoring; a corresponding trend for the 'move method' and 'move field' refactoring was found in 'fault-free' classes over the period while the add and remove parameter refactorings tended to remain constant. The research offers an insight into refactoring behaviour in light of faults (or no faults).

Keywords: Refactoring, faults, renaming, Eclipse, empirical.

1 Introduction

In the past ten or so years, the discipline of refactoring has become a mainstream software engineering activity by developers. While we know a relatively large amount about trends in refactoring across systems and the frequencies with which refactorings are applied to object-oriented systems [2, 3, 6, 7, 10] a feature of the area which still largely eludes the community is the relationship between refactoring and fault-proneness. In other words, questions such as which specific refactorings are applied to fault-prone classes and which to fault-free classes remain largely open. From a practical, industry perspective it may be of use for a developer or project manager to know which refactorings are applied to fault-free and fault-prone classes since that knowledge might guide and help target extra development effort in the future as well as help understand current effort distribution. Equally, understanding when certain refactorings are undertaken and the inter-relationships between refactorings (in the context of fault-free and fault-prone classes) may provide insights into the benefits or drawbacks of specific refactorings.

T. Dingsøyr et al. (Eds.): XP 2014 Workshops, LNBIP 199, pp. 136–147, 2014.

In this paper, we extracted up to sixty-five different refactorings between releases of the Eclipse system. The refactorings were extracted using the Ref-Finder tool [9]. Our research goal was to show that some refactorings were, or were not applied depending on whether there was at least one fault present in a class. Several trends in the data analysis emerged. Fault-prone classes tended to use the 'Rename method' refactoring more extensively; fault-free classes tended to use the 'Move method' and 'Move field' refactorings (and relatively little use of renaming). The 'Add parameter' refactoring remained consistently applied in each type of class. The results suggest that in the presence of faults, classes (and their methods) have different refactorings applied to them depending on the extent of their fault-proneness (in this case, a binary classification of 'yes – the class had faults, and 'no' it has not).

The remainder of the paper is structured as follows. In the next section, we present related work followed by preliminaries (Section 3) detailing how the refactorings were extracted and the approach taken. We then scrutinise the refactorings in the releases of Eclipse (Section 4) exploring the fault-prone classes and relationships with refactorings; we then contrast this analysis with fault-free classes (Section 5) before exploring threats to validity in Section 6. Finally, we conclude in Section 7 pointing to future work.

2   Related Work

In terms of seminal refactoring literature, it is well-cited that Opdyke first introduced the concept in his PhD Thesis [8]. Equally, that Fowler later proposed the set of seventy-two refactorings [5] in his seminal text and on which we draw from in this paper. There has been a wealth of refactoring studies exploring different aspects of the practice. In this paper, we will just look at studies of refactoring related to faults. Three other notable studies have explored the link between refactoring and fault-proneness in the recent past and are of direct relevance to the study presented.

Firstly, Weissgerber and Diehl [11] used versions of three open-source systems as an empirical basis of an investigation of the link between refactoring and faults; however, they only identified eight types of refactoring (we identify sixty-five refactoring types) and the time frame used was days rather than months and years (as we will use in our study). Secondly, Ratzinger et al., [10] analyzed whether refactoring history information was useful to support defect prediction and whether refactoring activities reduce the probability of software defects. They demonstrated that refactorings and defects had an inverse correlation: the number of software defects decreased if the number of refactorings increased. However, they did not distinguish among different kinds of refactoring operations; in addition, their detection process did not use source code analysis of version data. Finally, research by Bavota et al., [1] looked at the type of refactorings that induced faults. Results indicated that most types of refactorings were harmless. Others, however, such as those related to hierarchies caused faults more frequently. The study did not consider versions over which those refactorings were undertaken; it also viewed the fault profile of classes on a coarse-grained, binary basis – either a class has exhibited a fault or it has not and not with actual numbers.

3   Preliminaries

Our analysis is based on results between releases from each of three Eclipse projects: jdt.core, jdt.ui and jdt.uiworkbench; henceforth we refer to these as core, ui and workbench. Fault data was collected manually by one of the researchers and subsequently verified by another in order to ensure that, as far as possible, correct data was used in the study. We define a fault as an observed failure in the system and has been marked as such by Eclipse developers using the Bugzilla fault-tracking system and fixed. The Ref-Finder tool [9] was used to extract all refactorings between nine releases in total and is capable of identifying up to sixty-five refactorings of the original set of 72 proposed by Fowler [5]. The data reported thus relates to all classes that had been the subject of at least one refactoring between releases and all faults were therefore considered between the releases studied. For all refactored classes, we took into account faults between three releases for each project: 3.0 and 3.1, 3.1 and 3.2 and 3.2 and 3.3. We also collected classes for which no faults were reported between these releases. Eclipse was chosen because it is a well-known, long-lived project and was felt to be large enough to generate refactorings; it was also felt by the authors that it would provide a solid basis for extracting faults and being such a popular system would also facilitate further replication. (We note that the set of faults and refactorings collected as part of the study were disjoint across releases, i.e., double counting of either was not a threat. In other words, between releases, a unique set of faults and refactorings were identified.)

4   Data Analysis

4.1   All Fault-Prone Classes between Core_30_31

Table 1 shows the frequency of refactorings in the three most fault-prone classes of core_30_31 package (i.e., those between release 3.0 and 3.1), ordered alphabetically (note the tie between the 'Remove Parameter' and the 'Replace method with method object' refactorings). We chose the three most fault-prone classes because that gave us a large number of faults to work with. We have only shown the top five refactorings for clarity. So, the most frequently applied refactoring in the three most fault-prone classes was Rename Method, then Add parameter, etc. While the distribution of refactorings covers a relatively broad range, the Add Parameter (AP) with 56 occurrences and Rename Method (RM) with 228 occurrences dominate the list in terms of size.

The rationale behind using the RM refactoring is when the name of a method does not properly describe its purpose. The method name should be changed to reflect that purpose. The AP refactoring, on the other hand, should be used when a method is missing needed functionality and that can be provided with the addition of one or more parameters. We note that there were 1151 classes between core_30_31 releases to which at least one fault had been identified and then fixed.

Table 1. Refactorings applied to fault-prone classes (core_30_31 package)

Refactoring	Freq.
Add parameter	56
Extract method	27
Introduce explaining variable	25
Remove parameter	23
Rename method	228
Replace method with method object	23

One hypothesis as to why so many of both AP and RM refactorings were present is that if a method has to be changed significantly in the presence of multiple faults, then the method would ordinarily have to be changed to reflect the new function it fulfils. For a highly-faulty class, this could affect many methods in that class. As an explanation of the disproportionate number of AP and RM refactorings, we suggest that fault-prone classes would necessitate large changes to a class and this would also require the addition of significant numbers of parameters to the methods of a class. The 'Introduce explaining variable' refactoring is applied when an expression is complex and needs to be decomposed through the introduction of an additional variable (or variables).

4.2   All Fault-Prone Classes Between Core_31_32

Table 2 shows (for the set of classes undergoing at least one refactoring between these releases), the frequency of each refactoring type (in the same way as in Table 1 – *ordered alphabetically in each row when tied*) applied to the three most fault-prone classes between these releases. The contrast between Table 1 and 2 is noticeable; this version was relatively free of refactorings. That said, the AP and RM refactorings do feature and these have been bolded in the table. We note that there were 1029 classes between core_31_32 releases to which at least one fault had been identified and then fixed.

Table 2. Refactorings applied to fault-prone classes (core_31_32 package)

Refactoring	Freq.
Add parameter, Consolidate conditional duplicate fragments, Extract method, Inline temp, Introduce explaining variable, Remove assignment to parameters, Remove parameter, Replace nested conditional with guard clauses.	3
Hide delegate, Inline method, **Rename method**.	2
Consolidate conditional expression, Decompose conditional, Remove control flag, Replace data with object, Replace magic number with symbolic constant, Replace method with method object.	1

Interestingly from Tables 1 and 2, there appears to be only limited (if any) evidence of moving fields and/or methods around the class; we could tentatively suggest that application of this type of refactoring is used when methods are being maintained to aid comprehension and as perfective maintenance, but not necessarily when a class/method is faulty (as corrective maintenance); we will return to this hypothesis later in the paper.

4.3   All Fault-Prone Classes between Core_32_33

Table 3 shows the refactoring profile for the three classes with the most fault-prone profile between releases core_32_33. Again, it shows the top five refactorings in that category, ordered alphabetically. It is noticeable that the AP refactoring features strongly with 51 applied refactorings. The most common refactoring was the Extract Method refactoring with 105 applications between those two releases. We note that there are no occurrences in the top three classes of the RM refactoring, in contrast to the trend in the previous two tables (and, in particular, Table 1). In fact, scrutiny of the *entire* set of fault-prone classes revealed no application of this refactoring whatsoever. We can offer no concrete explanation as to why so few RM refactorings were applied. However, one plausible explanation might be that, in the context of so many Extract method refactorings being applied, application of Extract method acts as an alternative to renaming methods. Put another way, creating one or more new methods from one existing source method may eliminate the need to rename that source class altogether. We note that there were 254 classes between core_32_33 releases to which at least one fault had been identified and then fixed.

Table 3. Refactorings applied to fault-prone classes (core_32_33 package)

Refactoring	Freq.
Add parameter	51
Extract method	105
Move method	6
Remove parameter	21
Replace nested conditional with guard clauses	7

As *per* Tables 1 and 2, there seems to be limited evidence of moving features (only 6 Move method refactorings were observed between these two releases).

4.4   All Fault-Prone Classes between ui_30_31

Table 4 shows the same data as that contained in Tables 1-3, but between releases of package ui_30_31. In common with Table 1, the AP and RM refactorings again dominate the list with 55 and 183 refactorings, respectively. It is interesting that in each of the tables thus far the remove parameter refactoring has also featured. We note that there were 1489 classes between ui_30_31 releases in which at least one fault had been identified and then fixed.

Table 4. Refactorings applied to fault-prone classes (ui_30_31 package)

Refactoring	Freq.
Add parameter	55
Inline method	47
Move method	13
Remove parameter	42
Rename method	183

The 'Inline method' refactoring was also a feature of refactorings applied in this release. The purpose of this refactoring is where the body of a method is as clear as its name; they are amalgamated. The example of inline method taken from Fowler [5] is as follows:

```
int getRating() {
    return (moreThanFiveLateDeliveries()) ? 2 : 1;
}
boolean moreThanFiveLateDeliveries() {
    return _numberOfLateDeliveries > 5;
}
```

After refactoring, this becomes:

```
int getRating() {
    return (_numberOfLateDeliveries > 5) ? 2 : 1;
}
```

It is noteworthy that this refactoring is the opposite of the Extract method in the sense that the Extract method refactoring decomposes a method while inline method merges two (or more) methods. No evidence of that refactoring was found in this release. Looking at Table 3 also shows that when there were multiple occurrences of the Extract method refactoring, there were also no instances of the inline method. The evidence from Tables 1-4 suggests that the extract method refactoring may have many 'competing' and 'complementary' refactorings. It may be that when Inline method features, the Extract method refactoring does not.

4.5 All Fault-Prone Classes between ui_31_32

Table 5 shows the same data for ui _31_32 releases. Once again, the RM refactoring dominates the list with 18 occurrences. Clearly, fault-prone classes for the releases studied have a strong bind with this refactoring and even what we might consider as 'popular' refactorings (e.g., Add parameter) were applied relatively infrequently. We note that between these releases were 1187 classes which exhibited at least one fault.

Table 5. Refactorings applied to fault-prone classes (ui_31_32 package)

Refactoring	Freq.
Add parameter, Remove control flag, Remove parameter, Replace magic number with symbolic constant, Replace nested conditional with guard clauses, extract method, Introduce explaining variable.	2
Replace constructor with factory method, Consolidate conditional duplicate fragments.	5
Inline method, Replace method with method object.	3
Move method.	4
Rename method	18

4.6   All Fault-Prone Classes between ui_32_33

Table 6 shows the refactoring profile for the three most fault-prone classes between package ui_31_32 releases. Although there is evidence of a number of Move method refactorings (19), the AP refactoring still features strongly. Fewer RM refactorings (6) were observed between these two releases, however. We note that there were 1025 classes with at least one fault between these two releases.

Table 6. Refactorings applied to fault-prone classes (ui_32_33 package)

Refactoring	Freq.
Add parameter	**13**
Introduce explaining variable	7
Move method	**19**
Remove parameter	8
Rename method	6
Replace method with method object	**6**

It is interesting that the Introduce explaining variable refactoring has featured in 4 of the tables presented so far.

4.7   All Fault-Prone Classes between Workbench_30_31

Table 7 shows the most frequently applied refactorings for the workbench_31_32 package releases. In keeping with the previous tables, the RM refactoring is the most popular. In contrast to the previous tables however, there is evidence of the Move method refactoring (69 occurrences) but the RM refactoring still dominates. We note that there were 695 classes between these two releases where at least one fault had been identified and fixed.

Table 7. Refactorings applied to fault-prone classes (workbench_30_31 package)

Refactoring	Freq.
Add parameter	13
Extract method	22
Introduce explaining variable	13
Move method	69
Rename method	91
Replace method with method object	14

The 'Replace method with method object' has also featured in many tables reported. This refactoring occurs when [13]: 'You have a long method that uses local variables in such a way that you cannot apply Extract method. Turn the method into its own object so that all the local variables become fields on that object. You can then decompose the method into other methods on the same object'. This is an interesting refactoring, since the Extract method itself has been used relatively extensively, as evident from Table 7.

4.8 All Fault-Prone Classes between Workbench_31_32

Table 8 shows the same phenomenon as in many of the previous tables. The RM refactoring again dominates the set of refactorings with 25 occurrences. We note that there were 429 classes between these two releases where at least one fault had been identified and fixed.

Table 8. Refactorings applied to fault-prone classes (workbench_31_32 package)

Refactoring	Freq.
Extract method	10
Inline method	7
Move method	14
Rename method	**25**
Replace magic number with symbolic constant	6

The 'Replace magic number with symbolic constant' refactoring appears in three of the Tables 1-8. This refactoring is applied when [12]: 'You have a literal number with a particular meaning'. The solution is to: 'Create a constant, name it after the meaning, and replace the number with it'. Creating constants rather than hard-coding numbers in the body of code is a technique that every first-year Computer Science student learns as a basic programming skill and good practice; it would appear that not doing so may be the source of faults since, from the evidence so far, the refactoring has been associated with highly fault-prone classes. The example of this refactoring taken from Fowler [5] is:

```
double potentialEnergy(double mass, double height) {
   return mass * height * 9.81;
}
```

After refactoring, this becomes:

```
double potentialEnergy(double mass, double height) {
   return mass * GRAVITATIONAL_CONSTANT * height;
}
static final double GRAVITATIONAL_CONSTANT = 9.81;
```

4.9   All Fault-Prone Classes between Workbench_32_33

Finally, Table 9 shows the profile in refactorings for the three most fault-prone refactorings between releases in the workbench_32_33 package. Interestingly, in contrast to the other eight tables, the Move method refactoring dominates the profile with 90 refactorings. The AP and RM refactorings feature in a limited way only. There were 370 unique classes with at least one fault between these two releases.

Table 9. Refactorings applied to fault-prone classes (workbench_32_33 package)

Refactoring	Freq.
Add parameter	7
Inline temp	8
Introduce explaining variable	7
Move method	90
Rename method	10
Replace method with method object	20

The Inline temp refactoring (8 occurrences in Table 9) is similar in principle to the Inline method refactoring. It is used when [5]: "you have a temp that is assigned to once with a simple expression, and the temp is getting in the way of other refactorings". The solution is to replace all references to that temp with the expression. The example given in [5] is of code before the refactoring as follows:

```
double basePrice = anOrder.basePrice();
return (basePrice > 1000)
```

After the refactoring, the code becomes:

```
return (anOrder.basePrice() > 1000)
```

5   Fault-Free Class Analysis

One question that naturally arises from the analysis is whether there is a difference between the profiles of the three most fault-prone classes reported in Tables 1-9 and the set of classes which did not exhibit faults in the same set of releases. In other words, if we look at the total set of fault-free classes, do we find similar refactoring patterns? Table 10 shows, for each of the releases studied the two most popular refactorings in the set of fault-free classes. We chose two because that represented a significant percentage of the refactorings for the set of classes.

Table 10 shows the release name, the number of classes which were categorized as fault-free between those two releases, the two refactorings and, in the fourth column, (enclosed in brackets) a triple of: the number of the first refactoring, the number of the second refactoring and finally, the number of RM refactorings. For example, between releases core_30_31, there were 58 AP refactorings, 123 Remove parameter refactorings and just 10 RM refactorings.

Table 10. The most popular refactorings in set of fault-free classes

Package	No. Classes	Most popular two refactorings	Freq.
core_30_31	393	Add parameter, Remove parameter	(58, 123, 10)
core_31_32	130	Add parameter, Move method	(16, 15, 8)
core_32_33	169	Add parameter, Remove parameter	(76, 62, 0)
ui_30_31	1355	Add parameter, Move method	(137, 238, 112)
ui_31_32	846	Move field, Move method	(76, 224, 71)
ui_32_33	1652	Move field, Move method	(188, 477, 147)
workbench_30_31	423	Move field, Move method	(104, 147, 30)
workbench_31_32	229	Move field, Move method	(48, 83, 3)
workbench_32_33	174	Move field, Move method	(24, 90, 1)

Table 10 shows a clear difference in the composition of refactorings when compared with the profiles in Tables 1-9. In those tables, the RM was applied the most frequently in 5 of the 9 sets of releases scrutinized. From Table 10, there is some evidence of renaming (see, for example, ui_30_31 and ui_32_33). However, the Move field, Move method and AP refactorings tend to dominate the raw figures (particularly for the core package in the case of AP and the Move method and Move field refactoring in the case of the workbench and ui packages). Overall, there is some evidence to suggest that fault-prone classes have different refactorings applied to them when compared with fault-free classes. In particular that the RM refactoring is not applied as frequently in fault-free classes as it is in fault-prone classes. One could claim that maybe the RM refactoring was the third most popular refactoring from Table 10 which would suggest that it was a "close" third. However, in many of the Java packages, this was not the case.

6   Threats to Validity

In any empirical analysis, we need to consider the threats to the validity of the research [4]. In this paper, we have used multiple releases from one system only (Eclipse) and thus give limited scope for transferability of results. However, to counter this argument, we have used different packages from that system and although this is not an ideal solution to the threat, it does to a certain extent lessen that threat. A second threat is reflected in the methodology that we have adopted for our analysis. We chose the three most fault-prone refactorings between each pair of releases as a basis. Had we chosen the top ten most fault-prone classes, then it is possible that different results may have emerged. However, in our defense of this argument, it is possible that that the same refactorings would emerge anyway. Also, the question of 'how many should be chosen?' is an open question and not one that can be answered easily. A third threat is that we chose the top five refactorings within those three classes as data for the tables in the paper. The same argument applies here. It is possible that a different set of conclusions might have been drawn had we chosen for example, the top ten refactorings within the top three fault-prone classes. However, we feel that the same types of refactoring would emerge if we had widened our selection. A fourth threat is that the Ref-Finder is a tool subject to the criticism that there are tool extraction reliability rates (of precision and recall). However, the tool is well-trusted and has been used in various other empirical studies; any tool is subject to the same threat and we believe that this would have a negligible effect only on the results in the paper. Finally, our definition of a fault-free class is one that until the point of analysis is free of faults. It is possible that between subsequent releases that same class may experience one of more faults. However, as a snapshot of the system at a point, we feel this is a realistic assumption to take.

7   Conclusions and Future Work

In this exploratory study, we explored the differences from a refactoring perspective of fault-prone classes, *vis-à-vis* fault-free classes. Our main goal was to identify any differences in trends between refactorings applied to each type. Results showed an interesting and marked distinction between the two types; fault-prone classes tended to invite a large number of Rename method refactorings but relatively few movements of features (Move method and Move field). Fault-free classes invited many move operations suggesting that these types of refactoring were less to do with fixing faults and more to making classes easier to understand (in the true spirit of refactoring). Moving features around may be more in keeping with perfective maintenance than corrective maintenance. The overall implication of the preliminary research is that faults may cause developers to change methods significantly in response to faults and then *have* to rename them to preserve their meaning rather than moving features of the class around. Clearly, evidence suggests that the motivation for using refactoring changes depending on the context of the situation. The research therefore opens up a potentially new theme in refactoring and that relates to how developers actually apply refactoring in the context of faults. Future work will explore this facet more deeply and employ techniques such as association rules and time series analysis for establishing relationships between refactorings. In keeping with the threats to validity stated in the previous section, future work will also explore the same traits in different systems and widen the choice and selection of fault-prone classes and refactoring types. Finally, we have looked at the contrast between fault-free and fault-prone classes as a binary classification – i.e., that a class contains faults or it does not; however, it may be interesting to explore a scale of 'faultiness'. In other words, are there any differences between the refactorings applied depending on the actual extent (or scale) of their fault-proneness?

Acknowledgements. The research of Alessandro Murgia is sponsored by the Institute for the promotion of Innovation through Science and Technology in Flanders through a project entitled Change-centric Quality Assurance (CHAQ) with number120028.

References

1. Bavota, G., De Carluccio, B., De Lucia, A., Di Penta, M., Oliveto, R., Strollo, O.: When does a refactoring induce bugs? An Empirical Study. In: Proceedings of 12th IEEE International Working Conference on Source Code Analysis and Manipulation, Trento, Italy (2012)
2. Counsell, S., Hassoun, Y., Loizou, G., Najjar, R.: Common refactorings, a dependency graph and some code smells: An empirical study of Java OSS. In: International Symposium on Empirical Software Engineering (ISESE), Rio de Janeiro, pp. 288–296 (2006)
3. Demeyer, S., Ducasse, S., Nierstrasz, O.: Finding Refactorings via Change Metrics. In: Conference OO Programming Systems, Languages and Apps., pp. 166–177. ACM Press (2000)
4. Fenton, N.E., Pfleeger, S.L.: Software metrics - a practical and rigorous approach, 2nd edn. International Thomson (1996)
5. Fowler, M.: Refactoring: Improving the Design of Existing Code. Addison-Wesley Professional (1999)
6. Mens, T., Tourwe, T.: A Survey of Software Refactoring. IEEE Transactions on Software Engineering 30(2), 126–139 (2004)
7. Murphy-Hill, E., Parnin, C., Black, A.: How we refactor, and how we know it. IEEE Transactions on Software Engineering 38(1), 5–18 (2012)
8. Opdyke, W.: Refactoring object-oriented frameworks, PhD Thesis, University of Illinois at Urbana-Champaign (1992)
9. Prete, K., Rachatasumrit, N., Sudan, N., Kim, M.: Template-based reconstruction of complex refactorings. In: Intl. Conference Software Maintenance, Timisoara, Romania, pp. 1–10 (2010)
10. Ratzinger, J., Sigmund, T., Gall, H.C.: On the relation of refactorings and software defect prediction. In: Proceedings of the 2008 International Working Conference on Mining Software Repositories, pp. 35–38. ACM Press, Leipzig (2008)
11. Weissgerber, P., Diehl, S.: Are refactorings less error-prone than other changes? In: Proceedings of Workshop on Mining Software Repositories (MSR 2006), pp. 112–118 (2006)
12. http://www.refactoring.com
13. http://www.sourcemaking.com

Capturing Software Evolution and Change through Code Repository Smells

Francesca Arcelli Fontana, Matteo Rolla, and Marco Zanoni

Department of Informatics, Systems and Communication
University of Milano - Bicocca
{arcelli,zanoni}@disco.unimib.it, matteo.rolla@gmail.com
http://www.essere.disco.unimib.it

Abstract. In the last years we have seen the rise and the fall of many version control systems. These systems collect a large amount of data spanning from the path of the files involved in changes to the exact text changed in every file. This data can be exploited to produce an overview about how the system changed over time and evolved. We have developed a tool, called VCS-Analyzer, to use this information, both for data retrieval and analysis tasks. Currently, VCS-Analyzer implements six different analyses: two based on source code for the computation of metrics and the detection of code smells, and four original analysis based on repositories metadata, which are based on the concepts of Repository Metrics and Code Repository Smells. In this paper, we describe one smell and two metrics we have defined for source code repositories analysis.

Keywords: Code Repository smells, Repository analysis, Repository Metrics, Code changes.

1   Introduction

Code smells are well known in the literature [1], and researchers have been trying to automatically detect them, and to remove them through refactoring steps. Code smells are symptoms of deeper problems and are recognizable by considering the source code only. While searching problems in a system, not only a single code snapshot should be taken into account, but also its history that will eventually result into code smells, other problems, or symptoms of problems. Analyzing code changes taken from Version Control Systems (VCSs) is a natural way to track the code history. VCSs play a huge role in software development. There is no safe way of merging the work of several developers without using a VCS, and furthermore no developer nowadays would work on a project of some importance, size or value, without being able to revert changes when things become unmanageable. VCSs allow storing and exposing data on the contents, authors and times of the changes applied on a project repository.

In this paper, we show some ways in which these data, or part of them, can be used to extract symptoms of more deep-rooted problems. Since these symptoms are based on repositories, and for the analogy with Code Smells, they have

T. Dingsøyr et al. (Eds.): XP 2014 Workshops, LNBIP 199, pp. 148–165, 2014.

been called *Code Repository Smells*. In particular, we focus our attention on a Code Repository Smell, which we called *Code Bashing*. This smell refers to the situation in which changes made by several developers on several versions of a specified file gather in a narrow portion of the file itself.

Moreover, we have defined two new metrics, for data gathered from repositories, called the *Repository Stability* and the *File Volatility* metrics. Repository Stability is based on the concept of file closures and represents, at a given moment, the ratio between stable files and those that will be subjected to further modifications. File Volatility expresses how much the content of a file, or a portion of it, changes in relation to the number of its versions.

For our analyses, we have developed a tool, called VCS-Analyzer [2], that allows retrieving data needed for software analysis, by harvesting system repositories. It does not rely on any particular VCS, but instead it produces a model that abstracts and encapsulates all the data retrieved from such systems, guaranteeing complete independence. VCS-Analyzer needs only the identifier of the repository to be analyzed, and takes care of the retrieval of metadata or files, depending on the analysis to perform. It has been designed to allow simple plugging of new analyses and other VCSs, by decoupling the different aspects of repository crawling. The tool currently supports Git and SVN, which are the most used VCSs in the open source community, but others can be integrated if the need for them arises. VCS-Analyzer has been used to perform different analyses on many systems, e.g., JUnit, ElasticSearch, the Linux kernel. The detailed description of VCS-Analyzer and the analyses performed can be found in the Thesis of M. Rolla [3] and on the project's web page [1]. Currently the supported analyses exploit the detection of code smells, the computation of many metrics, change sizes and number of changes, as well as the information captured through the Code Repository Smell and Metrics defined in this paper.

In the paper, we first define the Code Bashing Smell and we describe the method we used to detect it. Our method is based on tracking line changes in source code repositories, through an algorithm we define. Then, we pose two Research Questions to understand if the information extracted by tracking line changes is actually different or similar from the one extracted by looking to file changes only. Moreover, other two Research Questions are posed to check if *i)* the number of changes per file and per line, and *ii)* the time interval between changes per file and per line, used for ranking files, highlight different files. Then, by using information regarding line changes, we define the File Volatility metric that we use to detect the Code Bashing smell. Finally, we define the Repository Stability metric, to evaluate the development activity and changes done on an entire repository, and in particular its degree of maturity.

The paper is organized through the following sections: In Section 2 we summarize some related work. In Section 3 we introduce the Code Bashing smell. In Section 4 we describe our line change tracking approach and in Section 5 we compare change measures based on files and lines, by posing and answering four different research questions. In Section 6 and Section 7 we introduce and

---

[1] http://essere.disco.unimib.it/reverse/VCSAnalyzer.html

describe the two new Repository Metrics. In Section 8 we describe the most relevant threats to the validity of our work. Finally, in Section 9, we conclude and outline some future developments.

2 Related Work

At the best of our knowledge, the literature does not report a concept similar to the *Code Bashing* smell, as defined in this paper; the same holds for the identified Repository Metrics, i.e., *File Volatility* and *Repository Stability*.

Regarding the different analysis on the evolution of software repositories, as those we can perform with VCS-Analyzer, many works have been proposed in the literature, as the papers in the Proceedings of Mining Software Repositories Conferences [4] and many others [5,6,7,8].

In this paper, we describe and apply a technique for tracking lines changes along the evolution of a repository. Many works have been proposed in the literature describing different analyses on file changes [6,7,9]. Many of these works measure and exploit file changes for making different kinds of inference about the quality or the evolution of software projects. At the best of our knowledge, the literature reports only few analyses based on line changes. Zimmermann et al. [10] introduce line change tracking, and the usage of annotation graphs to track the complete history of each line of the analyzed project. The approach they used for recognizing line changes is very similar to the one we describe. The technique is applied to compute the coupling among lines in the Eclipse project. Canfora et al. [11] propose a more advanced algorithm to achieve better performances in line tracking. The algorithm addresses problems like file renaming or line reordering, and computes the similarity among lines to support line tracking.

The File Volatility metric defined in this paper measures the maximum change density of a file in a repository, exploiting the line tracking technique we define. Other metrics address the measurement of the amount of changes received by a file. For example, a largely studied metric, which considers the amount the changed lines, is code churn [8]. Despite their similarities, the two metrics have different goals, and in Section 6 we demonstrate that they produce different results.

Regarding other systems similar to VCS-Analyzer, different works have been proposed in the literature. A first example is *Churrasco* [12], which provides software evolution modeling, analysis and visualization through a web interface. This tool takes as input the URL of a Subversion repository to be analyzed, processes the project and automatically creates and stores an evolutionary model in a centralized relational database. Another example is *Kenyon* [13], a system designed to facilitate software evolution research by providing a common set of solutions to common problems. *Kenyon*'s authors used the tool for processing source-code data from 12 systems of different sizes and domains, archived in 3 different types of VCS. *Kenyon* extracts each source code change from the input repositories and stores information into a relational database. In addition to extracting changes, users can add their own plug-ins to perform desirable tasks. All tasks are configurable through a web interface based on the Hudson build framework[2]. Another example is CodeVizard [14]. This tool allows analyzing CVS or Subversion repositories, and to display different kinds of information, at different granularities, over a timeline. It supports Java and C#. The tool computes over 70 software metrics of each version of the analyzed project, and can use this information to detect code smells. An example of the views it can provide is the *System View*, where each file in a repository is represented with a timeline, and file properties, e.g., code smells are encoded with different colors. The view allows visualizing the evolution of specific properties in the life of all files of the analyzed project. Other tools exist with more specific aims, e.g., the visualization of software evolution [15,16].

The aim of VCS-Analyzer is different from the above tools. Currently, the tool implements the computation of code related metrics and the detection of code smells as well, but its main focus is supporting any software assessment process by analyzing data exposed by the VCSs. In this regards, Kenyon, is the most similar related work we described.

3   Code Bashing Smell

Code is rarely completely right at first writing: it undergoes several changes and optimizations, which are natural during its evolution. When a portion of code keeps changing frequently it may point out a deeper problem in the system structure or design. Nevertheless, when developers reiteratively edit the same portion of code, it is sign of a problem: e.g., either the requirement specifications were not exhaustive and subject to frequent change, or the code is too complex for the developer to be fully understood. Moreover, once a piece of code is considered stable enough, changes involving it should be in a limited number, following the principle of single responsibility [17] which states that every class should have a single reason to change, because it has a single responsibility. Even in agile methods, where changes are normal and welcome, an excessive number of changes to the same piece (or single line) of code can be suspicious. A region of code is affected by *Code Bashing* when it has been changed a disproportionate amount of times during its life. Clearly, depending on the repository branches and conventions, the evaluation of the amount of changes can have different interpretations. A local development branch will be by far more unstable than an official stable/release branch. It often happens that local branches are used to experiment different solutions, and files get almost totally changed from time to time. On mature projects, instead, there is usually a branch which receives only tested and approved code. When too many changes are made to this last kind of code, it is often the sign that a problem happened.

To be able to detect the Code Bashing smell, we need first to be able to measure the amount of changes made to single code regions. The simplest measure is the change count. Whenever a code region is changed, its change counter is

---

incremented. Since code regions cannot be defined in advance, unless we consider and parse the grammar of the analyzed file, we consider the changes applied to each single line of code. Single lines can be grouped back to regions, if needed, in a later stage. What we would like to have is a *Change Intensity* metric (defined below), telling how many changes each line received during a considered time interval. The *Change Intensity* metric is used to compute File Volatility (see Section 6).

4 Tracking Line Changes

We defined a technique to track changes made to the lines of each file in a repository. The algorithm we implemented in VCS-Analyzer populates an array of descriptors for each text file in the repository, where each cell represents a line of the respective file, and contains the list of changes made to the line, keeping track of the timestamp, the version identifier, the author, and the position of the changed line.

To track changes, the algorithm analyzes the differences between the same file in consecutive versions, using the patch texts provided by the VCS[3]. All major VCSs embrace the unified diff format. The lines of a diff can be grouped into three categories:

- *Neutral blocks*: composed of lines serving as context and not taking part in changing the file.
- *Additive blocks*: composed of lines marked with the plus sign (+) by the diff; these are the lines added in the new version of the file.
- *Subtractive blocks*: composed of lines that are marked by the minus sign (-); they represent the lines that will not be present in the new version.

The algorithm splits the diff text and the file in blocks, reassembling them in a way that the result is a sequence of additive, subtractive and neutral blocks. Then the vector containing the change descriptors of the previous version of the file is updated, according to the changes represented by the different blocks. Changes in the unified diff format are in form of additions and deletions only. Edits are represented by the deletion of lines followed by the addition of the former lines, incorporating the change. The way the changes are assigned to lines is guided by simple rules we defined. We manage different cases:

- isolated additive block: inserted lines are assigned a descriptor, tracking their initial revision;
- isolated subtractive block: deleted lines descriptors are discarded;
- subtractive block followed by additive block, representing a change; in this case, the initial lines of the additive block are tracked as changes to the respective line in the subtractive block, adding a descriptor to the respective list; the remaining lines are considered deleted or added, depending if the subtractive block is longer or shorter than the additive one.

---

[3] Actually, by the library used to access the VCS data. See Section 8 for further explanations.

Listing 1.1. Original file

```
1 package org.jsoup.parser;
1
1 /**
1 */
1 public class ParseError {
1     private String errorMsg;
1     private int pos;
1     private char c;
1     private TokeniserState tokeniserState;
1     private TreeBuilderState treeBuilderState;
1     private Token token;
1
1     public ParseError(String errorMsg, char c, Tokeniser[...]
1         this.errorMsg = errorMsg;
1         this.c = c;
1         this.tokeniserState = tokeniserState;
1         this.pos = pos;
1     }
1
1     public ParseError(String errorMsg, TokeniserState[...]
1         this.errorMsg = errorMsg;
1         this.tokeniserState = tokeniserState;
1         this.pos = pos;
1     }
        [...]
1 }
```

The defined rule allows tracking changes made to single lines, with a degree of approximation, due to the availability of different diff algorithms and the usage of line positions in diff blocks for tracking changes. Possible enhancements to this procedure are discussed in Section 9.

In the following, we report an example of the application of the score assignment schema. The example is taken from the JSoup project, and shown the application of the score assignment schema on a the `ParserError` class. In Listing 1.1, Listing 1.3 and Listing 1.2, we show the corresponding file before and after a change, and the diff file for the change. Each line of the file has an associated score, before and after the change. The score represents the number of changes received by the line. The [...] placeholders in the listings represent some text that we removed for space reasons.

5   Experiments on Tracking Line Changes

We described, in the previous section, a line tracking algorithm we used to derive a strategy for the detection of the Code Bashing smell. Since we have no previous information about the properties of measures derived from line changes, we set up an experiment to compare line changes to file changes.

Listing 1.2. Difference between the two files

```
diff --git a/src/main/java/org/jsoup/parser/ParseError.ja[...]
index 01dec6e..2656c00 100644
--- a/src/main/java/org/jsoup/parser/ParseError.java
+++ b/src/main/java/org/jsoup/parser/ParseError.java
@@ -1,8 +1,10 @@
 package org.jsoup.parser;


 /**
+ * A Parse Error records an error in the input HTML that[...]
  */
-public class ParseError {
+// todo: currently not ready for public consumption. [...]
+class ParseError {
     private String errorMsg;
     private int pos;
     private char c;
@@ -10,36 +12,36 @@ public class ParseError {
     private TreeBuilderState treeBuilderState;
     private Token token;

-    public ParseError(String errorMsg, char c, Tokeniser[...]
+    ParseError(String errorMsg, char c, TokeniserState [...]
         this.errorMsg = errorMsg;
         this.c = c;
         this.tokeniserState = tokeniserState;
         this.pos = pos;
     }

-    public ParseError(String errorMsg, TokeniserState [...]
+    ParseError(String errorMsg, TokeniserState [...]
         this.errorMsg = errorMsg;
         this.tokeniserState = tokeniserState;
         this.pos = pos;
     }
     [...]
 }
```

We pose and try to answer the following research questions:

RQ1. Does the number of changes per file provide the same information as the number of changes per line?

RQ2. Does the time interval between file changes provide the same information as the time interval between line changes?

RQ3. Can the number of changes per file and the number of changes per line, used for ranking files, highlight different files?

RQ4. Can the time interval between changes per file and per line, used for ranking files, highlight different files?

Listing 1.3. Resulting file

```
1 package org.jsoup.parser;
1
1 /**
1  * A Parse Error records an error in the input HTML that[...]
1  */
2 // todo: currently not ready for public consumption. [...]
1 class ParseError {
1     private String errorMsg;
1     private int pos;
1     private char c;
1     private TokeniserState tokeniserState;
1     private TreeBuilderState treeBuilderState;
1     private Token token;
1
2     ParseError(String errorMsg, char c, Tokeniser[...]
1         this.errorMsg = errorMsg;
1         this.c = c;
1         this.tokeniserState = tokeniserState;
1         this.pos = pos;
1     }
1
2     ParseError(String errorMsg, TokeniserState[...]
1         this.errorMsg = errorMsg;
1         this.tokeniserState = tokeniserState;
1         this.pos = pos;
1     }
       [...]
1 }
```

We defined a set of possible analyses leveraging the extracted data, for answering the research questions we made. We applied our line change tracking algorithm to a set of open source repositories. Table 1 lists the projects we analyzed. We made the choice of using Git repositories only because Git repositories are copied to the local machine, speeding up the computation. For our experiments, we used the whole history of the considered projects.

Research questions RQ1 and RQ2 are posed to understand if the information extracted by tracking line changes is actually different from the one extracted by looking to file changes only.

For answering question RQ1, we compute the number of changes for each file, and also the number of changes for each of the lines of each file. To summarize the line changes, for each file we compute the maximum and the median of the number of changes of each line. We do not consider the minimum because it is less interesting, and its value is almost always 1. For both lines and files, we consider only the ones having at least one change after their creation.

Figure 1 shows a boxplot of the Kendall τ correlation obtained between the number of file changes and the maximum and median number of line changes for the respective file. The number of file changes is equal to the maximum number

Table 1. Analyzed projects

Project name	Repository URL
JSoup	`https://github.com/jhy/jsoup.git`
ElasticSearch	`https://github.com/elasticsearch/elasticsearch.git`
Tomcat	`https://github.com/apache/tomcat.git`
Wildfly	`https://github.com/wildfly/wildfly.git`
Linux kernel	`git://git.kernel.org/pub/scm/linux/kernel/git/torvalds/linux.git`
JUnit	`https://github.com/junit-team/junit.git`
Checkstyle	`https://github.com/checkstyle/checkstyle.git`
PMD	`https://github.com/pmd/pmd.git`

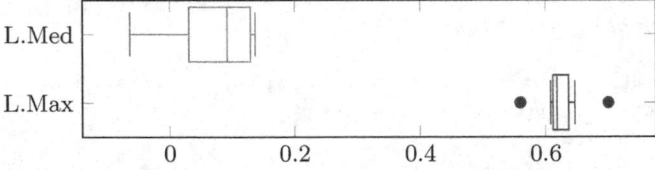

Fig. 1. Num. file and line changes (correlation)

of changes per line only when a line was changed in every file change. In fact, the diagram shows a good, but not perfect correlation (around 0.65) between the two measures. The median, instead, has low correlation with the number of file changes. This means that there is a tendency of some lines to be changed more, while most of them are rarely updated.

For answering question RQ2, we compute the time distance between subsequent changes for each file, and for each of the lines of each file. To summarize time distances on files, we compute the minimum and the median of time distances of each file. To summarize time distances on lines, for each line we compute the minimum and the median of the change time distance. Then, for each file, we compute the minimum and the median of the previous two values. The resulting measures for lines are the four combinations {min, med} × {min, med}. For example, med-min is the median of the change time per lines, which is obtained as the minimum of change times of each line. For both lines and files, we consider only the ones having at least one change after their creation.

Figure 2 and 3 show the boxplot of the Kendall τ correlation among the minimum and median (respectively) of time between changes in files, and the different combination of minimum and median of time between changes in lines. The minimum time change for each file has a 0.6–0.7 correlation with min-min and min-med. The values are very similar to the ones found for the number of changes. The median of file change times, has better correlation with all the median line measures, and slightly worse with minimum line measures.

The answer to RQ1 and RQ2 is that considering the number and time between changes (in files and in lines) provide similar, but different information. In particular, the extreme indicators (min time between changes and max number of

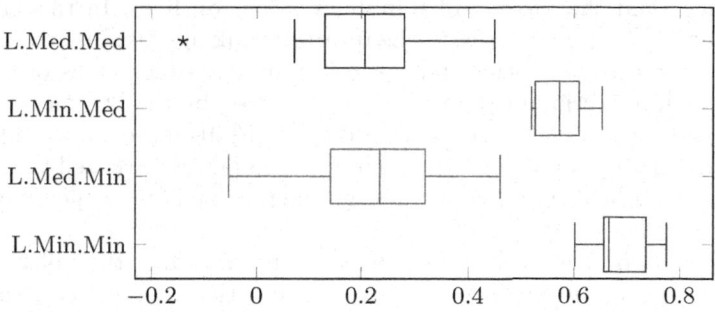

Fig. 2. Correlation among the minimum change time distance in files and different change time distance measures in lines

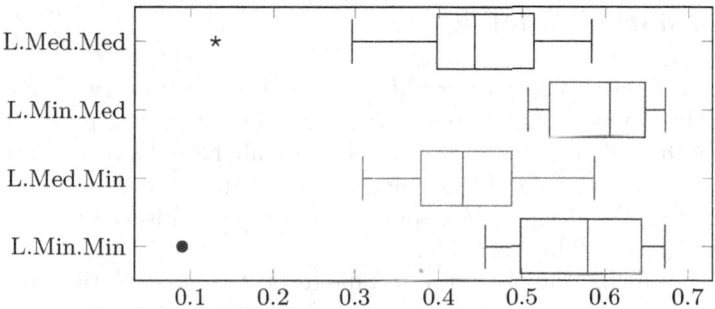

Fig. 3. Correlation among the median of change time distances in files and different change time distance measures in lines

changes) have good, but not perfect correlation with the respective measures on files. These indicators are among the most interesting for investigating anomalies; the fact that these very similar measures, taken considering file and line granularity are not fully correlated, means that there is some masked information when considering file granularity.

To answer RQ3 and RQ4, we take an example of the top files obtained by sorting the file list of each project by the different measures produced in RQ1 and RQ2. We are looking for differences in the file appearance or rank, when using different measures. In particular, we want to understand if some files having high rank using file measures get lower measures with line measures, or viceversa. With respect to RQ3, in most cases, build files and changelogs are the ones with the higher number of file changes. By considering the max number of changes per line, instead, these files get lower ranks. In Linux, e.g., the MAINTAINERS file received 1772 changes, but with a maximum number of changes per line of 6. This changes its rank from 1 to 231. The file lists the maintainers of the kernel modules, and lines are rarely changed, but people are added or removed from the list. For the time between changes (RQ4), we take as an example the median values on files and the median of minimum values on lines. In this case, it is more difficult to assign semantics to the returned rankings, because the measures should be combined with other indicators for making other kinds of inference. We made the intersection of the top 50 file returned by the two measures. The size of the intersections spans nearly the complete 0–50 on the analyzed projects. It seems that there is no particular rule in this case, but we can tell that the two measures are highlighting different files, in different amounts depending on the project.

We cannot report here a complete experiment regarding the different ranks provided by the tested measures, but we can use the obtained correlations as guidelines. The correlation index we used, in fact, is based on the rank of the compared values. This gives also an idea of the amount of changes obtained by sorting files using the different measures.

6   File Volatility Metric

File Volatility is the first Repository Metric we defined[4]. At every moment during its life, each line of each file has associated a list of change descriptors, calculated with the method described in Section 4. We call here *Change Intensity* the number of elements of each of those list, i.e., the number of changes received by each line of each file. Each file is associated to a Change Intensity vector, having one element for each line of the file.

We can then define the *volatility* of a file respect to its evolution, as the ratio between the maximum value in the Change Intensity vector and the number of changes to the file since its creation. More precisely, File Volatility is defined as:

$$FileVolatitily(f) = \frac{max(ChangeIntensity(f))}{Changes(f)}$$

where:

- $ChangeIntensity(f)$ is an array containing all the Change Intensity of each line of file f;
- $Change(f)$ is the number of changes received by file f.

This value compares the change frequency of single pieces of code contained in a file with the change frequency of the file in the same time interval. A value close to 1 that means in the file there is a portion of the code that has been involved in changes from the beginning until the last version. This behavior is clearly not desirable, or at least points to a peculiar situation. Figure 4 represents the plot of the *File Volatility* of the file `pom.xml` in the ElasticSearch[5] project. In an ideal situation, the value of the metric decreases in time, starting from 1. When a file is created its File Volatility is 1, and at each change it keeps close to 1

---

[4] At the end of the section, we outline the differences with other existing metrics like code churn.

[5] `https://github.com/elasticsearch/elasticsearch`

if the changes are applied to the same region of code. Otherwise, the value of the metric tends to be lower. In the example, the value of the metric quickly decreases to smaller values, meaning that the changes involved different regions of the file. In that particular file, the only line of code having a high Change Intensity is the one representing the version of the system. In fact, the same line has been edited every time the system changed its version number.

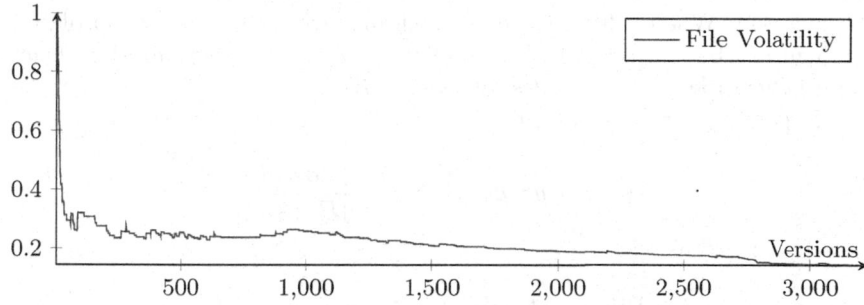

Fig. 4. Evolution of the File Volatility metric

Code refactoring techniques like *Move Method*, *Extract Method* and *Extract Class* can greatly affect the value of the metric. Consider for example the case of problematic code in a method, which is subjected to many changes for several reasons and was not even supposed to be in that particular class. It could be a case, e.g., of a *Feature Envy* method. To remove such smell, the refactoring to apply could consist in moving that method elsewhere in the code base. If that method had, into its body, lines with the highest values of Change Intensity in the file, then its removal would dramatically drop the volatility metric value. The same statement holds w.r.t. every refactoring technique that implies the removal of a considerable portion of the code, as well as deleting code for other reasons.

File Volatility is different from other existing metrics measuring code changes. Two widely investigated change measures are the number of file changes and code churn [8]. File Volatility expresses a different measure than the number of file changes. In fact, it summarizes the changes of the single lines, relative to the number of file changes. We also assessed in Section 4 that line changes are not totally correlated with file changes, so the ratio of the two measures can carry meaningful information. For example, a file receiving 10 new lines in 10 versions, one line per versions, has a number of changes value of 10. Its File Volatility, instead is 1/10 (assuming no other lines have ever been changed). The code churn (in its simplest form) for the same file will be (absolute form) 10, or (relative form) the average of 1/LOC for each of the 10 versions. File Volatility is a measure evaluating the peaks of line changes in files, while code churn is related to the size of every change made to the file, without recognizing the identity of the single lines.

7   Repository Stability Metric

The second Repository Metric we defined is Repository Stability. Following the principle of single responsibility, when a piece of code reaches enough maturity, the chances of it being changed are extremely low. M. Feathers defined that a class can be considered closed [18] at time t if no further modifications will happen from t to present. The same concept can be extended to files: a file can be considered closed when no further development is done on it from a version to the last one. When a file reaches enough maturity, there is high probability that it will not be subjected to future changes. Given this assumption, tracked files can be grouped in *active files* and *closed files*.

The Repository Stability of a repository at version v is defined as:

$$RepositoryStability(v) = \frac{|Closed(v)|}{|Files(v)|}$$

where:

- $Closed(v) = \{f \in Files(v)| \; \nexists v'(v' > v \land f \in Changed(v'))\}$;
- $Files(v)$: files existing in the repository in version v;
- $Changed(v)$: files changed, added or removed in version v;
- $v \in \mathbb{N}$: version v is the number of the version of the system; $v' > v$ means that v' is a version more recent than v.

To give a graphical immediate representation of the concept of *file closures* described above, we report, as an example, the values computed on JUnit, chosen for its long change and development history. JUnit's repository[6] is managed by Git, after the migration from CVS. Figure 5 shows the amount of files involved in every single commit.

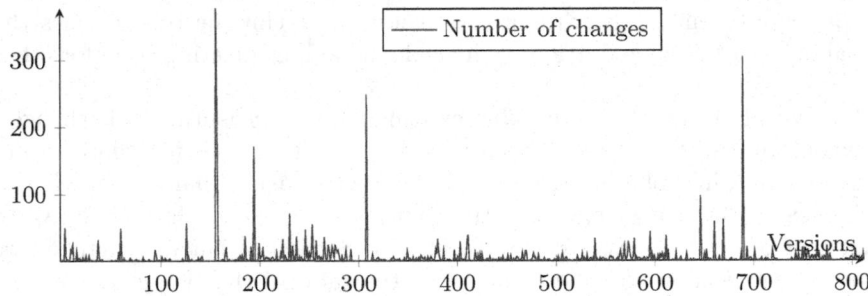

Fig. 5. Number of files changed in JUnit for each version

We can see that there are few commits that really stand out from the average and especially the last one, as we will see later, has a remarkable impact on the value of the metric. In Figure 6, we can see a comparison of the evolution of total and closed files.

---

[6] https://github.com/junit-team/junit

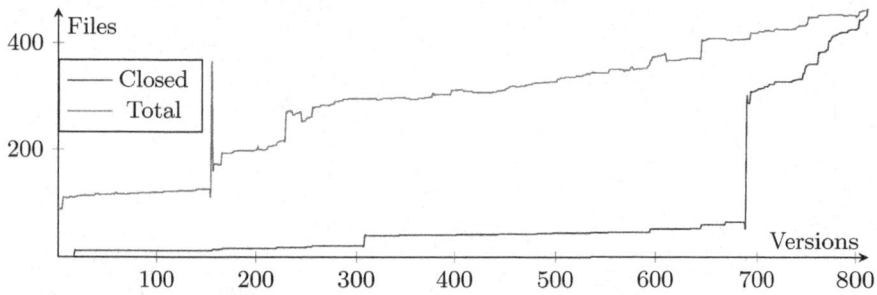

Fig. 6. Evolution of closed and total files in JUnit

The commit near the end represents the reason why the metric keeps low values for almost the entire life span of the repository, except for the last two hundreds versions. The development team decided to apply new coding conventions to the code base. This decision resulted in a huge number of files involved into the change. Hence, only the files not interested by the new standards could be considered closed. Just after the commit, the number of closed files suddenly increases and keeps increasing until the end of the timeline. In the last commit, the number of closed and total files are the same. This is due to the fact that, by construction, the odds of finding a file contained in a change set decrease proportionally with the progress in the history of commits. At last commit, none of the files can be found at a later stage. The desired development behavior is to focus on single functionalities and then move to others when the implementation is mature enough. By looking at the Repository Stability evolution graph, one can immediately judge if developers are following this principle. The Repository Stability evolution graph (Figure 7 shows the one for JUnit) for a given interval, should keep growing as time advances and the gap between active and closed files should be as narrow as possible. Even in agile development environments with short release cycles and incremental refactoring, there is a time when code has to stop changing and become stable. Obviously, code cannot be mature from the start, but it should be at some time in the future.

From the experience we had while testing the Repository Stability metric we found some opportunities to improve it. One possibility would be to define change categories we filter out of the computation. For example, we found many cases where licences or other disclaimer were changed in all source files at once. This kind of change could be automatically ignored in the computation, because it has no associated semantics. It could be possible also to ignore any change involving only comments. This last option can be more debatable, because comments are part of the system and its evolution, in a sense. It will be interesting comparing results obtained by applying this filter or not. Another possibility would be to compute Repository Stability at the line level, counting both the closed lines of code and the total lines of code for every version. The result would be a smoother view of the evolution of the system, but it will hide the modularity existing in the project.

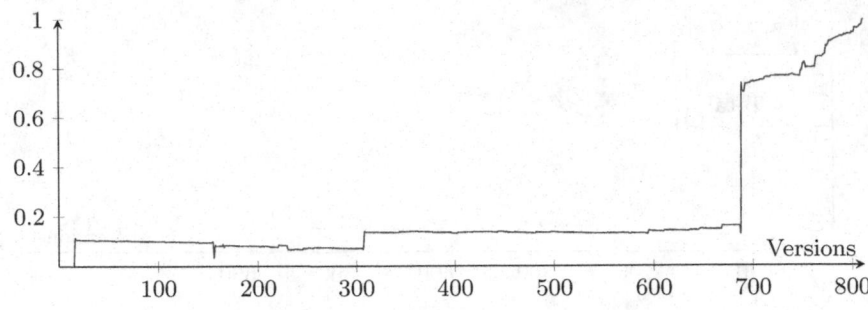

Fig. 7. Evolution of the Repository Stability metric in JUnit

8   Threats to Validity

A threat to the internal validity of our analysis is related to the extraction of single line changes. In the unified diff format, changes are represented as sequences of lines additions and removals. This format does not tell exactly which line was replaced by another line. Our algorithm uses line indexes as an approximation for mapping changed lines. This approximation can lead to some distortion in the line tracking. However, distortions are limited to the single diff block.

Moreover, different diff algorithms can lead to different diff sequences and, consequently, different scores. We currently rely on the diff algorithm provided by the `dulwich` library, which is the one from python's `libdiff`.

Threats to external validity of the analysis procedure are mainly related to the characteristics of the analyzed projects. Different VCS technologies, programming languages, and development communities may lead to different results.

9   Conclusions and Discussions

In this paper, we focused our attention on analyzing software evolution by harvesting system repository. With this goal, we defined a Code Repository Smell, called Code Bashing, and two Repository Metrics, called File Volatility and Repository Stability.

The Code Bashing Smell is useful to highlight code regions that received more attention than others. When a code region receives too many changes, it can be a sign of bad development practices, or unstable code. Therefore, detecting Code Bashing can help locating issues hidden in the development history.

While the two Repository Metrics are useful to give a quick overview of the level of maturity of single files and of an entire repository. In particular, File Volatility assigns to each file a score, telling how much changes are concentrated on particular lines, revealing code regions that needed more attention than others, and could need more in the future. File Volatility can be applied to detect Code Bashing. To be able to measure File Volatility, we defined an algorithm for tracking changes on single lines of code in a VCS repository. We evaluated the number of changes per line and the periods of time passed among line changes with respect to the equivalent measures on files.

By answering the four research questions posed in Section 5, we found that the correlation among the produced measures is good, but not complete. This means that the measurement of line changes gives different information than using file changes. We also have shown cases in which some files get very different rankings considering line and file changes. File Volatility exploits this differences to reveal the balance between the changes received by files and the ones received by their inner lines.

We think that the measures that can be produced by line change tracking could be helpful in the same areas where file change measures have been applied, e.g., change or defect prediction. In many cases, line changes can be a more precise indicator than file changes. Source code, in fact, is often organized in structured files, where different parts of the same file can have an independent evolution.

The second metric we defined, Repository Stability, instead, can summarize the portion of repository which did not need to be changed since an instant in its development history; repositories where most files change over time can suffer from organizational or design issues, so this metric can reveal potential quality problems. In our experiments, by plotting the metric value over the system history, we revealed large spread modifications in the analyzed repositories.

Information characterizing the evolution of software repositories can be exploited for software maintenance and quality assessment. For example, the selection of a third party open source component can be aided with measures characterizing the maturity of the project, as well as other issues related to its development process.

We already analyzed different projects, i.e., Mozilla Rhino, JUnit, JSoup, ElasticSearch, Hibernate, Tomcat, Wildfly, XBMC, and the Linux kernel. The results of these analysis are available in a web page[7] that we will keep updated with results obtained on new projects.

In the past, we focused our attention on code smell detection and assessment [19]. Now we aim to focus on finding smells tied to software evolution and repository analysis, to extend our experimentation with the Repository Smells and discovering new ones. Moreover, through VCS-Analyzer we intend to perform different empirical analysis for assessing the quality of software projects, starting from their development history. Another possible future work is addressing the issue highlighted in Section 8 regarding the accuracy of line change tracking. There are other less-exploited diff algorithms that work at the word level, and could be exploited to have a more precise estimation of the lines that were changed. This kind of diff needs more effort for its interpretation and has less tool support, i.e., Git can provide it, but other VCSs may not, requiring external processing.

---

[7] http://essere.disco.unimib.it/VCSAnalyzerResults.html

References

1. Fowler, M.: Refactoring: Improving the Design of Existing Code. Addison-Wesley, Boston (1999)
2. Arcelli Fontana, F., Rolla, M., Zanoni, M.: VCS-analyzer for software evolution empirical analysis. In: Proceedings of the 8th International Symposium on Empirical Software Engineering and Measurement (ESEM 2014). IEEE, Torino (September 2014)
3. Rolla, M.: Empirical analysis for software assessment. Master's thesis, University of Milano-Bicocca, Viale Sarca, 336, Milano, Italy (January 2014)
4. Zimmermann, T., Di Penta, M., Kim, S. (eds.): Proc. 10th Working Conference on Mining Software Repositories (MSR 2013). IEEE/ACM, San Francisco, CA (2013)
5. Peters, R., Zaidman, A.: Evaluating the lifespan of code smells using software repository mining. In: Proceedings of the 16th European Conference on Software Maintenance and Reengineering (CSMR 2012), pp. 411–416 (2012)
6. Kagdi, H., Collard, M.L., Maletic, J.I.: A survey and taxonomy of approaches for mining software repositories in the context of software evolution. J. Softw. Maint. Evol. 19(2), 77–131 (2007)
7. Zimmermann, T., Zeller, A., Weissgerber, P., Diehl, S.: Mining version histories to guide software changes, 31(6), 429–445 (2005)
8. Nagappan, N., Ball, T.: Use of relative code churn measures to predict system defect density. In: Proc. 27th International Conference on Software Engineering (ICSE 2005), pp. 284–292 (May 2005)
9. Ying, A., Murphy, G., Ng, R., Chu-Carroll, M.: Predicting source code changes by mining change history 30(9), 574–586 (2004)
10. Zimmermann, T., Kim, S., Zeller, A., Whitehead Jr., E.J.: Mining version archives for co-changed lines. In: Proc. Int.l Workshop on Mining Software Repositories (MSR 2006), pp. 72–75. ACM, Shanghai (2006)
11. Canfora, G., Cerulo, L., Di Penta, M.: Identifying changed source code lines from version repositories. In: Proc. 4th Int.l Workshop Mining Software Repositories (MSR 2007), p. 14. IEEE (May 2007)
12. D'Ambros, M., Lanza, M.: Distributed and collaborative software evolution analysis with churrasco. Science of Computer Programming 75(4), 276–287 (2010), Experimental Software and Toolkits (EST 3): A special issue of the Workshop on Academic Software Development Tools and Techniques (WASDeTT 2008)
13. Bevan, J., Whitehead Jr., E.J., Kim, S., Godfrey, M.: Facilitating software evolution research with kenyon. In: Proc. 10th European Software Eng. Conf. Held Jointly with 13th ACM SIGSOFT Int.l Symp. Foundations of Software Eng. (ESEC/FSE 2013), pp. 177–186. ACM, Lisbon (2005)
14. Zazworka, N., Ackermann, C.: CodeVizard: A tool to aid the analysis of software evolution. In: Proc. ACM-IEEE International Symposium on Empirical Software Engineering and Measurement (ESEM 2010), p. 63:1. ACM, Bolzano (2010)
15. Voinea, L., Telea, A., van Wijk, J.J.: CVSscan: Visualization of code evolution. In: Proceedings of the 2005 ACM Symposium on Software Visualization (SoftVis 2005), pp. 47–56. ACM, St. Louis (2005)
16. D'Ambros, M., Lanza, M.: BugCrawler: Visualizing evolving software systems. In: Proceedings of the 11th European Conference on Software Maintenance and Reengineering (CSMR 2007), pp. 333–334 (March 2007)
17. Martin, R.C.: Chapter 9 — SRP: The Single Responsibility Principle. In: The Principles of OOD (February 2002),
   http://www.objectmentor.com/resources/articles/srp.pdf

18. Feathers, M.: Working Effectively with Legacy Code. Robert C. Martin Series. Pearson Education (2004)
19. Arcelli Fontana, F., Braione, P., Zanoni, M.: Automatic detection of bad smells in code: An experimental assessment. J. Object Technology 11(2), 5:1–38 (2012)

Considering Polymorphism
in Change-Based Test Suite Reduction

Ali Parsai, Quinten David Soetens, Alessandro Murgia, and Serge Demeyer

University of Antwerp, Antwerpen, Belgium
ali.parsai@student.uantwerpen.be,
{quinten.soetens,alessandro.murgia,serge.demeyer}@uantwerpen.be

Abstract. With the increasing popularity of continuous integration, algorithms for selecting the minimal test-suite to cover a given set of changes are in order. This paper reports on how polymorphism can handle false negatives in a previous algorithm which uses method-level changes in the base-code to deduce which tests need to be rerun. We compare the approach with and without polymorphism on two distinct cases —PMD and CruiseControl— and discovered an interesting trade-off: incorporating polymorphism results in more relevant tests to be included in the test suite (hence improves accuracy), however comes at the cost of a larger test suite (hence increases the time to run the minimal test-suite).

Keywords: test selection, unit-testing, change-based test selection, polymorphism, ChEOPSJ.

1 Introduction

The advent of agile processes with their emphasis on test-driven development [2] and continuous integration [9] implies that developers want (and need) to test their newly changed or modified classes or components early and often [12]. Yet, as Runeson observed in a series of workshops with testing teams, some unit test suites take hours to run [15]. In such a situation, a *"retest all"* approach which maximizes the chances of verifying if (i) the new functionalities introduced are working properly and (ii) the refactoring of the previous ones do not break the code, takes too long to provide rapid feedback in a normal edit-compile-run cycle.

A series of interviews we conducted with developers working in different agile teams confirmed that rapid feedback in the presence of a large suite of unit-tests is critically important. When developers address a change-request, they make a chain of changes in the code base, fire a manually selected subset of the unit tests to confirm the system still functions as expected, commit their changes to the code base, run the continuos integration build —the developers we interviewed reported that a "retest-all" takes between 8 and 10 hours— and in the meantime proceed with the next change request. Most of the time this works fine, but in some occasions the continuous integration build reveals a regression fault and then developers must switch contexts to resolve the fault. One team leader determined that it takes at least 10 minutes before a developer

T. Dingsøyr et al. (Eds.): XP 2014 Workshops, LNBIP 199, pp. 166–181, 2014.

mentally reconstituted the context; since each failed integration build involves several context switches it follows that they easily add an extra half hour just to get a developer in the right frame of mind. Another team leader pointed out that as a system grows and becomes more complex, it is more difficult to identify a suitable test subset hence failed integration builds occur more frequently. A back-of-the-envelope estimation based on their latest quarterly release, revealed that failed integration builds add at least two extra hours per working day.

Essentially, there are three possible strategies to achieve a rapid feedback cycle in the presence of a large suite of unit tests: (a) *parallelisation*, i.e. perform a "retest all" on a battery of dedicated test servers to reduce the time to execute the test; (b) *smoke tests*, i.e. define a few representative tests as a quick and dirty verification; (c) *test selection*, i.e. select the subset of the complete test suite covering the last changes made. In this paper, we focus on the latter, however point out that from a pragmatic point of view, a combination of the three strategies is desirable.

Test selection is the problem to "*determine which test-cases need to be re-executed [...] in order to verify the behavior of modified software*" [6]. It has been the subject of intense research in the area of regression testing, however is recently also studied in the context of agile approaches. We refer the interested reader to a survey by Engström et. al, for an overview of the former [6] while Hurdugaci et al. [11], Zaidman et al. [21] are some examples of the latter.

We ourselves experimented with one particular test selection technique and reported about it during the CSMR 2013 conference [18]. In essence, the algorithm builds a series of dependencies between methods that have been changed —all of which are captured by the ChEOPSJ tool [17]— and from that deduces all tests which directly or indirectly invoke those methods. Our results showed that given a list of methods which changed since the latest commit, we could select a subset of the entire test suite which is significantly smaller. The selected subset is not safe as it occasionally misses a few relevant tests. However it is *adequate* since the test-coverage —expressed as "percentage of mutations that were killed" [1])— remained the same.

Nevertheless, the algorithm explained in [18] made one simplifying assumption, namely that developers would refrain from using polymorphism, i.e. invocations of overridden methods, abstract methods or methods declared in interfaces [3, Ch. 2]. This simplifying assumption did not hold in one of the cases (namely PMD) and as a result our algorithm missed several relevant tests. For this reason, we decided to repeat the previous experiment to address the following research question:

RQ. *Does considering polymorphism improve the quality of the reduced test suite in a realistic situation?*

In this experiment, we applied the improved algorithm on the two cases used in the original experiment: PMD and CruiseControl.

The rest of this paper is structured as follows. In section 2, we describe the approach for test selection and the test selection algorithm. In section 3 we explain the experimental setup. In section 4, we present the results of the experiment. In section 5, we describe which factors may jeopardize the validity of our analysis. In section 6, we summarize the related work. Finally, in section 7 we wrap up the work with a summary and conclusions.

2   Supporting Code Change and Test Selection

This section describes how we introduced the concept of polymorphism in the test suite reduction algorithm of ChEOPSJ. We start by introducing ChEOPSJ and then its test selection algorithm[1].

ChEOPSJ[2] is a proof of concept system able to extract and model software changes. This tool is implemented as a series of Eclipse plugins. Figure 1 shows the overview of its structure. At the center of the tool we have a plugin that contains and maintains the change model. There are two plugins that are responsible for populating the change model. The *Logger* generates change objects by recording actions a developer makes in the main editor during a development session, while the *Distiller* obtains the change objects by mining a Subversion repository. Once the change model is populated with first class change objects, many applications can be built on top of ChEOPSJ that can use them for their own purpose. Our TestSelection plugin is one such application.

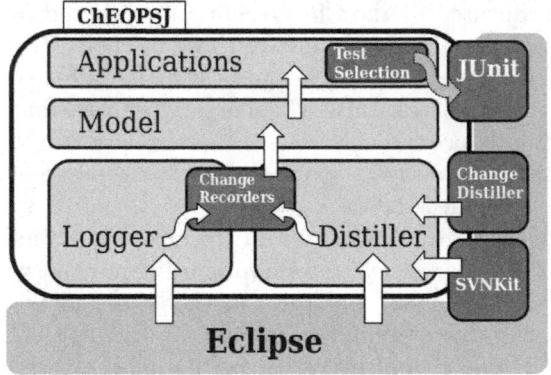

Fig. 1. The layered design of ChEOPSJ

Our approach for change-based test selection uses the first class change-objects of ChEOPSJ. We define a *Change* as an object representing an action that

---

[1]   The proposed procedure is easily generalizable for any object oriented system. There are commercial tools (e.g. Visual Studio) which try to solve the same problem for a specific language, but does not publicly provide the used technique.

[2]   The acronym ChEOPSJ stands for: Change ad Evolution Oriented Programming Support for Java.

changes a software system. As such, a change becomes a tangible entity that we can analyze and manipulate. We define three kinds of *Atomic Changes*: `Add`, `Modify` and `Remove`. These changes act upon a *Subject* representing an actual source code entity. For these subjects we can use any model that is capable of representing source code entities. We chose the FAMIX model as defined in [5] since its model is usable to describe many object oriented programming languages. As such our approach is applicable in any object oriented setting.

Our model also defines dependencies between the changes. These are deduced from the FAMIX model, which imposes a number of invariants to which each model must adhere. For instance, there is an invariant that states that each method needs to be contained in a class. This means that there is a precondition for the change (m_{Add}) that adds a method m to a class c. There should exist a change (c_{Add}) that adds the class c and there is no change that removes the class c. We can then say that the change m_{Add} depends on the change c_{Add}. More generally we can say that a change object c_1 depends on another change object c_2 if the application of c_1 without c_2 would violate the system invariants.

The change based test selection heavily relies on these dependencies, as it traces them from a selected change to the additions of test methods. To calculate the reduced test suites we execute Algorithm 1.

Algorithm 1. select relevant tests

Input: A *ChangeModel*, A set *SelectedChanges*
Output: A Map that maps each selected change to a set of relevant tests.
foreach *c in SelectedChanges* **do**
    calledMethod = findMethodAddition(hierarchicalDependencies(*c*));
    invocations = invocationalDependees(*calledMethod*);
    foreach *i in invocations* **do**
        invokedBy = findMethodAddition(hierarchicalDependencies(*i*));
        foreach *m in invokedBy* **do**
            if *m is a test* **then**
                add *m* to *relevantTests*;
            else
                if *m was not previously analyzed* **then**
                    tests = selectRelevantTests(*m*);
                    add *tests* to *relevantTests*;
    map *c* to *relevantTests*;

In this algorithm, we iterate all selected changes and map each change to their set of relevant tests. We start by finding the change that adds the method in which the change was performed. We can find this change, by following the chain of hierarchical dependencies and stop at the change that adds a method. In Algorithm 1 this is presented by a call to the procedure `findMethodAddition`. After this call `calledMethod` will be the change that adds the method in which the change c took place. Next we need to find all changes that add an invocation to this method. These are found by looking for `invocationalDependencies`. For each of these changes, we again look for the change that adds the method in which these invocations were added. And thus we find the set of all changes that add a method that invokes the method that contains our selected change. We then iterate these method additions and check whether these changes added a test method. If this was the case we consider this test method as a relevant test for the originally selected change. If on the other hand the added method was not a test method, then we need to find the relevant tests of this method and that set of tests needs to be added to the set of relevant tests for the selected change.

Polymorphism during test selection. In our original approach, the change model assumed that invocations were a one to one relationship between the caller and the callee. As such the addition of an invocation was dependant on the addition of the caller method as well as on the addition of the callee method. We could statically determine the latter based on the type of the variable on which the method was invoked. However with polymorphism this is not necessarily the case, as a method invocation might invoke any of a number of possible methods.

Take for instance the code in Figure 2, here we have a class `Foo` that declares a method `foo` and a subclass `Bar` that declares a polymorphic version of that same method. Our test invokes the method `foo` on a variable `f` of type `Foo`, hence our algorithm would state that this test is relevant for all changes in the method `Foo.foo()`. However in the `setUp` method, the variable `f` is instantiated as an object of type `Bar` so this test is in fact also relevant for the method `Bar.foo()`, which is a link that our test selection algorithm missed. Hence our algorithm did not take into account actual methods that are invoked at runtime like polymorphic methods, abstract methods or methods declared in interfaces.

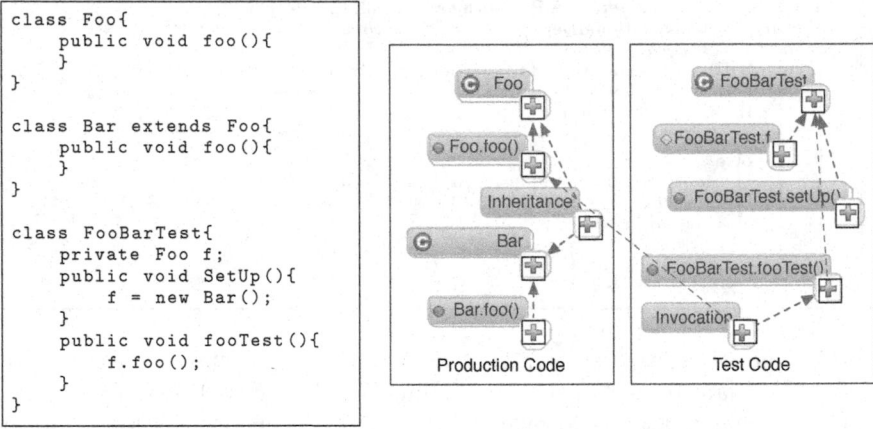

Fig. 2. Example of changes with polymorphic call

As a simple workaround, we slightly changed our change model so that an addition of an invocation is dependant of all additions of methods that this invocation can possibly be referring to, based on its identifier and parameter list. So when a method invocation is added, this addition now depends on all method additions that add a method with this same identifier. This would change the model of the changes in Figure 2 to the model represented in Figure 3. Note that in the new model, there is an added dependency from addition of the invocation

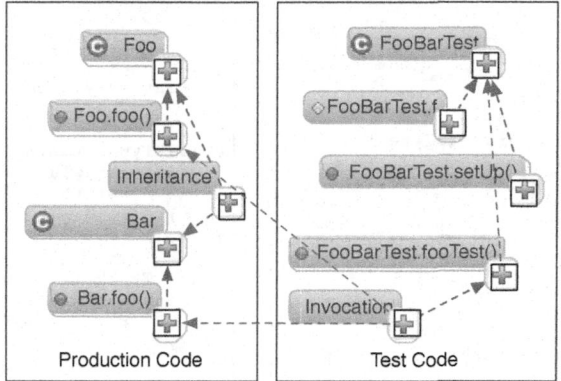

Fig. 3. Updated model with dependency from invocation to all possible methods with same identifer

in the test method to the addition of the method `Bar.foo`. So now our test selection algorithm will say that the test `FooBarTest.fooTest()` is relevant for changes in both the methods `Foo.foo()` and `Bar.foo()`.

We report another example in Figure 4: the refactoring REPLACECONDITION-ALWITHPOLYMORPHISM. In this example the class `Base` contains a method `getValue` which uses a conditional to determine its actual runtime type and based on that will perform a different action. The refactoring then involves the creation of polymorphic versions of this method in the two subtypes that perform the type specific actions. We show the change model of this code before and after the refactoring in Figures 5. The test of this code, invokes the method `getValue` on the superclass, which results in a dependency from the test to the addition of that method. This means that this test is relevant to all changes in the `getValue()` method. In the version before refactoring this would be correct, however in the post-refactored class without polymorphic support, a test containing an invocation of *getValue* on an object of class *Base* will not be selected for objects of types *Type1* and *Type2*; Because, the addition of the invocation of *getValue* in class *Test* is dependent on the addition of the abstract method *Base.getValue* and not the addition of methods *Type1.getValue* and *Type2.getValue*. Whereas, with the polymorphic support *Test* will be selected, because as shown in Figure 5 there is a dependency from the invocation to all methods with the identifier "getValue".

3   Experimental Setup

We use mutation testing to estimate the real-life behavior of the reduced test suite. We replicated a previous study to evaluate the benefits of the introduction of polymorphism [18] .

```
class Base{
    int getValue(){
        switch (_type){
            case Type1:
                return getType1Value();
            case Type2:
                return getType2Value();
        }
    }
}

class Type1 extends Base{
}

class Type2 extends Base{
}
```

```
class Base{
    int getValue();
}

class Type1 extends Base{
    int getValue(){
        return getType1Value();
    }
}

class Type2 extends Base{
    int getValue(){
        return getType2Value();
    }
}
```

Fig. 4. Replace Conditional with Polymorphism refactoring

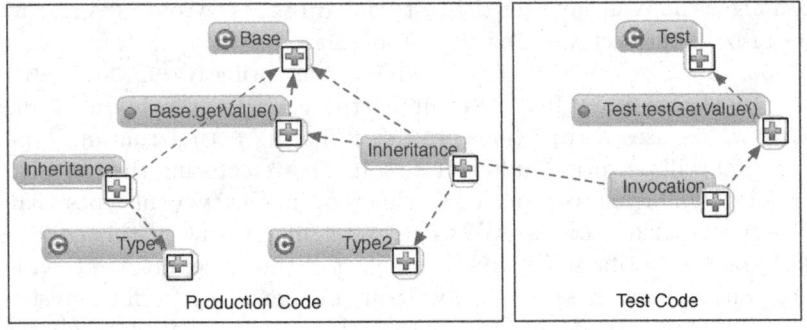

Before refactoring

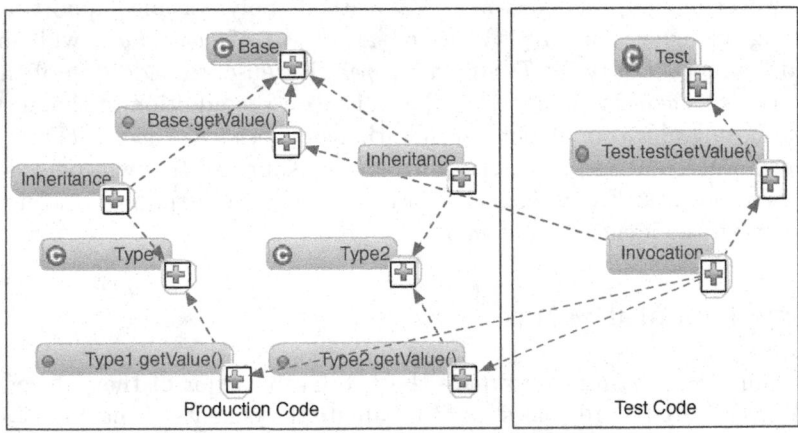

After refactoring

Fig. 5. Model state before and after the refactoring

3.1   Mutation Testing

Mutation testing[3] provides a workaround to measure the quality of a test suite and identify its weak points [1]. In mutation testing intentional faults are put inside a fault-free program by applying mutation operators (or mutators). Mutators are chosen according to a fault model so that the generated faults correspond to a realistic situation. A mutation is *killed* if it causes a test to fail, while if it does not fail any tests, it has *survived* the experiment. We can then consider the mutation coverage, which is a ratio between the number of mutants that were killed over the number of mutants that were introduced. Mutation coverage provides a reliable metric to measure the quality of a test suite [1]. A higher mutation coverage, means that more of the introduced mutants were killed and consequently that your test suite is of better quality.

In the previous experiment, PIT[4] was used as the main means for mutation testing. In this experiment, we use the same configuration of PIT used in the previous study [18]. PIT provides byte code mutation testing by integration into the build procedure —either Ant or Maven— of the target software. To get a base measurement of the quality of the test suites, PIT is run considering all classes and the full test suite. Then separate build files were generated for each class which included only the tests ChEOPSJ deemed relevant to the class in question. We compare the mutation coverage of each reduced test suite with the mutation coverage of the full test suite by looking at the mutants that survived the reduced suite but that were killed in the full suite. Ideally the mutation coverage of the reduced test suite should equal the mutation coverage of the entire test suite. When the mutation coverage is lower, it means that we have missed some relevant tests in our selection.

The results of this mutation coverage analysis (using polymorphism) is then compared to the results of our previous experiment (where polymorphism was not taken into account).

3.2   Selected Cases

To be able to measure the impact of supporting polymorphism in ChEOPSJ, we examined the same cases (PMD[5] and CruiseControl[6]) as the previous study [18]. Moreover, we use the same revisions of both projects to reliably repeat the experiment. CruiseControl is a continuous integration tool and an extensible framework for creating a custom continuous build process. PMD is a source code analyzer which finds common programming flaws like unused variables, empty catch blocks, unnecessary object creation. These projects are open-source, written in Java and accessible through SVN.

The sizes of these projects and the selected revisions are shown in Table 1.

---

[3] The interested reader may refer to [4, Ch. 7] for more information regarding mutation testing.

[4] http://pitest.org

[5] http://pmd.sourceforge.net

[6] http://cruisecontrol.sourceforge.net

Table 1. Number of 1000 Lines of Code (KLOC) and Number of Classes (NOC) for both source code and test code (measured with InFusion 7.2.7).

Project	Version analyzed	Src KLOC	Src NOC	Test KLOC	Test NOC	Build Process
Cruisecontrol	rev. 4601	26.5	376	24.5	295	ant
PMD	rev. 7706	46	804	9	215	maven

4   Results and Discussion

This section analyses the results of the test selection algorithm. We compute for all classes —in the full test suite and in the reduced one— the mutants generated. Then, we count the number of mutants killed and the number of classes involved. Moreover, we compare our results with those achieved with the previous version of ChEOPSJ.

4.1   PMD

The test suite of PMD covers 665 classes and with PIT we generate mutants on each one of them. Using PIT on the reduced test suite, we generated mutants for 607 classes[7]. When comparing this to the previous experiment we have a significant improvement, as the previous version generated mutants for only 144 classes.

In Figure 6b we compare the mutation coverage of the reduced test suites with the full test suite. We find that the reduced test suites of 47% of the classes have the same mutation coverage as the full test suite. This matches the results of the previous experiment [18], where there were 50% of reduced test suites that had an equal number of mutants killed compared to the mutation coverage of the full test suite.

We also observed another improvement with respect to the experiment made with the previous version of ChEOPSJ. In both experiments, the reduced test suites have 128 common classes with 4908 mutations. In the previous experiment the reduced test suites killed 2114 mutants, whereas in our current experiment the reduced test suites killed a total of 2327 mutants. This means that our improved approach killed 213 more mutants than before. So considering polymorphism resulted in an improvement of 4.3% in the quality of the reduced test suite. In Figure 6a we report the percentage of classes with improved mutation coverage. In the case of PMD, 33% of the classes have improved mutation coverage while 8% have worsened coverage.

Finally, to inquire to what extent there is an improvement on the number of killed mutants, we compare them with respect to the total number of mutants generated for any class. This is reported in Figure 7 where the X axis is the number of generated mutants and the Y axis is the difference in number of

---

[7] PIT does not generate mutations in a class if the given test suite has no coverage over that class.

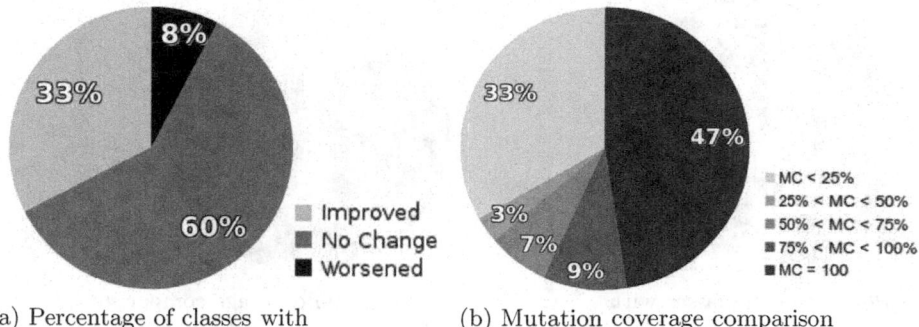

(a) Percentage of classes with
improved mutation coverage

(b) Mutation coverage comparison
between all tests and selected tests

Fig. 6. Mutation coverage on PMD

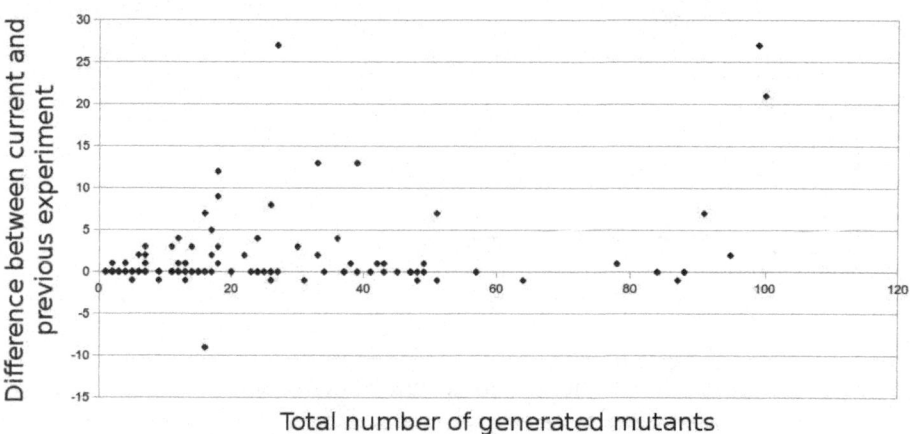

Fig. 7. Difference in killed mutants for PMD

killed mutants for each class in the two experiments. Given a class, we have an
improvement of the test suite reduction whenever the number of killed mutants is
higher than before. Therefore, the accumulation of points near the Y axis means
that those classes with small number of mutants have been impacted more and
their mutation coverage is significantly improved.

4.2   CruiseControl

PIT generates mutants in 246 classes covered by the full test suite of CruiseC-
ontrol and in 231 classes covered by the reduced test suites. From a total of
6860 mutants generated, 3627 were killed. This is the same number of generated
mutants as in the previous experiment and the new reduced test suites kill only
4 more mutants than the old reduced test suites. This means that the addition

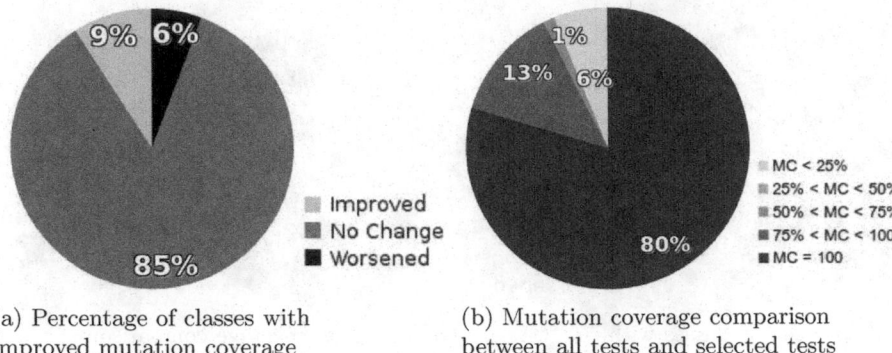

(a) Percentage of classes with improved mutation coverage

(b) Mutation coverage comparison between all tests and selected tests

Fig. 8. Mutation coverage on CruiseControl

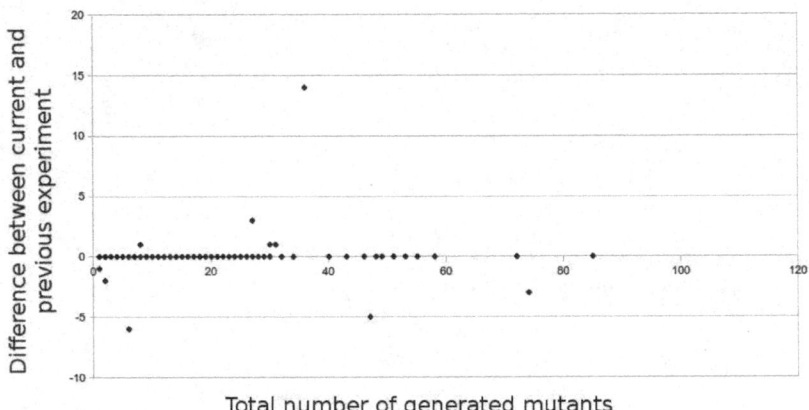

Fig. 9. Difference in killed mutants for CruiseControl

of polymorphism had nearly no effect on the results in the case of CruiseControl. This is also confirmed by Figure 8a. This Figure shows that the percentage of classes with improved mutation coverage is 9% compared to 6% for classes with worsened mutation coverage. Also, almost all of the classes have the same mutation coverage as before; and only one class has a significantly better coverage than before. On the other hand, the quality of the whole test suite remains similar to the previous experiment when 80% of classes have the exact same mutation coverage as running the whole test suite as can be seen in Figure 8b.

Figure 9 reports the difference in number of killed mutants in the two experiments for each class by the total number of mutants generated. As we can see the quality of the test suites remain the same with few exceptions. Meanwhile, those classes with worsened coverage have only slightly less mutation coverage than in the previous experiment.

RQ. *Does considering polymorphism improve the quality of the reduced test suite in any realistic situation?*

In a realistic situation the effect of the addition of polymorphism to the test selection must be considered case-by-case. In the case of PMD, the project's heavy reliance on polymorphic structures means that the results for the mutation coverage have improved greatly by considering this concept. However, there are a lot of tests that are not being selected for different reasons. For example, PMD uses XML files as input for *rule-based tests*. This kind of tests do not result in any invocations, and therefore are not detected and selected by ChEOPSJ. As a consequence, the results are less than optimal, considering the fact that such tests are a huge part of the whole test suite. In the case of CruiseControl, the effects on the mutation coverage are minimal. This is due to two reasons: (i) the project does not use polymorphism extensively, and (ii) in the original experiment the mutation coverage was already good [18].

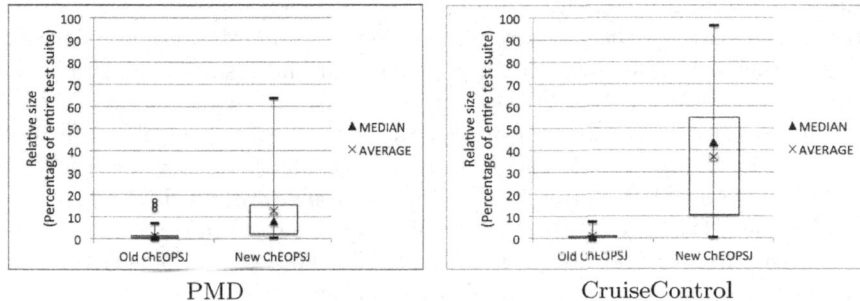

PMD   CruiseControl

Fig. 10. Comparison of reduced test suite size between previous and current experiments for CruiseControl and PMD

For PMD and CruiseControl, we compute the test size reduction as the percentage of test classes in the selected subset against the number of test classes in the entire test suite (Figure 10). In both cases, we observe that the size of the reduced test suite is much larger when the polymorphism is considered. This means that there is a trade-off between size reduction and considering polymorphism. The size of this trade-off is determined on a case-by-case basis. For example, in the case of PMD, the reduced test suite is still good enough to be useful in a realistic situation. However, in CruiseControl the reduction in size may not be enough to promote the adoption of polymorphism.

As conclusion, to improve the quality of test selection, the adoption of polymorphism should be provided as an option. However, if the developer does not have enough knowledge of software characteristics, a workaround would be the creation of a heuristic function that detects the reliance of the software system on polymorphism.

5   Threats to Validity

In this section we present the threats to validity of our study according to the guidelines reported in [20].

Threats to internal validity concern confounding factors that can influence the obtained results. In this study we used the code base of ChEOPSJ which does not include constructor invocations. As a consequence we may erroneously miss relevant tests. We could fix this problem incorporating these language constructs in the change model of ChEOPSJ.

Threats to construct validity focus on how accurately the observations describe the phenomena of interest. For our experiment, the elements of interest are (1) the test suite reduction and (2) the number of missing faults due to not-retested code. We measure the first one as the ratio between number test classes in the reduced test suite versus the complete test suite. The second one is computed as the number of mutants killed. Both approaches are used in literature for the same purpose [18]. However, other methods are suitable for evaluating the test suite reduction and number of missing faults.

Threats to external validity correspond to the generalizability of our experimental results. We use the projects CruiseControl and PMD. Even if both systems are sufficiently different, yet more projects are necessary to generalize our findings.

Threats to reliability validity correspond to the degree to which the result dependent on the used tools. To implement the algorithm we use the baseline offered by ChEOPSJ (which relies on Eclipse's internal Java mode) and ChangeDistiller. Both systems are reliable and used to perform research studies [8,18]. For the mutation testing we used PIT. This system is actively being developed and improved and can be considered reliable.

6   Related Work

Regression testing aims to test code changes to ensure that the correct behavior of the system is preserved [14]. In this context, test suite reduction is crucial in continuous integration environments or test-driven development [2,9], namely whenever software development has frequent re-testing activities. Regression testing is also useful during code refactoring since refactoring may reverberate on the test suite [10,19].

Test suite reduction is an active research field [6,7]. It mainly focuses on evaluating the trade-offs between executing a subset of tests and the risk of missing some faults sneaked into not-retested code sections. The test selection problem has been handled in many different manners. In the context of static approaches, common used heuristics are naming conventions, fixture element types, static call graph, lexical analysis, co-evolution [13]. Nevertheless, none of previous approaches handle shortcomings related to code polymorphism. In this work, we explore this aspect evaluating how test suite reduction algorithms may be adapted to deal with invocations of polymorphic methods, abstract methods and methods declared in interfaces.

Integration of the testing activity within the IDE environment is critically important to achieve a "continuous testing" system [16]. Moreover, providing ad-hoc plugins for test selection is already common in academic research (e.g. TestNForce [11]) or among commercial vendors (e.g. Visual Studio's Test Impact Analysis). The second author embedded a test selection algorithms within the Eclipse's plugin and performed few empirical studies to show its performances [17,18]. In this work, we extended this plugin to make it able to deal with polymorphism.

7   Conclusion

We replicated an experiment that we did in [18] to analyzes the effects of polymorphism for test suite reduction using a change-based model.

Our goal was to answer the research question:

RQ. *Does considering polymorphism improve the quality of the reduced test suite in a realistic situation?*

Our results show that polymorphism may have different relevance on PMD and CruiseControl from the point of view of mutation coverage analysis and test suite reduction.

In PMD, one third of the classes had an improved mutation coverage. Relevant tests were found for more classes than before with the same statistical probability for killing mutants. Overall, a 4% increase in the rate of total killed mutants is observed. Having the possibility to retrieve *rule-based tests*, our results would probably be better.

On the other hand, for CruiseControl the differences between the two experiments were minimal. This can be attributed to the fact that PMD uses polymorphism in the code extensively and there are some abstract core entities which are used throughout the whole project. The use of polymorphism in CruiseControl is limited and therefore the effects of considering polymorphism would remain minimal.

From the point of view of the test suite reduction the introduction of polymorphism increases the size of the test suite. This is a normal trade-off we have to accept if we increase the number of potential relevant tests of our suite. A possible workaround would be to determine the level of adaption of polymorphism in the project and then decide if it is valuable to include it during test suite reduction. As such the adoption of polymorphism in the test selection process should be provided as an optional feature for the developers to choose from.

Contributions. We made the following contributions:

- We improved our tool prototype ChEOPSJ to incorporate polymorphism.
- Using this improved platform we replicated a previous experiment and confirmed our previous findings.
- Finally, we found that there is a tradeoff between the accuracy of our approach and the size of the reduced test suite.

Future Work. We will improve the support of common architectural design concepts that are used widely in software systems. We will focus on test generation techniques that use XML specifications and polymorphic tests which use the same abstract entities to provide many tests.

Additionally we will perform more replications in an industrial setting. Will developers be more inclined to run their developer tests more frequently with test selection enabled? Will this result in fewer (regression) faults later in the life-cycle? This to assess the real significance of test selection in a realistic scenario.

Acknowledgments. This work is sponsored by the Institute for the Promotion of Innovation through Science and Technology in Flanders through a project entitled Change-centric Quality Assurance (CHAQ) with number 120028.

References

1. Andrews, J.H., Briand, L.C., Labiche, Y.: Is mutation an appropriate tool for testing experiments (software testing). In: Proceedings of the 27th International Conference on Software Engineering, ICSE 2005, pp. 402–411 (2005)
2. Beck, K.: Test Driven Development: By Example. Addison-Wesley Longman Publishing Co., Inc., Boston (2002)
3. Booch, G.: Object Oriented Analysis and Design with Application. Pearson Education India (2006)
4. Dasso, A., Funes, A.: Verification, Validation And Testing in Software Engineering. Idea Group Publishing (2007)
5. Demeyer, S., Tichelaar, S., Steyaert, P.: FAMIX 2.0 - The FAMOOS information exchange model. Technical report, University of Berne (1999)
6. Engström, E., Runeson, P., Skoglund, M.: A systematic review on regression test selection techniques. Journal Information and Software Technology 52(1), 14–30 (2010)
7. Engström, E., Skoglund, M., Runeson, P.: Empirical evaluations of regression test selection techniques: A systematic review. In: Proceedings of the Second ACM-IEEE International Symposium on Empirical Software Engineering and Measurement, ESEM 2008, pp. 22–31. ACM, New York (2008)
8. Fluri, B., Wuersch, M., PInzger, M., Gall, H.: Change distilling: Tree differencing for fine-grained source code change extraction. IEEE Transactions on Software Engineering 33(11), 725–743 (2007)
9. Fowler, M.: Continuous integration. Technical report (May 2006), http://www.martinfowler.com/
10. Hayes, J.H., Dekhtyar, A., Janzen, D.S.: Towards traceable test-driven development. In: Proceedings of the 2009 ICSE Workshop on Traceability in Emerging Forms of Software Engineering, TEFSE 200, pp. 26–30. IEEE Computer Society, Washington, DC (2009)
11. Hurdugaci, V., Zaidman, A.: Aiding software developers to maintain developer tests. In: Proceedings of the 2012 16th European Conference on Software Maintenance and Reengineering, CSMR 2012, pp. 11–20. IEEE Computer Society, Washington, DC (2012)
12. McGregor, J.D.: Test early, test often (2007)
13. Van Rompaey, B., Demeyer, S.: Establishing traceability links between unit test cases and units under test. In: Proceedings of the 2009 European Conference on Software Maintenance and Reengineering, CSMR 2009, pp. 209–218. IEEE Computer Society, Washington, DC (2009)
14. Rothermel, G., Harrold, M.J.: Analyzing regression test selection techniques. IEEE Transactions on Software Engineering 22(8), 529–551 (1996)

15. Runeson, P.: A survey of unit testing practices. IEEE Software 23(4), 22–29 (2006)
16. Saff, D., Ernst, M.D.: An experimental evaluation of continuous testing during development. In: ISSTA 2004, Proceedings of the 2004 International Symposium on Software Testing and Analysis, Boston, MA, USA, July 12-14, pp. 76–85 (2004)
17. Soetens, Q.D., Demeyer, S.: Cheopsj: Change-based test optimization. In: Proceedings of the 16th European Conference on Software Maintenance and Reengineering (CSMR), pp. 535–538 (March 2012)
18. Soetens, Q.D., Demeyer, S., Zaidman, A.: Change-based test selection in the presence of developer tests. In: Proceedings of the 17th European Conference on Software Maintenance and Reengineering (CSMR), pp. 101–110 (March 2013)
19. van Deursen, A., Moonen, L.: The video store revisited – thoughts on refactoring and testing. In: Proceedings of the Int'l Conf. eXtreme Programming and Flexible Processes in Software Engineering (XP), Sardinia, Italy, pp. 71–76 (2002)
20. Yin, R.K.: Case Study Research: Design and Methods. Applied Social Research Methods. SAGE Publications (2003)
21. Zaidman, A., Rompaey, B., Deursen, A., Demeyer, S.: Studying the co-evolution of production and test code in open source and industrial developer test processes through repository mining. Empirical Software Engineering 16(3), 325–364 (2011)

Effort Estimation in Agile Global
Software Development Context

Ricardo Britto, Muhammad Usman, and Emilia Mendes

Department of Software Engineering, Faculty of Computing,
Blekinge Institute of Technology, 371 79, Karlskrona, Sweden
{ricardo.britto,muhammad.usman,emilia.mendes}@bth.se

Abstract. Both Agile Software Development (ASD) and Global Software Development (GSD) are 21st century trends in the software industry. Many studies are reported in the literature wherein software companies have applied an agile method or practice GSD. Given that effort estimation plays a remarkable role in software project management, how do companies perform effort estimation when they use agile method in a GSD context? Based on two effort estimation Systematic Literature Reviews (SLR) - one in within the ASD context and the other in a GSD context, this paper reports a study in which we combined the results of these SLRs to report the state of the art of effort estimation in agile global software development (ASD) context.

Keywords: Agile Software Development, Global Software Development, Effort Estimation.

1   Introduction

The software industry is greatly impacted by globalization of world economies in 21st century. Software companies are increasingly engaging themselves in Global Software Development (GSD) in order to gain benefits such as cost savings, access to global resource pool, round the clock development [1]. Due to temporal, cultural and geographical boundaries, GSD also poses some challenges e.g. communication and coordination issues, project management, knowledge management [1]. In parallel with the GSD trend, software industry is also shifting to agile methods during last ten years or so. ASD [2] and GSD are 21st century trends in software industry. Studies have been conducted to investigate the adoption of agile methods and practices in GSD context, also called by Agile Global Software Development (AGSD) [3].

Jalali *et al.* [4] conducted a systematic literature review in order to find the state of the art of applying agile methods and practices in GSD context. In this SLR both inshore and offshore-distributed development settings were considered. The authors found that most of the existing literature consists of industrial experience reports. The authors also identified the most used agile practices in the context of GSD.

Hossain *et al.* [5] performed a systematic literature review that identified challenges and risk factors related to the use of Scrum practices in globally distributed projects. Strategies and practices to deal with the identified challenges and risk factors

T. Dingsøyr et al. (Eds.): XP 2014 Workshops, LNBIP 199, pp. 182–192, 2014.

were also investigated. The authors found out that in order to be applied in a global context, Scrum practices must be adapted to deal with the additional difficulties regarding communication, coordination and collaboration processes in a globally distributed software project.

Project management is an important task in both agile and global software development contexts. Estimation is at the core of efficient project management as it guides the formulation, execution and adjustment of project plans. It is important to see what software estimation techniques or predictors or metrics have been used with agile methods when they are applied in GSD context i.e. Agile Global Software Development (AGSD). To date, no work has tried to aggregate the evidence regarding effort estimation in the context of AGSD. The aim of this paper is to report the state of the art on effort estimation in AGSD. Rest of the paper is organized as follows: Section 2 describes the research methodology; results are presented in Section 3,; Section 4 states the validity threats and conclusion is described in Section 5.

2   Methodology

As previously mentioned, to carry out this study we combined the outcomes of two systematic literature reviews performed by the authors of this paper ([6], [7]). So, in this section we explain the methodology used to conduct this study.

2.1   Research Questions

The research questions of the two SLRs were combined in order to guide this work. They are as follows:

- **Question 1** - What methods/techniques have been used to estimate effort in AGSD?
  - o   **1a** - What metrics have been used to measure the accuracy of effort estimation methods/techniques in AGSD projects?
  - o   **1b** - What are the accuracy levels for the observed estimation methods?
- **Question 2** - What effort predictors (cost drivers/size metrics) have been used to estimate effort in AGSD?
- **Question 3** - What are the characteristics of the datasets used for effort estimation in AGSD?
  - o   **3a** - What are the domains represented in the dataset (academia/industry projects)?
  - o   **3b** - What are the types represented in the dataset (single-company/cross-company)?
  - o   **3c** - What are the application types represented in the dataset (web-based/traditional)?
- **Question 4** - Which software development phases were considered during effort estimation process?

- **Question 5** – What sourcing strategies (offshore outsourcing/offshore insourcing) are used?
  - o   **5a** - Which countries involved?
  - o   **5b** - How many sites are involved?
- **Question 6** – Which agile methods have been used?

2.2   Study Selection and Data Extraction

Both SLRs ([6], [7]) have used same databases/search engines for applying the search strings. These databases/search engines were:

1. Scopus.
2. IEEExplore.
3. ACM Digital Library.
4. ScienceDirect.
5. Compendex.
6. Inspec.
7. Web of Science.

Both SLRs have similar inclusion exclusion criteria with the only difference being that one was about agile and other was about global software development. The study selection process was applied in two phases. In the first phase, the inclusion and exclusion criteria were applied on titles and abstracts and in the second phase the criteria were applied on the papers' full text. The final lists of each SLR have respectively 5 papers [6] and 20 papers (25 studies) [7]. From these final lists we selected for this study those papers that:

1. Have investigated effort estimation methods or size metrics or accuracy metrics or cost drivers and
2. Have used an agile method as software development process and
3. Are carried out in a GSD context.

The application of above criteria resulted in the selection of four papers from Britto *et al.* [6], identified as G1 [8], G2 [9], G3 [10] and G4 [11] each reporting a single study; and one paper [12] from Usman *et al.* [7] reporting results from four projects identified as A1a to A1d. Therefore this study includes a total of 5 papers reporting 8 projects.

Most of the required data were available from the data extraction steps of two SLRs to carry out the study. However, since the questions 5, 5a, 5c and 5b were considered just for Britto *et al.* [6] and question 6 was considered only for Usman *et al.* [7] we had to extract the remaining data from the selected papers, in order to address all research questions.

3   Results and Discussion

In this section, first we provide a brief description, contexts and settings of the included primary studies. Later, results for each of the research questions are described and discussed.

3.1   Study Summaries

Study G1 reports a survey that was conducted to understand the state of the practice of effort estimation in GSD projects. Survey was applied in a large multinational IT organization that has operations in countries like USA, Brazil, India etc. The software development in this organization is performed using both onshore and offshore insourcing strategies. Out of a total of 3595 employees, 551 answered the survey. Study describes that the organization uses both agile and plan-driven development processes but it does not describe the name of the agile method followed in the organization. It was concluded in this study that the teams do not have a clear criterion to select a suitable effort estimation technique in a given context.

Study G2 reports a case study that was conducted at ABB[1] group of companies to understand the factors that impact the management of GSD projects. Seven projects (six at ABB and one at another company) were included in this case study wherein all projects were carried out in a single company setting i.e. offshore insourcing. Study describes that three out of seven projects applied an agile method but it does not specify the name of the agile method used. It also does not describe the development method used in other four projects. Data collection was performed by means of interviews (31 participants) and an online questionnaire (40 participants) wherein participants were from different ABB sites across the globe. The study identified number of factors (cost drivers) for GSD projects and mechanisms to mitigate the risk related to each identified factor.

Study G3 also reports a case study that was conducted at three different Indian software companies, which work in development of financial service, retail, manufacturing and telecommunication software systems. These software companies apply the offshore insourcing strategy for distributed development. Participatory action research approach was applied to collect the data from these three companies. It involved 75 brainstorming sessions with study participants that lead to the identification of several cost drivers. It is interesting to note that this study considered process model (agile or otherwise) as a cost driver. Applying the identified cost drivers, case base reasoning approach was used to estimate the effort of 219 projects. The study analyzed the impact of "the knowledge about client", "the work dispersion across sites" and "the understanding of technology" on the development effort. The authors compared their customized case based reasoning approach with standard regression based approach for estimation and found that case based reasoning approach performed better than regression for the studied projects. It is important to note that the study does not describe the exact development process applied.

Study G4 reports a qualitative study in which authors proposed a formal model for task allocation and effort estimation in GSD. The model includes the estimation technique and cost drivers. However, the authors only validated the cost drivers by means of semi-structured interviews with four project managers that lead to the better understanding of the identified cost drivers. Process model (agile or plan-driven) is one of cost drivers that impact the development effort. Since the proposed estimation technique was not validated, we did not include it in our analysis. It is important to

---

[1] ABB is a leading company in power and automation sector (www.abb.com).

note that the study does not clearly describe the sourcing strategy and exact development process applied.

Study A1 reports a case study consisting of four projects to investigate effort estimation for testing phase in an agile software development context. Study presented a customized version of use case points estimation method for estimating testing effort only. A1 was performed in an offshore outsourcing context wherein Scrum was applied as the development method. The authors found that the new method (modified use case points method) was more accurate than the expert judgment and the original use case points method.

The details from these summarized studies are described in the following subsections.

3.2   Estimation Methods

Table 1 lists the estimation methods used in an AGSD context, showing that the methods used the most were expert judgment, use case points (UCP), planning poker and Delphi. Note that the use case point method is used differently – in one paper it was used to size the application and in another to estimate the testing effort. We also note that some of these 'effort estimation' methods are in fact size metrics, which are used in combination with some sort of productivity metrics, or cost per hour measure, to obtain the effort/cost relating to an application. Traditional algorithmic models such as COCOMO were not identified in any of the AGSD studies.

Table 1. Identified effort estimation methods

Estimation method	Study ID
Case-based reasoning	G3
Planning poker	G1
Function point count	G1
Use case point count	G1, A1a to A1d
Use case point test effort estimation model	A1a to A1d
Expert judgment	G1, A1a to A1d
Delphi	G1
No estimation approach	G2, G4

3.3   Accuracy Metrics and Levels

Table 2 lists the accuracy metrics used in the selected papers and projects therein. Three studies (G1, G2, G3) did not report usage of any accuracy metric. Two papers (A1, G3) have used the magnitude of relative error (MRE) or its variation to assess the estimation accuracy of their techniques. Only one study (G3) has used multiple metrics (MMRE, MdMRE and Pred(25)).

Table 2. Identified accuracy metrics

Accuracy metric	Study ID
MMRE	G3
MdMRE	G3
Pred(25)	G3
MRE	A1a to A1d
No accuracy metrics	G1, G2, G4

Only two papers (G3, A1) reported accuracy levels related to the estimation techniques being investigated. These values are reported in Table 3, where we can also see that case base reasoning and UC point test effort estimation model present good accuracy values [13]. MRE values for UCP method, for all four projects in study A1, are also below 25%.

Table 3. Identified accuracy levels

Estimation method	Study ID	Accuracy (%)
Case-based reasoning	G3	MMRE: 15.99 MdMRE: 11.67 Pred(25): 84.12
Use case point test effort estimation model	A1	Project1 – MRE:11; Project2 – MRE:2; Project3 – MRE:3; Project4 – MRE:6.
Expert judgment	A1	Project1 – MRE:32; Project2 – MRE:30; Project3 – MRE:8; Project4 – MRE:21.
Use case point	A1	Project1 – MRE:21; Project2 – MRE:20; Project3 – MRE:21; Project4 – MRE:10.

3.4   Cost Drivers and Size Metrics

Table 4 lists the cost drivers that were identified from the primary studies. Time, language and cultural differences are the most frequently reported cost drivers in an AGSD context. When we move from collocated development to GSD, global barriers, e.g. temporal, geographical and cultural, arise as fundamental challenges. These global challenges make communication and coordination tasks more difficult which in turn impacts all development activities (e.g. RE, estimation etc.) [1].

In addition, the process model is also reported by two studies as a cost driver. This may be due to the fact that papers in this study are applying or investigating the applicability of a different process model, e.g. agile methods, in a GSD context.

The size metrics identified in the five primary studies are listed in Table 5. Function points, LOC and UC points are used in two papers. Overall, point-based size metrics (function or UC or story points) were used in three out of five studies.

Table 4. Identified cost drivers

Cost driver	Study ID
Time zone	G2, G3, G4
Language and cultural differences	G2, G3, G4
Process model	G3, G4
Communication	G4
Competence level	G2
Requirements legibility	G2
Process compliance	G2
Communication infrastructure	G2
Communication process	G2
Work dispersion	G3
Range of parallel-sequential work handover	G3
Client-specific knowledge	G3
Client involvement	G3
Design and technology newness	G3
Team size	G3
Project effort	G3
Development productivity	G3
Defect density	G3
Rework	G3
Reuse	G3
Project management effort	G3
Travel	G4
Tester efficiency factor	A1
Tester risk factor	A1

Table 5. Identified size metrics

Size metric	Study ID
Function points	G1, G4
Lines of code	G3, G4
Use case points	G1, A1
Story points	G1
No size metric used	G2

3.5   Dataset Domain and Type

All primary studies used industrial datasets to evaluate the estimation methods. This is viewed as a positive sign given that the use of industrial datasets may increase the external validity of the results.

Another issue attached with the use of a dataset is the dataset type, which could be single company or cross company dataset. Three papers (G2, G3 and A1) used single company datasets, while two did not state the type of their datasets.

Table 6. Identified dataset domains

Domain	Study ID
Industry	G1, G2, G3, G4, A1
Academia	none

Table 7. Identified dataset types

Type	Study ID
Single-company	G2, G3, A1
Not stated	G1, G4

3.6   Application Type

Application type is only documented in one primary study (A1). In A1, two projects were Web-based systems while the other two were mobile applications.

Table 8. Identified application types

Type	Study ID
Web-based	A1a, A1c
Mobile	A1b, A1d
Not stated	G1, G2, G3, G4

3.7   Sourcing Strategies and Countries

Three primary studies reported studies (G1, G2, G3) that are conducted in offshore insourcing environments, i.e. same company had multiple development sites in different parts of the world. Only one paper reports projects that are conducted in offshore outsourcing arrangements, i.e. the multiple sites involved in GSD project belong to different companies. Table 9 lists the sourcing strategies identified in the five selected papers.

Table 9. Identified sourcing strategies

Sourcing strategy	Study ID
Offshore insourcing	G1, G2, G3
Offshore outsourcing	A1
Not stated	G4

Three studies did not report the number of countries (or sites) involved in GSD projects. GSD projects in Study G1 and G2 were considerably complex as they included seven and ten countries respectively.

Table 10. Identified number of involved countries

Number	Study ID
7	G2
10	G1
Not stated	G3, G4, A1

Three studies did not state the name of the countries where development sites were located, while USA, China and India were reported by two studies. Additionally, primary study G1 reported UK, Malaysia, Japan, Taiwan, Ireland, Brazil and Slovak Republic. Finally, primary study G2 reported Finland, Germany, Norway and Sweden.

Table 11. Identified countries

Name	Study ID
USA	G1, G2
China	G1, G2
India	G1, G2
Not stated	G3, G4, A1

3.8   Development Phase

Which software development phase or activity is being estimated is also an important concern. Four out of five selected papers did not state the development phase or activity being estimated. One possible explanation for not stating the development phase could be that all development activities are being estimated. Only one paper (A1) clearly states that testing effort is being estimated. Table 12 provides the breakdown for this facet.

Table 12. Considered phases in the effort estimation process

Phase	Study ID
Requirements	none
Design	none
Coding	none
Testing	A1
Transition	none
Not stated	G1, G2, G3, G4

3.9   Agile Method

Another important facet is to see what agile methods are being investigated in estimation studies in AGSD context. Table 13 gives the breakup of studies with respect to the agile method used. Only one paper (A1) states the agile method used

(Scrum in this case) in its projects. Other studies only mention that they are using agile software development but did not specify the exact method. We are not sure why a study would only state that they are following an agile software development without disclosing the exact method used.

It is also interesting to note that two primary studies (G3, G4) considered the usage of agile method as a cost driver. However, those studies did not explain the impact on the effort estimation process of the usage of agile methods.

Table 13. Identified agile methodologies

Agile methodology	Study ID
Scrum	A1
Not stated	G1, G2, G3, G4

4   Threats to Validity

We believe that the main threat to the validity of this work is related to the coverage of the available literature on effort estimation in agile global software development. We applied very comprehensive search strategies in both SLRs, which were used as basis for this work. However, Britto *et al.* [6] just considered effort estimation in GSD context and Usman *et al.* [7] just looked at effort estimation in the ASD context.

Another possible threat relates to the external validity of our findings. As we only have five papers (8 projects) in this study, it is not reasonable to generalize our findings outside the context of the projects that were presented herein. Nevertheless, given the number of companies embarking on GSD and agile practices, we refrain from taking the stance that companies may not combine both approaches; rather, we believe that such results may suggest the need for researchers to amplify the number of studies within the context of AGSD, so we can understand much better not only effort estimation but also other aspects relating to software development and management under such context.

5   Conclusions

This paper presents a study on effort estimation in AGSD by combining the results from two SLRs respectively on effort estimation in agile contexts and effort estimation in global software development contexts. Five papers, from the list of primary studies of both SLRs, fulfilled AGSD criteria set up for this study.

We found that most of the studies did not document some aspects such as the agile method applied, the GSD strategy used, the number of development sites, the countries involved, and the development phase being estimated. Methods such as expert judgment are used in multiple studies. Global barriers of time and culture are the most frequently reported cost drivers in an AGSD context.

It is interesting to note a positive pattern, where all studies used industrial data sets to validate the estimation techniques. Offshore insourcing is the most frequently used GSD strategy in effort estimation studies in AGSD context.

Acknowledgments. We would like to thank CNPq and INES, for partially supporting this work.

References

1. Herbsleb, J., Moitra, D.: Global software development. IEEE Softw. 18, 16–20 (2001)
2. Schwaber, K., Beedle, M.: Agile Software Development with Scrum. Prentice Hall (2001)
3. Kamaruddin, N., Arshad, K., Mohamed, N.H., Chaos, A.: issues on communication in agile global software development. In: Proceedings of IEEE Business, Engineering and Industrial Applications Colloquium, BEIAC 2012, pp. 394–398 (2012)
4. Jalali, S., Wohlin, C.: Global software engineering and agile practices: A systematic review. J. Softw. Evol. Process. 24, 643–659 (2012)
5. Hossain, E., Ali Babar, M., Paik, H.-Y.: Using scrum in global software development: A systematic literature review. In: Proceedings of 4th IEEE International Conference on Global Software Engineering, ICGSE 2009, Limerick, Ireland, pp. 175–184 (2009)
6. Britto, R., Freitas, V., Mendes, E., Usman, M.: Effort Estimation in Global Software Development: A Systematic Literature Review. In: Proceedings of 9th IEEE International Conference on Global Software Engineering, ICGSE 2014, Shanghai, China (2014)
7. Usman, M., Mendes, E., Weidt, F., Britto, R.: Effort Estimation in Agile Software Development: A Systematic Literature Review. In: Proceedings of 10th International Conference on Predictive Models in Software Engineering, PROMISE 2014, Turin, Italy, pp. 82–91 (2014)
8. Peixoto, C.E.L., Audy, J.L.N., Prikladnicki, R.: Effort Estimation in Global Software Development Projects: Preliminary Results from a Survey. In: Proceedings of 5th IEEE International Conference on Global Software Engineering, ICGSE 2010, pp. 123–127. IEEE, Princeton (2010)
9. Björndal, P., Smiley, K., Mohapatra, P.: Global Software Project Management: A Case Study. In: Nordio, M., Joseph, M., Meyer, B., Terekhov, A. (eds.) SEAFOOD 2010. LNBIP, vol. 54, pp. 64–70. Springer, Heidelberg (2010)
10. Ramasubbu, N., Balan, R.K.: Overcoming the challenges in cost estimation for distributed software projects. In: Proceedings of 34th International Conference on Software Engineering, ICSE 2012, pp. 91–101. IEEE, Zurich (2012)
11. Narendra, N.C., Ponnalagu, K., Zhou, N., Gifford, W.M.: Towards a Formal Model for Optimal Task-Site Allocation and Effort Estimation in Global Software Development. In: Proceedings of 2012 Service Research and Innovation Institute Global Conference, pp. 470–477. IEEE, California (2012)
12. Parvez, A.W.M.M.: Efficiency factor and risk factor based user case point test effort estimation model compatible with agile software development. In: Proceedings of the International Conference on Information Technology and Electrical Engineering, ICITEE 2013, Yogyakarta, Indonesia, pp. 113–118 (2013)
13. Conte, S.D., Dunsmore, H.E., Shen, V.Y.: Software Engineering Metrics and Models. Benjamin-Cummings Publishing (1986)

Early Software Project Estimation the Six Sigma Way

Thomas Michael Fehlmann[1] and Eberhard Kranich[2]

[1] Euro Project Office AG, Zurich
8032 Zürich, Switzerland
thomas.fehlmann@e-p-o.com
[2] Euro Project Office, Duisburg
47051 Duisburg, Germany
eberhard.kranich@e-p-o.com

Abstract. The Buglione-Trudel matrix is a tool that provides agile teams with immediate feedback whether their priorities meet customer needs. Functional size measurement yields a transfer function mapping user stories to *Functional User Requirements* (FUR), and business impact of non-functional requirements yield another transfer function mapping the same user stories onto customer's *Business Drivers*.

Normally, transfer functions in Six Sigma are based on measurements; however, they can be predicted with the *Quality Function Deployment* (QFD) method, applicable early in the project life cycle and based on expert's estimation rather than measurements. The *Convergence Gap* indicates prediction accuracy. These tools allow early project estimation by predicting what agile teams likely will identify as additional requirements for the customer during the sprints, based on his values and business drivers. Precondition is that business drivers and an initial set of customer's FUR are known when estimating the project.

As an added benefit, the method allows mapping story points to functional size and in a second step, to effort, based on benchmarking data,.

Keywords: Lean Six Sigma, Agile Software Development, Functional Sizing, Story Points, Project Estimation, Transfer Functions, Software Benchmarking.

1 Why Is Software Project Estimation So Difficult?

Today's lean and agile software developers use *Story Points* to predict the effort required for implementation, and plan sprints. Agile development methods outperform older approaches because they embrace requirements elicitation. Developing software is a knowledge acquisition process. However, it is hard to predict how long such a knowledge acquisition process will last, and what its cost will be.

Nevertheless, the need for software increases and *Information & Communication Technology* (ICT) has become essential for all but very few industries. Thus, getting reliable predictions what software will cost at the end is mission-critical for many organizations. Agile methodologies have but limited ways answering this challenging question.

T. Dingsøyr et al. (Eds.): XP 2014 Workshops, LNBIP 199, pp. 193–208, 2014.
© Springer International Publishing Switzerland 2014

1.1   The Difficulty with Applying Traditional Estimation Approaches to Agile

Traditionally, estimators use either macro or micro estimation approaches. Macro estimations rely on historical benchmarking data such as the ISBSG database [1]. Parametric tools such as Galorath or QSM allow fitting historical data to today's projects. Micro estimation try to identify all tasks needed to get the work done in a *Work Breakdown Structure* (WBS), size them, estimate the effort, and then add risk avoidance, mitigation and retention tasks as needed. In either case, functional size measurement provides the base for any decent estimation method; see the AACE International Recommended Practice No. 74R-13 [2].

The family of international risk management standards ISO/IEC 31000 defines risk as the "effect of uncertainty on objectives" [3], thus causing the word "risk" to refer to positive possibilities as well as negative ones. Project managers add the cost of the selected risk reduction strategies and risk contingency to the project budget to cope with risk exposure, for instance following the recommended practice [4]. Usually such an approach works well if the domain is sufficiently well known and the project scope known in advance.

However, in most software projects, requirements elicitation is part of the project, and requirements change while performing the project. The amount of change is unknown in advance and difficult to predict using risk management techniques. Attempts to identify cost drivers for ICT projects are promising [5]; however, predicting or even measuring cost drivers is hard and requires sophisticated techniques [6].

1.2   Effort Prediction in Agile Methodologies

If there is no plan, there cannot be an estimate for the planned project. However, from Cohn [7] the agile community learned how to deal with the uncertainty of projects without help of a plan. The basic learnings are that a) how to use story points to predict effort for a *Story Card*, or work item, in a sprint, and b) that ideal size and effort are somewhat orthogonal, and not to be confounded. The driver for setting priorities and story card selection should be the value created for the customer. In Scrum, it is the task of the sponsor to decide what value creation means. Throughout this paper, story card refers always to a work item that fits into one single sprint. User stories might split into more than one story card, if they do not fit into one sprint.

Agile masterminds like Cohn [7] spread the idea that focusing on customer needs and business value avoids producing waste; however, reality is that project sponsors often find it difficult identifying value. New research (Bakalova [8]) has shown that identifying value creation in agile projects is not as easy or straightforward as it might appear. While values remain stable, the value creation process changes over the lifetime of a project. That makes prediction of total effort even harder. For instance, the value of being able to move physically remains equally high over time. However, it depends on the means deemed suitable, how such value is created: Horse carriages in the 19th century, cars and planes in the 20th and high-speed trains for the 21st. Software projects face the same kind of technical evolution; however, in years not centuries.

Combining effort prediction methods with measuring business value or customer needs thus becomes interesting. Six Sigma has a long experience in uncovering and measuring customer needs, even hidden needs and requirements not (yet) consciously expressed and outspoken by customers. The *Quality Function Deployment* (QFD) discipline is the tool of choice in the Six Sigma toolbox for defining market strategy, for product management and improvement, requirements elicitation, and other aspects of customer orientation [9]. QFD was developed as a method for product development by Yōji Akao and Shigeru Mizuno more than 30 years ago, see e.g., [9], [10], [11].

2 Voice of the Customer (VoC)

For QFD, many techniques exist, among them "Gemba" and NPS Surveys. These two VoC techniques are most relevant for agile software development.

2.1 Go to the Gemba

Gemba, (現場 *genba*), is a Japanese term meaning "*the real place*". Gemba refers to the place where value is created: the factory floor, the sales point or where the service provider interacts directly with the customer [12]. For mobile apps, Gemba is the street where people walk [13], or the metro where they stand, consulting their smartphone. For traditional software, it might be some traditional office. According Glenn Mazur, Gemba denotes the customer's place of business or lifestyle [14].

However, Gemba visits for services provided are not always possible and not always available for assessing customer's experiences. For such software, usability tests have been widely accepted as a kind of Gemba visits, although testers usually conduct tests in lab environments. They aim improving human interaction design.

2.2 Net Promoter® Score Surveys

Many opportunities for Gemba visits exist in the *Big Data* space: helpdesk tickets and feedback from support interventions. Helpdesk tickets describe an unintended use of some product or service, and thus contain a treasure of information for the supplier to understand growth opportunities for future business. Analyzing the *Ultimate Question* approach for surveys [15] introduced by Fred Reichheld is a standard QFD technique. Net Promoter® is a registered trademark held by Satmetrix, Inc. and Fred Reichheld. The authors of this paper explained the use of Six Sigma transfer functions for uncovering customer needs using Net Promoter surveys in various papers, e.g., [16].

2.3 Business Drivers and Customer Needs

Result of the VoC analysis is a *Priority Profile*. A priority profile is a vector in the space of topics that are of interest to the business, or customer. It shows the relative priorities among the topics of interest; see the example Fig. 2. Profile for Helpdesk Business Drivers.

For software development, topics of interest can be functionality of software, or other rather non-functional characteristics that contribute to the success of the software product. The term customer needs often refers to functionality, whereas business drivers has been introduced by Denney [17] to denote primarily non-functional aspects needed to make a product successful. However, the distinction is fluent: non-functional software requirements regularly become functional requirements, when implemented, and account for a significant part of the so-called scope creep that affects almost all software projects. The advantage of the agile approach is the ability to cope with scope creep in a sensible way.

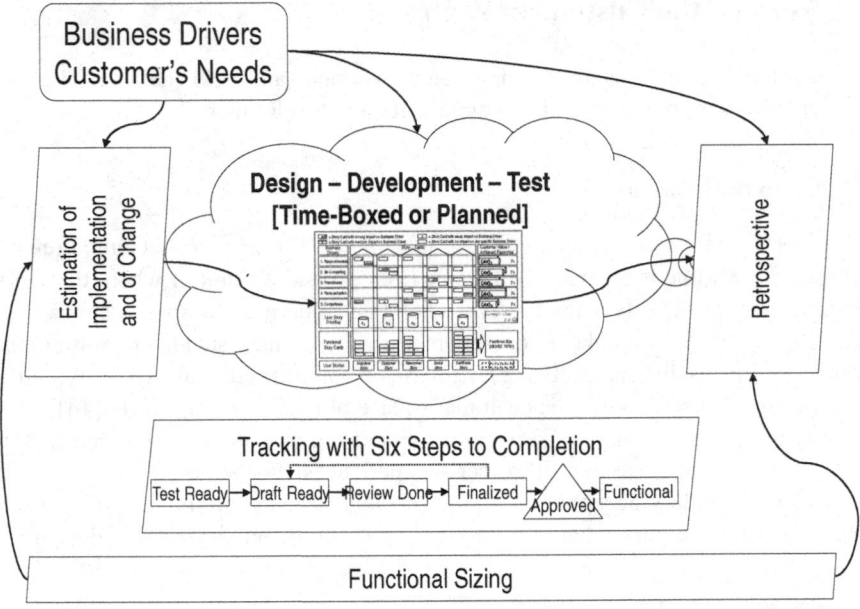

Fig. 1. Business Drivers govern an ICT project from Estimation to Tracking to Completion

Fig. 1 shows an overview how customer needs and business drivers influence a software development project. Business drivers tend to increase the project's scope during development life cycle, but also make some of the initially required functionality obsolete.

3   Lean Six Sigma Software Development

Lean means avoiding waste. In software development, lean means identifying require-ments and user stories that later will lose value well in time before the team implements them. Agile alone is not good enough – if the team has no means identifying sustainable business value, no protection against setting wrong priorities exists.

3.1   A Sample Agile Project

The sample project has been introduced by the authors in 2011 [18] in order to explain how to use ISO/IEC 19761 COSMIC for sizing UML sequence diagrams. For simplicity, we reuse this example again, this time for early effort estimation.

Assume a transportation company – railway or airline – wants to enhance their helpdesk operations and make them fit for today's social media environment. To start with, they consider the following five user stories for implementation:

- *Helpdesk Story*: As a helpdesk staff, I want to identify a client without having to ask for the name or get credentials, regardless whether calling by phone, e-mail, or by chat, such that I can charge service fees or ticket sold according the clients' preferred payment method.
- *Customer Story*: As a registered customer of the travel company, I expect that the helpdesk will recognize me based on the SIM card in my mobile phone, so I can pay my travel with the payment method recorded in my user profile.
- *Newcomer Story*: As a non-registered customer, I want to be able to enroll me quickly and easily with my credit card and my mobile phone such that I can use the services of my travel service provider immediately.
- *Social Story*: As a socially committed person I would like to plan, book and amend my travels on short notice, and cancel, at any time day or night maybe, in order to be where I have just the most fun or best work to do.
- *Certificate Story*: As a user of e-mail on a computer, laptop, tablet or smartphone I want to store my SIM certificate that I need for authentication in the usual certificate store provided by my operating system, so that I can sign my e-mail when contacting the helpdesk and identify myself as easily as when calling via smartphone.

The user stories employ the *Grant Rule* format [19].

3.2   Business Drivers

Business drivers are non-functional requirements, stating customer's values and needs for running the business. Assume the transportation company has identified the profile for customer's values by a suitable method (e.g., Net Promoter® Score, see [16]).

	Business Drivers Topics	**Profile**	
Help Desk	BD1 Responsiveness	0.33	
	BD2 Be Compelling	0.51	
	BD3 Friendliness	0.43	
	BD4 Personalization	0.55	
	BD5 Competence	0.38	

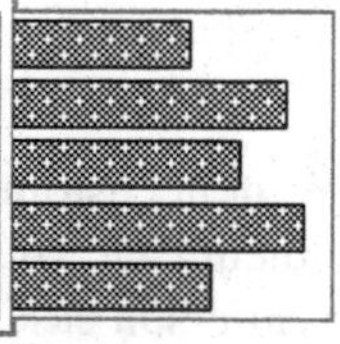

Fig. 2. Profile for Helpdesk Business Drivers

The result is a goal profile for customer's business drivers as shown in Fig. 2. It shows that BD4: Personalization is a key issue for the transportation company, to make their helpdesk a competitive advantage. Thus, they need to know who is calling – or contacting via e-Mail or chat – and what their customer's travel plans are. The caller travel plans they know from electronic bookings via web or mobile; for the caller's identity they need to investigate the *Subscriber Identification Module* (SIM) card with the help of the issuer, the telecom company providing connectivity on the go.

3.3   Kanban Approach

As usual, Kanban charts collect user stories – or epics – selected for implementation. User stories might not yet be ready for implementation; they typically split into *Story Cards*: work items that fit into one sprint. The team members move the story cards through the various stages from vision to implemented functionality.

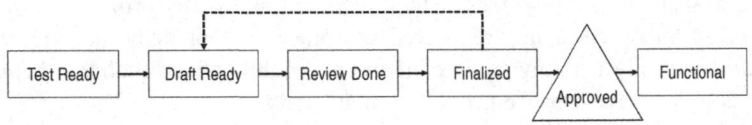

Fig. 3. Six Steps to Completion

In Lean Six Sigma, the *Definition of Done* is slightly different from traditional agile. First, in Six Sigma we always use the *Test-Driven* (TDD) approach; the first step is creating unit tests to work out the idea. Next, drafts, reviews and executing tests are in a separate column; most teams also use a separate column for the finalization needed after review findings. The team has to approve story cards for completion. These principles in Six Sigma for Software are known as *Six Steps to Completion* [20]. The Kanban principles apply: team members must not have more than one story card in the *Draft Ready* column at a time, working on one story card only at a time.

3.4   Story Cards

User stories translate into a number of story cards. There are two different kind:

1. Story Cards that predominantly implement functionality
2. Story Cards that predominantly implement non-functional qualities

FUR implement customer needs. One FUR arises from the need to contact the SIM card and authenticate with the issuer, the telecom service provider. The need to authenticate callers in case additional payments are agreed requires more functionality than usual. It is not enough to see the caller's mobile number and to retrieve her or his profile; to make sure the phone is not stolen, the issuer must approve the SIM card; see Fig. 4.

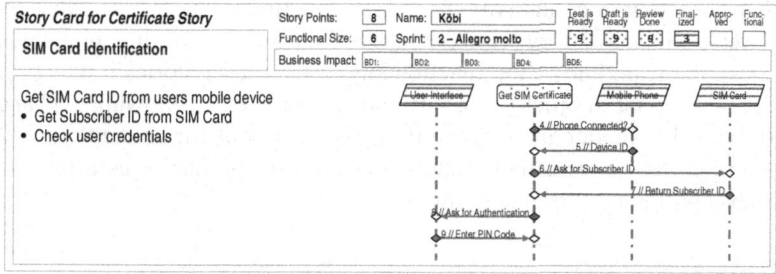

Fig. 4. Sample Functional Story Card

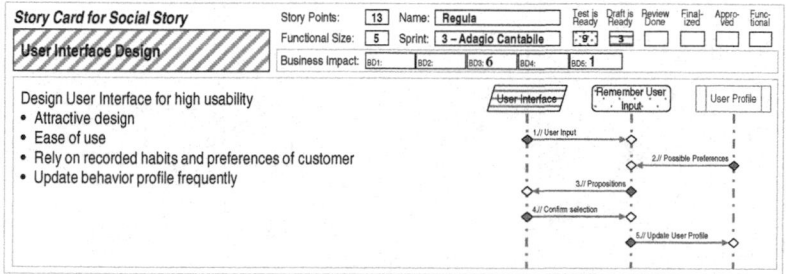

Fig. 5. Sample Non-functional Story Card

Story cards record a task description as short as possible, the agile team assigns story points and impact on business drivers; while functional size is automatically counted with ISO/IEC 19761 COSMIC.

The team defines business impact as the contribution of some story card to one of the business drivers. It might be zero, if the task is purely functional – a must-be task – or if contribution is not specific to one of the business drivers identified (Fig. 2). Other story cards might address the opposite: dedicated effort, often not including any functionality. If the team detected additional FUR during the sprint, needed for meeting business drivers of the customer, then they add it to the story card and to the total functional size. Business impact is weighted, for instance with 1 to 6 points, to distinguish between low and high impact. The team can agree on whatever scale.

3.5   The Kanban Chart

Six Steps to Completion steps yield burndown charts but also *Kanban*; see Fig. 6. It organizes, assigns and tracks sprints with the development team.

The *Waiting* column consist of story cards that already have been sized and estimated and are ready to be implemented, but are not yet included in the current sprint. One sprint consists of the story cards in the five columns *Test Ready* until *Approved*.

The *Backlog* column contains user stories, sometimes called *Epics*, that the team has not yet split into story cards and are not yet ready for implementation. Nevertheless, the team knows the functionality of these user stories if they performed a functional size count in order to identify functionality, e.g., following [21] and [22].

The story cards generate the input to the sprint matrix chart; unlike Scrum [23], we need to story cards for visualizing additional information, and thus a purely paper-based Kanban will not do for this purpose.

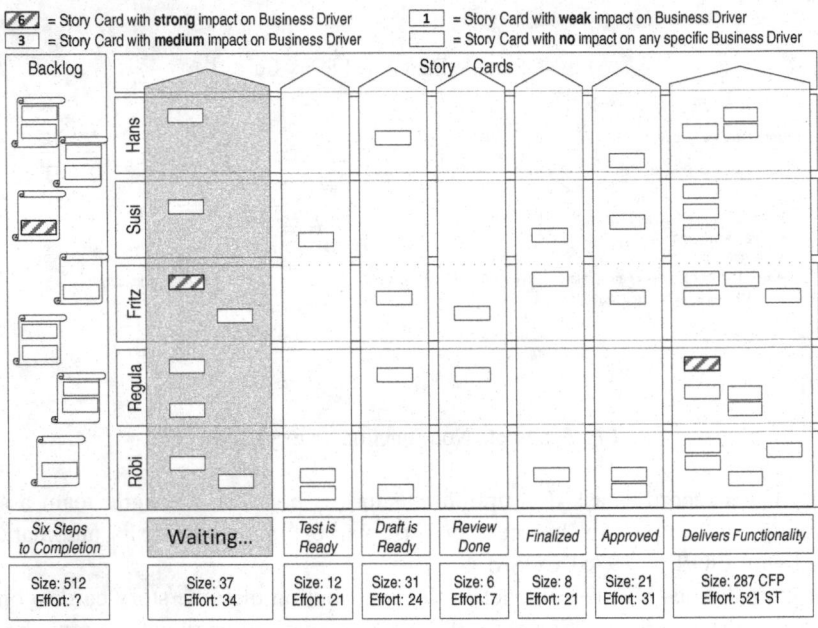

Fig. 6. Kanban Board for the Helpdesk Project

3.6   The Buglione-Trudel Matrix for Agile Software Development

The *Buglione-Trudel Matrix* (BT-matrix) is another view on story cards. It combines functional and non-functional aspects of software development, as explained in [19] and [22]. This combination allows tracking software cost by considering non-functional or quality tasks, as represented by the vector $c = \langle c_1, c_2, \ldots c_5 \rangle$ in Fig. 7. The c_i represent the sum of story points assigned to each of the story cards per column. They have not the same profile as the priority vector x; it is not weighted by business drivers. Many of these tasks will become apparent when requirement elicitation and ongoing changes during the software development project reflect the project team's improved understanding of customer needs and business drivers. Traditional effort estimations cannot handle such values and therefore rapidly become obsolete. Fehlmann has detailed this out in [19].

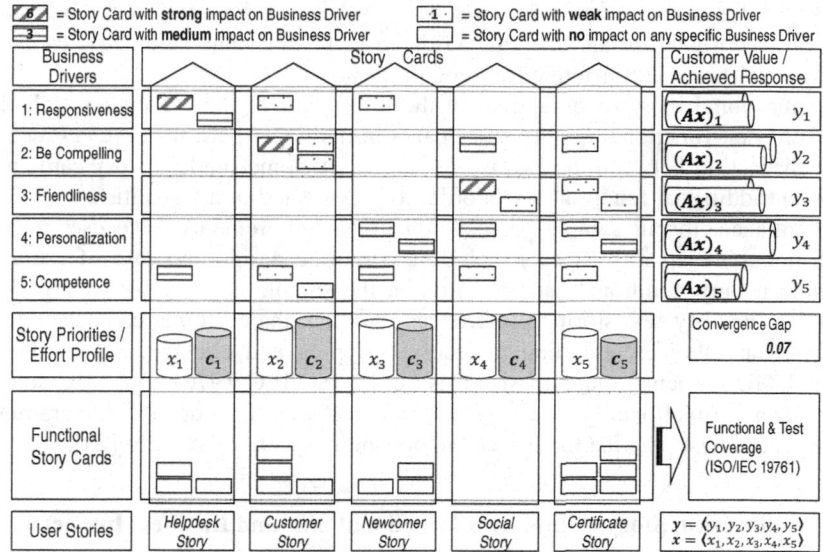

Fig. 7. Buglione-Trudel Matrix for the Helpdesk Project solving $Ax = y$

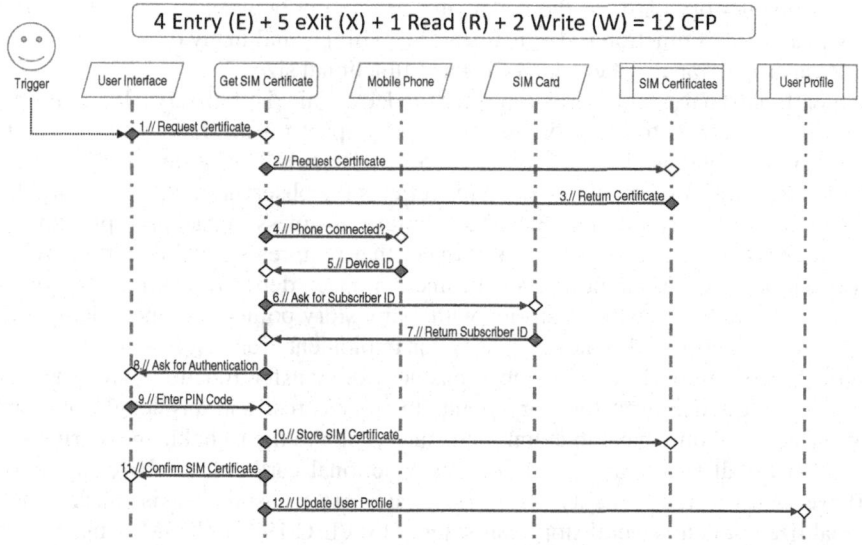

Fig. 8. Sample Sequence Diagram for Getting SIM Certificate, with COSMIC Count

The BT-matrix results from a workshop at the IWSM conference in Stuttgart 2010. It consists of two QFD transfer functions, one mapping user stories into FURs by means of the functional coverage transfer function (see Fig. 10), and another one mapping user stories into business drivers by means of the business impact recorded on story cards (see Fig. 9). This paper looks at the second transfer function only, because for functional story cards, we have cost estimations with known accuracy based on functional size and the ISBSG database [1], or some parametric estimation tool using it. This is not different for agile projects.

The functional story cards appear in the lower part of the BT-matrix, called the *Cellar*, the non-functional quality story cards in the upper half, the *Sundeck*, see Fig. 7. The distinction between the two is not very strict: some sundeck story cards might implement additional functionality in order to provide additional qualities.

For instance, in our sample project, functional requirements drive user interface design not alone; quality aspects including corporate design and ease of use are as important as any additional functionality. In the sample case shown in Fig. 5, the added functionality was storing preferences such that the customer can select entries from previous choices, avoiding unnecessary typing and clicking. Fig. 8 shows a sample UML sequence diagram sized using the ISO/IEC 19761 COSMIC standard [24]. Sizing functionality is a free side effect of sequence diagramming, recommended best practice for agile development by Scott W. Ambler [25].

3.7   Calibrating Story Points with Functional Size and Business Impact

A few initial story card tasks of the functional type can calibrate story points as a team-individual metric, and business impact per story card is an expert criteria measured on some ratio scale agreed by the team, e.g., 0 to 6.

For functional story cards in the cellar, the correlation between effort – estimated by story points – and functional size is linear. See Hill [1] and many others for studies that confirm proportionality between effort and functional size.

For non-functional story cards on the sundeck, this is unlikely. In contrary, business impact relates to story points. Business impact on the ratio scale 1, …, 6 correspond to the Fibonacci sequence 1, 2, 3, 5, 8, 13, 21 … Thus a story card with 13 story points has business impact of six. This reflects the observation that doubling the effort does not necessarily double the effect. In turn, business impact can split among various business drivers; this is the only aspect that requires special attention. What further underpins the assumption that business impact depends from story points alone is the observation that user stories with many story points, no functionality and low business impact probably never qualify for implementation. This is another Lean aspect of the approach. Thanks to the robustness of transfer functions, this metrics work for any sequence used for story points in story cards, and any length of story point sequence. We only have to count them, and assign to the right business driver.

Thus, functional story cards calibrate non-functional cards. This obviously work only if we measure functionality with a software size measure that is linear, since functional size splits to several story cards. Only ISO/IEC 19761 COSMIC meets that criterion. Both story cards and functional size refer to data movements.

4   Controlling Agile Development Using Transfer Functions

The placement of cards identifies two matrices or transfer functions: the sundeck maps the user stories onto business drivers, and the cellar maps the same user stories onto FUR. Thus, the *Convergence Gap* is the method of choice to calculate the degree of achievement for both matrices [26].

4.1   What Is the Convergence Gap?

Lean Six Sigma transfer functions map controls onto responses [26]. In most cases, and in all cases relating to software quality, these transfer functions are linear, or can be linearized, according an outspoken remark of Dr. Walter Wintersteiger: "Quality is linear". If the transfer functions are linear, they can be represented as matrices and calculated with linear algebra [27]. The problem statement is a fixed-point equation

$$Ax = y \tag{1}$$

where y is the observable response vector, x the unknown solution, and A is the transfer function represented as a matrix $A = [\alpha_{i,j}]$, the indices i and j running over the dimensions of the response and the solution vector. The preferred method for solving fixed-point equations in linear algebra is the *Eigenvector* method; a well-known method because for instance Google search uses it, see [28] and [29].

If AA^T is positive definite, i.e., all cell components of the composed matrix are positive, the principal eigenvector of AA^T exists and algorithms exit to calculate them. To solve equation (1), the calculation of the normalized principal eigenvector y' of AA^T is required. This requires solving equation (2)

$$AA^Ty' = \lambda y' \tag{2}$$

where A^T is the transpose of A. By setting $\lambda = 1$ through normalization, $x = A^Ty'$ solves (1), and the convergence gap is

$$\|Ax - y\| \tag{3}$$

where $\|\cdots\|$ denotes the vector length in the Euclidian coordinate system.

Note that cell values in the QFD transfer function A are not limited to the traditional 0,1,3,9 scale. A ratio scale is required. Negative cell values in A are admissible as long as AA^T remains positive definite. Moreover, the solution profile x represents the customer's priorities regarding user stories. If A represents the agile implementation process, selecting the solution profile x guarantees the value profile Ax delivered.

4.2   Meeting Customer's Business Drivers

The sundeck transfer function maps the business impact of user stories onto business drivers. Business impact are the reasons why non-functional story cards have been included to the user story during one of the sprints. The team chooses and agrees these detailed reasons with the customer, as part of requirements elicitation. They were unknown before in full detail.

The convergence gap measures how well the chosen story cards match the business driver's goal profile. If the gap opens, the team can identify which aspects need more attention, and place additional story cards. In contrary, if some aspects are over-fulfilled, planned story cards can be removed or new, brilliant ideas rejected just on the fact that they apparently do not add new value for the customer. The sundeck of the BT-matrix serves for balancing the efforts with the needs of the customer, in a well-understood, visual manner. This makes agile software development lean. It blocks waste effectively from becoming part of a sprint.

4.3   Meeting Functional User Requirements

The cellar is different. Data movements implement FURs, not business impact. Data movements from a sequence diagram describe the functionality needed. The transfer function is simply measurable by counting the number of ISO/IEC 19761 COSMIC data movements that contribute to some FUR in a user story. The total number of data movement counts in the cells of the cellar matrix is larger than the total functional size, as there are many data movements serving more than one FUR.

Such a transfer function implements the set of user stories by data movements as necessary. The cellar shows to what extend goals meet FUR priority. Waste planned functionality opens the convergence gap widely. If so, there is the possibility to save effort by removing part of the functionality as originally planned. Usually the cellar is more predictable and stable than the sundeck and less prone to adding or changing requirements. The sequence diagram in Fig. 8 shows a part of the cellar, referring to the functionality needed for the helpdesk and the certificate story. Part of the data movements appear on Fig. 1 as well.

5   Early Estimation by a QFD Workshop

Tracking agile projects includes tracking efforts because of the dependency between effort and business impact on the sundeck, and effort and functional size in the cellar.

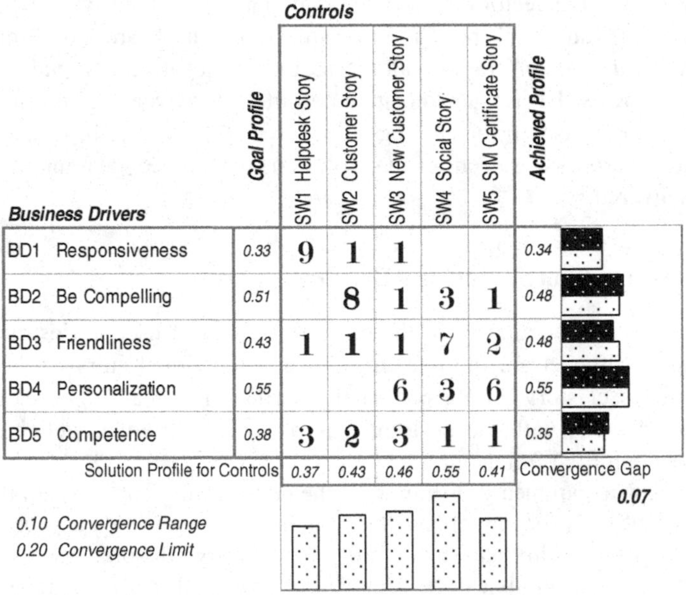

Fig. 9. Sample Sundeck Prediction QFD

Note that the matrix cells in Fig. 9 represent impact per user story in business drivers. Thus, before starting a project, experts from both business and development can predict the sundeck of the BT-matrix using classical QFD workshop techniques, while the cellar is predicable by sizing user stories, and using a benchmark database. The experts agree on numbers in all matrix cells, representing the business impact needed per user story for the sundeck without bothering for the unknown details that later will be written into story cards.

Per matrix cell, the business impact roughly equals the effort needed, as seen in Fig. 7. Thus summing up the columns indicates the expected cost for implementing non-functional requirements, long before these requirements are known in detail.

5.1   The Sundeck Matrix Prediction

Fig. 9 shows a sample sundeck QFD, showing a matrix that corresponds to the sundeck part of Fig. 7. The total business impact value per story card yield the cell value in the transfer function, thus the cell numbers represent total business impact. Experts can predict business impact using standard QFD workshop techniques.

The convergence gap shows the vector length differences between the goal profile vector and the effective profile vector, represented in the graph on the right. Thus, the convergence gap tells the experts whether they considered all influencing factors.

5.2   The Cellar Matrix Prediction

Fig. 10 shows a sample transfer function for the cellar, where the cells contain the data movement counts as needed by the respective user stories to meet the FUR. The FUR goal profile to the right is its solution profile. Fig. 7 does not show the details of the cellar matrix – for simplicity, but also because normally developers do not need

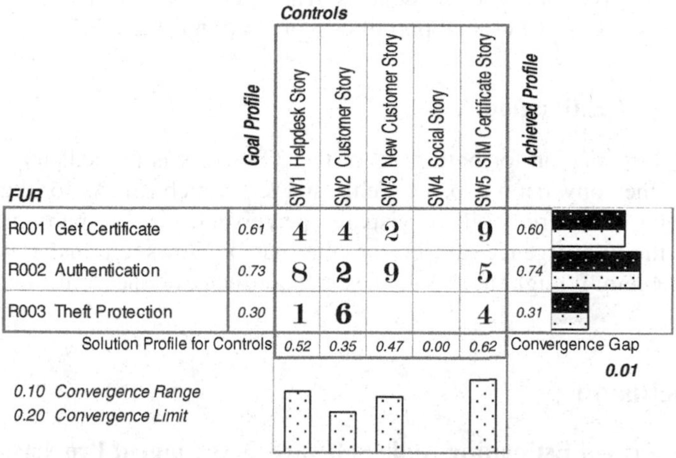

FUR	Goal Profile	SW1 Helpdesk Story	SW2 Customer Story	SW3 New Customer Story	SW4 Social Story	SW5 SIM Certificate Story	Achieved Profile
R001 Get Certificate	0.61	4	4	2		9	0.60
R002 Authentication	0.73	8	2	9		5	0.74
R003 Theft Protection	0.30	1	6			4	0.31
Solution Profile for Controls		0.52	0.35	0.47	0.00	0.62	Convergence Gap

0.10 Convergence Range
0.20 Convergence Limit

Convergence Gap 0.01

Fig. 10. Sample Cellar Measurement Transfer Function (extract)

looking at it. It is significantly simpler, as there is no business impact prediction by experts. It is sufficient to assign data movements in a UML sequence diagram to one of the FUR. Following ISO/IEC 19761 COSMIC, this is a side effect of the count. The matrix shows only a small part of all FUR, focused on the "Get Certificate" functionality. Since the user story "SW4: Social Story" requires no specific functionality, it does not contribute to FURs. The cell numbers in Fig. 10 represent data movements' counts.

Again, the convergence gap is an important indicator, this time it shows that the user stories effectively deliver the FURs requested without waste. For Lean Six Sigma in software development, this tool is indispensable in order to avoid excess and waste functionality be included in a software project. For more details on Lean Six Sigma software development, see [19]. For understanding, how COSMIC supports requirement elicitation, consult Trudel [30].

5.3   Preconditions for Early Estimations Based on QFD

The preconditions are:

- Knowing the user stories (epics);
- Knowing the business driver's goal profile;
- Knowing FUR and their goal profile;
- Knowing the team's velocity, i.e., how many story points fit into one sprint;
- Have story points calibrated to functional size.

The last point refers to *Story Point Delivery Rate*: the number of story points needed to implement one COSMIC function point, i.e., one data movement. If data movements touch different environments, e.g., when exchanging data with the SIM card provider, calibration might not equal among all data movement sin the project. The ISBSG database provides guidance in identifying the various types of industry and application environment dependencies. The exact relation how business impact corresponds to effort is the crucial part of cost prediction using QFD.

5.4   Quality of Estimation

The quality of estimation for both parts of the BT-matrix is immediately perceivable by looking at the conversion gap, see Fehlmann & Kranich [6]. As for the developers when planning the sprints, it is visually perceivable which parts need special attention. If the convergence gap closes, the matrix shows a transfer function that solves the problem. It might not be the best one, or the only one, or the cheapest but it is a solution.

6   Conclusion

6.1   New Ways of Estimating Agile Software Development Projects

Estimating the number of sprints needed to implement a software product vision is decisive when investing large amounts in software development. The proposed method utilizes Lean Six Sigma and QFD tolls that agile teams are nor familiar with. Bringing these disciplines together, especially for sensitive issues as if early project estimation is a challenge but certainly worth trying.

Estimations based on predicting what additional requirements agile teams are likely to discover during development is a completely new approach. However, the time is ripe for it; micro estimation based on work breakdown structure and Gantt charts is no longer state of the art and obsolete.

6.2   Open Points

The conversion of business impact, and of functional size, require practical experience providing evidence with both kind of prediction matrices. It might be necessary to use additional Six Sigma statistical methods to assess the correlation level.

Moreover, separating functional and non-functional story card might not always be as straightforward as shown here. Non-functional story cards tend to exhibit additional functionality as shown in Fig. 5 when analyzed in full detail. There is a grey zone, when functionality is the major business driver of some customer of a software product. In this case, the two QFDs might collapse and result in a standard single QFD.

References

[1] Hill, P.: Practical Software Project Estimation, 3rd edn. McGraw-Hill, New York (2010)
[2] American Association of Cost Estimators, Basis of Estimate - as Applied for the Software Services Industries. AACE Recommended Practices, Morgantown, WV (2014)
[3] International Standards Organization, ISO/IEC 31010:2009 - Risk Management - Risk Assessment Techniques. International Standards Organization, Geneva, Switzerland (2009)
[4] American Association of Cost Estimators, Risk Analysis and Contingency Determination Using Range Estimating. ACE International Recommended Practices, Morgantown, WV (2008)
[5] Santillo, L., Moretto, G.: A general taxonomy of productivity impact factors. In: Proceedings of the IWSM/MetriKon/Mensura 2010, Stuttgart, Germany (2010)
[6] Fehlmann, T.M., Kranich, E.: Quality of Estimations. In: Proceedings of the IWSM/Mensura, Assisi, Italy (2012)
[7] Cohn, M.: Agile estimating and planning. Prentice Hall, New Jersey (2005)
[8] Bakalova, Z.: Towards Understanding the Value-Creation in Agile Projects, vols. 13-288. CTIT Dissertation Series, Enschede (2014)
[9] Akao, Y. (ed.): Quality Function Deployment - Integrating Customer Requirements into Product Design. Productivity Press, Portland (1990)
[10] Mizuno, S., Akao, Y.: QFD: The Customer-Driven Approach to Quality Planning and Deployment, translated by Glenn Mazur. In: Mizuno, S., Akao, Y. (eds.) Quality Function Deployment. Asian Productivity Institute, Tokyo (1994)
[11] Herzwurm, G., Schockert, S., Mellis, W.: Joint Requirements Engineering. QFD for Rapid Customer Focused Software and Internet-Development. Vieweg, Braunschweig (2000)

[12] Imai, M.: Gemba Kaizen: A Commonsense, Low-Cost Approach to Management. McGraw-Hill, New York (1997)
[13] Womack, J.: Gemba Walks - Expanded, 2nd edn. Lean Enterprise Institute, Inc., Barters Island (2013)
[14] Mazur, G., Bylund, N.: Globalizing Gemba Visits for Multinationals, Savannah, GA, USA (2009)
[15] Reichheld, F.: The Ultimate Question: Driving Good Profits and True Growth. Harvard Business School Press, Boston (2007)
[16] Fehlmann, T.M., Kranich, E.: Using Six Sigma Transfer Functions for Analysing Customer's Voice. In: Fourth International Conference on Lean Six Sigma, Glasgow, UK (2012)
[17] Denney, R.: Succeeding with Use Cases – Working Smart to Deliver Quality. Booch–Jacobson–Rumbaugh – Series. Addison-Wesley, New York (2005)
[18] Fehlmann, T.M., Kranich, E.: COSMIC Functional Sizing based on UML Sequence Diagrams. In: MetriKon 2011, Kaiserslautern (2011)
[19] Fehlmann, T.M.: Agile Software Projects with Six Sigma. In: Proceedings of the 3rd European Research Conference on Lean Six Sigma, Glasgow, UK (2011)
[20] Fehlmann, T.M.: Six Sigma in der SW-Entwicklung. Vieweg, Wiesbaden (2005)
[21] Buglione, L., Gencel, Ç.: Impact of Base Functional Component Types on Software Size Based Effort Estimation. In: Jedlitschka, A., Salo, O. (eds.) PROFES 2008. LNCS, vol. 5089, pp. 75–89. Springer, Heidelberg (2008)
[22] Buglione, L., Trudel, S.: Guideline for sizing agile projects with COSMIC. In: Proceedings of the IWSM/MetriKon/Mensura, Stuttgart, Germany (2010)
[23] Schwaber, K., Beedle, M.: Agile software development with Scrum. Prentice Hall (2002)
[24] Jenner, M.S.: Automation of Counting of Functional Size Using COSMIC FFP in UML. In: COSMIC Function Points - Theory and Advanced Practices, pp. 276–283. CRC Press - Auerbach, Boca Raton, FL (2011)
[25] Ambler, S.W.: The Object Primer: Agile Model–Driven Development With UML 2.0, 3rd edn. Cambridge University Press, New York (2004)
[26] Fehlmann, T.M., Kranich, E.: Transfer Functions, Eigenvectors and QFD in Concert. In: Proceedings of the ISQFD 2011, Stuttgart, Germany (2011)
[27] Lang, E.: Linear Algebra, 3rd edn. Springer-Verlag New York Inc., New York (1973)
[28] Kressner, D.: Numerical Methods for General and Structured Eigenvalue Problems. LNCSE, vol. 46. Springer, Heidelberg (2015)
[29] Gallardo, P.F.: Google's Secret and Linear Algebra. EMS Newsletter 63, 10–15 (2007)
[30] Trudel, S.: Using the COSMIC Functional Size Measurement Method (ISO 19761) as a Software Requirements Improvement Mechanism. École de Technologie Supérieure - Université du Québec, Montréal, Canada (2012)

Author Index